VAUDEVILLE MELODIES

VAUDEVILLE MELODIES

Popular Musicians and Mass Entertainment
in American Culture, 1870–1929

NICHOLAS GEBHARDT

THE UNIVERSITY OF CHICAGO PRESS
CHICAGO AND LONDON

The University of Chicago Press, Chicago 60637
The University of Chicago Press, Ltd., London
© 2017 by The University of Chicago
Published 2017.
Printed in the United States of America

26 25 24 23 22 21 20 19 18 17   1 2 3 4 5

ISBN-13: 978-0-226-44855-8 (cloth)
ISBN-13: 978-0-226-44869-5 (paper)
ISBN-13: 978-0-226-44872-5 (e-book)
DOI: 10.7208/chicago/9780226448725.001.0001

Library of Congress Cataloging-in-Publication Data

Names: Gebhardt, Nicholas, author.
Title: Vaudeville melodies : popular musicians and mass entertainment in American
    culture, 1870–1929 / Nicholas Gebhardt.
Description: Chicago ; London : The University of Chicago Press, 2017. | Includes
    bibliographical references and index.
Identifiers: LCCN 2016034775| ISBN 9780226448558 (cloth : alk. paper) | ISBN
    9780226448695 (pbk. : alk. paper) | ISBN 9780226448725 (e-book)
Subjects: LCSH: Vaudeville—United States. | Revues—United States. | Music-halls
    (Variety-theaters, cabarets, etc.)—United States. | Popular music—United States.
Classification: LCC PN1968.U5 G43 2017 | DDC 792.70973—dc23 LC record available
    at https://lccn.loc.gov/2016034775

♾ This paper meets the requirements of ANSI/NISO Z39.48-1992 (Permanence of
Paper).

For Matilda . . . a class act

We have asked nothing of vaudeville simply because we haven't sus-
pected what it had to give.
—Gilbert Seldes

I was born on the road. Not on the Orpheum, the Pantages, Keith, or any
other of the circuits I've travelled since. The road I mean is a long, rutted
track that leads away from Russia across Poland to the Baltic.
—Sophie Tucker

A holiday to an American is a serious affair . . .
—Edwin Royle

I never trust a man I can't buy.
—Benjamin Franklin Keith

CONTENTS

ACKNOWLEDGMENTS

This book has proven to be quite a journey, and many people have contributed to its final form. Most of the research was undertaken at four libraries: the Rare Book and Manuscript Library at Columbia University in New York, the New York Public Library for the Performing Arts, the British Library in London, and Lancaster University Library. I want to thank the many librarians from those institutions who over the years made this project possible. I also received generous financial support for this research from the Faculty of Arts and Social Sciences at Lancaster University and the Faculty of Arts, Design and Media at Birmingham City University.

I have benefited a great deal from my colleagues at Lancaster University and Birmingham City University. In particular, I want to thank Simon Barber, Oliver Carter, Jez Collins, Kirsten Forkett, Janine Grenfell, Patrick Hagopian, Timothy Hickman, Paul Long, John Mercer, Jonathan Munby, Annette Naudin, Nicolas Pillai, Loes Rusch, Dima Saber, Deborah Sutton, Tim Wall, and Nick Webber. I am also grateful to those people who have played a formative role in my scholarly career, including George McKay, Maureen McNeil, Ronald Radano, Derek Scott, Walter van de Leur, and Shane White. More recently, my graduate writing group at Birmingham City University has been a model of collaborative work and imaginative discussion on the problem of getting things done.

At the University of Chicago Press, Douglas Mitchell's encouragement and support has kept this project on course when all seemed to be lost, and for that he has my deepest thanks. Not only that; his dedication to music and to scholarship is truly a source of inspiration. It has also been a pleasure to work with Doug's assistants, Tim McGovern and Kyle Wagner, who kept the whole show on the road. I am likewise thankful for the chance to work with such a supportive editorial team. Therese Boyd reminded me of why

I set out to write this book in the first place, while Joel Score, Ryan Li, Ben Balskus, Ashley Pierce, and Jan Worrell guided it ever so smoothly to completion.

For more than a decade now I have benefited from intellectual exchanges with Richard Rushton and Tony Whyton. I could not possibly have ended up where I have without their contribution and friendship. Finally, I want to thank Jory Debenham. Without her remarkable creativity, intellect, sense of humor, and companionship, this book would never have seen the light of day.

Introduction

This book is about the changes that took place in popular music in the United States, in the period from 1870 until 1929. It explores the context for those changes and offers an explanation for why they happened. Above all, it aims to tell a particular kind of story about popular musicians, one that foregrounds their relationship to new conceptions of wealth, power, and social order. Central to this story is the transformation of musical values, practices, repertoires, and institutions that occurred because of the corporate reconstruction of American culture. Although the early signs of this transformation were evident by the mid-nineteenth century, especially as a result of the international achievements of the minstrel show, it was not until the 1890s that a new musical culture came into view. The major objective of this study is to clarify some of the ways in which the economic, political, and moral authority of corporate capitalism was able to reshape this musical culture so dramatically, and with such long-lasting effect. Because popular musicians were such active participants in this process, I primarily want to examine their efforts to open up creative spaces within those institutions most closely identified with the emerging amusement industries.

My main focus will be on the structure and significance of American vaudeville. There are two reasons for this. First, the performance practices established on the vaudeville stage remain essential to our assumptions about popular music today, especially in terms of what it means to entertain an audience. Second, for performers, composers, and lyricists seeking popular success in this period, vaudeville was the context in which they were most likely to achieve it. "It was to vaudeville, more than any other branch of musical theatre," notes historian David Ewen, "that the Tin Pan Alley [composers and publishers] of 1890 and the early 1900s owed [their]

greatest debt. The history of vaudeville and Tin Pan Alley overlaps so frequently that it is hardly possible to speak of one without discussing the
other."[1] Later in the book, I shall discuss how that overlapping history provided a framework for the emergence of a specific set of practices for the
production of popular melodies for vaudeville audiences.

From the 1890s until the 1920s, vaudeville was the dominant context
for popular entertainment in the United States, and was synonymous with
names such as Tony Pastor, B. F. Keith, Al Jolson, Nora Bayes, Bert Williams, William Morris, Eva Tanguay, Harry Houdini, E. F. Albee, Sarah Bernhardt, Sophie Tucker, the Great Sandow, James Corbett, and many others.
By 1915 its reach extended across the globe, taking in every continent and
performance tradition, and incorporating thousands of performers from
every branch of show business. Its phenomenal success relied on a huge
network of theaters, each one part of a circuit and administered from centralized booking offices, most of which were based in cities such as New
York, Chicago, San Francisco, London, and Paris.

The shows were made up of a continuous sequence of self-contained
acts, each of which appeared anywhere from three to six times a day and
up to seven days a week, depending on whether a theater was part of a big-
time or small-time circuit and whether it offered a full- or split-week booking. Acts were designed to appeal to the broadest possible audience, and
those that failed were either quickly modified or dropped altogether from
the weekly bill. The range of acts included solo singers and instrumental-
ists, song-and-dance acts, comics, animal acts, jugglers, monologists, one-
act playlets, musical ensembles, strongmen, female impersonators, contor-
tionists, sportsmen and -women, dancers, and magicians. While audience
figures vary from city to city, by 1910 the total seating capacity of New
York City's theaters and movie houses approached 2 million, while similar
venues in San Francisco averaged audiences of more than half a million
every week.[2]

The most important studies of vaudeville have focused attention on
how it mediated the changes to a predominantly urban-industrial society in
the United States. The first such analysis was Albert McLean's *American
Vaudeville as Ritual*, which was published in the mid-1960s and drew heavily on the theories of symbolic action and mythic consciousness developed
by the philosophers Ernst Cassirer and Suzanne Langer. Wrote McLean,

> Viewed from the mythic perspective, vaudeville becomes not merely an
> "amusement" or means of killing leisure time—a preoccupation quite
> apart from the main business of American society. Nor was it just a fan-

tasy in motley improvised by a clique of ambitious showmen and performers who foisted upon the public their artificial and eclectic medley of songs, monologues, dances, feats of skill, and exhibitions of the extraordinary. To the contrary, once the blinders of custom, sentiment, and nostalgia are removed, a pattern of social significance begins to emerge. Beneath the dazzle and the frenzy of the performances, a symbolism is revealed which not only increases our comprehension of the vaudeville era but also illuminates the entire development of mass entertainment within modern culture.[3]

McLean's argument focuses on vaudeville's role in articulating what he describes as the American "Myth of Success." Through its symbolism, he says,

vaudeville sought to allay those common tensions among city-dwellers brought about by their crowded lives, by their worries over employment and scarcity, by the growing depersonalisation of their occupations, and by the erosion of simple moral values. But the symbolising process went even further in pointing out continuously the positive goals of city life and giving life to the dream that someday all these affronts to sanity and dignity would be dissolved. The Myth of Success was both an escape from the moment and a tangible promise for the future.[4]

McLean concludes that although highly rationalized at the level of management and production, vaudeville was ultimately a "ritualistic expression of inchoate emotions and half-understood ideas."[5] Its audiences were no more aware than its artists were of the ways in which it was reshaping and revaluing their experience of the world and the values they ascribed to it.

Until the early 1970s, McLean's study remained the single most important scholarly treatment of vaudeville as a cultural form. The publication of John DiMeglio's *Vaudeville U.S.A.*, however, which was based primarily on interviews with ex-vaudevillians, marked a new phase, as well as a telling shift in emphasis. Written in the context of Vietnam and Watergate, DiMeglio saw in vaudeville the last vestiges of a genuinely democratic art, in which performers and audiences were bound by a shared vision of the possibilities of American culture. Whereas McLean had focused on the ritual aspects of vaudeville and its relationship to an emergent urban-industrial society, DiMeglio was more interested in how the show reflected and encompassed the cultural diversity of the American national experience. "Vaudeville, vaudevillians, and their audiences," he claimed, "were

America in microcosm. Unlike legitimate theatre, opera and concert halls, where patronage was smaller and socially more selective, vaudeville drew from all walks of life. A typical vaudeville audience covered the spectrum of American society." Even though DiMeglio's focus was on the practicalities of the medium he, too, understood vaudeville's appeal to be primarily a mythic one: "The expansiveness of vaudeville . . . where novelty acts, animal acts, impersonators, acrobats, variety acts, magicians, soloists, monologists, comedy teams, drama sketches, dancers, and even chasers, all got billing and did their separate, highly individual parts, yet all somehow integrating into the whole, served as a symbol of Americanism."[6]

More recently, historians such as Richard Busch, Susan Glenn, Henry Jenkins, Alison Kibler, David Nasaw, Kathryn Oberdeck, and Robert Snyder have questioned these kinds of claims, arguing instead that vaudeville was primarily a medium through which urban Americans, many of them recent immigrants, challenged dominant cultural values and ideals and, in the process, negotiated complex issues of identity such as gender, race, class, and cultural inheritance. Through vaudeville, artists and audiences alike were able to both question and redefine the possibilities for participation in the public sphere.[7] In this view, vaudeville did not simply symbolize the American experience; rather, it was an arena of intense cultural conflict over what that experience meant and whom controlled such meanings to begin with.[8]

What unites these authors is their claim that vaudeville has something important to tell us about the value of entertainment for Americans.[9] Much of what follows in this study will be taken up with this same goal. I want to emphasize, however, that this is not a book about the history of musical genres on the vaudeville stage. My principal focus is on the subjective experiences of performers, and the sense in which they came to recognize themselves, and so relate to their audiences, as popular artists for whom music was their primary medium of communication.

Let me summarize the journey ahead. Chapter 1 opens with a discussion of Ted Snyder, Bert Kalmar, and Edgar Leslie's hit song "I Work Eight Hours, I Sleep Eight Hours, That Leaves Eight Hours for Love," which the famous singer Nora Bayes added to her act in 1914. The song introduces the central theme in this book: becoming a popular entertainer. To set this up, I discuss several scenes in two of the most influential Hollywood backstage musicals: Stanley Donen and Gene Kelly's *Singin' in the Rain* (1952) and Vincente Minnelli's *The Band Wagon* (1953). Both films take vaudeville as a key reference point in the claims they want to make about the popular artist's connection to her audience. This framework is particularly important to the case I want to make here: that vaudeville brought an entirely new set of relationships into being between the performers, managers, and audiences that affected popular music in ways we have yet to fully appreciate. Each of the subsequent chapters opens up a different perspective on this process, including the daily rituals of life on the road, the business practices developed by the vaudeville managers, and the stagecraft involved in creating a successful act.

In chapter 2 I explore how the circuits shaped performers' view of vaudeville and their place within it, insofar as they began to conceive of themselves, and relate to each other and their audiences, as popular artists. This part of the book introduces some of the principal performers who populate the story I want to tell. Chapter 3 focuses on the ritual passages that performers took as they went from being anonymous audience members at a show to becoming stars on the vaudeville stage, while in the following chapter I ask why it became so important for vaudeville performers to identify show business with a life that was unlike any other. In chapter 5 I examine in more detail those principles that the vaudeville owners developed in their efforts to systematize the amusement business. In the next chapter, I reconstruct a performance history of vaudeville and explore some of the basic issues involved in developing an act. In particular, I concentrate on how a performer's sense of artistic worth derived from the continual practice of appealing to an audience and holding its attention. This is especially significant if we want to account for changing tastes and expectations within show business.

Chapter 8 is in many ways the most important chapter of the book. It is here that I set out a theory of vaudeville melodies and relate their production to the performance practices that had come to characterize vaudeville acts. In chapter 9 I return to the narratives and images of popular success and explore some of the ways in which they were connected to the broader mythology of modernization that was taking shape in the United States in the late nineteenth century. In the concluding chapter, I argue that vaudeville raises some important questions about how we account for the value of popular music in American society.

My intention in this book is to provide an overview of the practices by which vaudeville performers came to understand what it meant to entertain an audience. In order to do this, I focus primarily on the conditions in which they worked, the institutions they relied upon, and the artistic values that they thought were essential to their success. Beyond that, I have also tried to remain alive to the creative possibilities that vaudeville offered them in this period. William Dean Howells, the editor of *Harper's Monthly*, saw this very clearly. "To hold its own," he wrote, "vaudeville . . . must venture into regions yet unexplored. It must seize not only the fleeting moments, but the enduring moments of experience; it should be wise not only to the whims and moods, but the passions, the feelings, the natures of men; for it appeals to a public not sophisticated by mistaken ideals of art, but instantly responsive to representations of life. Nothing is lost upon the vaudeville audience."[10] Let's take a seat in the darkened theater and decide if he was right.

CHAPTER ONE

That's Entertainment

In 1914 Nora Bayes added a new song by Ted Snyder, Bert Kalmar, and Edgar Leslie to her successful "Single Woman" act.[1] "I Work Eight Hours, I Sleep Eight Hours, That Leaves Eight Hours for Love" was a lilting up-tempo waltz that told the story of Danny Maloney, a "real ladies' man" who worked in a store and spent most of his time trying to "date up" the young girls who shopped there. Aware of his reputation, one of Danny's sweethearts asks him how he has the time to fit it all in. As he "hangs up his hat in the hall," he replies:

> I work eight hours, I sleep eight hours, that leaves eight hours for love
> Eight long hours with nothing to do
> Thing of the fun if I spend them with you
> To prove I love ya
> I'll sit and hug ya
> And if you want an encore
> My sleep I'll be sure tonight
> Even stop workin'
> So I can love you some more.

While the verses of "I Work Eight Hours . . ." relied on well-established comic conventions for an Irish character song, as well as other familiar narrative devices, the chorus raised the more complicated issue of the relationship between work and pleasure. Its opening phrase deftly parodied the large number of protest songs that had appeared in support of the American labor movement's long campaign for a shorter working day, which began to gather momentum in the mid-1860s, following the Civil War, and culminated in huge May Day demonstrations in 1886. The most popular of these was "Eight Hours," which was first published in the *Labor Standard* in July 1878. Based on an 1866 poem written by I. G. Blanchard for the *Working-man's Advocate*, it was set to music by the Reverend Jesse H. Jones and by the 1880s had become the official song of the eight-hour movement.[2] "Eight hours for work, eight hours for rest, eight hours for what we will!" went the chorus, quickly becoming the movement's rallying cry.[3] For Jones and Blanchard, the struggle over the form and contents of the working day held out the promise that workers' free time would remain their own, and that those hours were sufficient in and of themselves.

Although Snyder, Kalmar, and Leslie satirized the demands of the Eight Hour movement to some extent, they also articulated some of the deeper issues at stake in the social struggle over the form and contents of the working day. In particular, they dramatized the problem of what people actually do when they are not at work or at home resting, asking their listeners to think about the significance they attached to their activities during those hours. Moreover, in the second line of the chorus, the conjunction of "eight *long* hours" (emphasis added) and "with *nothing* to do" (emphasis added) underlined the extent to which the rationalization and exploitation of labor in this period also required the moralization and organization of leisure. "I Work Eight Hours . . ." claimed that productivity in the factory or office depended on workers having access to their own time outside of work. They required this free time to renew themselves, to restore their labor power for the next day's work. The great fear of moral reformers and workers' associations, however, was that if left unregulated and unfilled by meaningful activity, those eight long hours "for what we will" would become ends in themselves. And sure enough, by the end of the song, Danny Maloney offers to give up work for the sake of love.

Dreams of escape and renewal were central themes within vaudeville production, and informed much of the critical commentary that attempted to explain its influence. For example, in an 1893 article for *Harper's Magazine*, Charles Davis suggested that vaudeville was the "sort of amusement which makes a sleep easier and the next day's work less like work after all."[4] Likewise, in 1899, in an article in *Scribner's Magazine*, the actor Edwin Royle wrote that vaudeville "appeals to our businessman, tired and worn, who drops in for half an hour on his way home; to the person who has an hour or two before a train goes, or before a business appointment; to the woman who is wearied of shopping; to the children who love animals and acrobats; to the man with his sweetheart or sister; to the individual who wants to be diverted but doesn't want to think or feel."[5] What both of these comments suggest is that if we want to know more about why popular music began to sound so different in the early decades of the twentieth century, then we need a specific kind of historical and critical account of the ways in which vaudeville was related to those "eight long hours with nothing to do." Such an account, in my view, begins with what we might describe as the problem of entertainment. What did it mean to entertain the vaudeville audience?

Answers to this question can be found in two well-known Hollywood backstage musicals from the 1950s, which seem to me to offer a particularly rich perspective on the problem of entertainment.[6] What I take from these films is something along the lines proposed by Stanley Cavell, in an essay on what he calls the thought of movies. For Cavell, movies present us with ways of thinking about "things that ordinary human beings cannot help thinking about, or anyway cannot help having occur to them . . . such things, for example, as whether we can know the world as it is in itself, or whether others really know the nature of one's own experiences, or whether good and bad are relative, or whether we might not now be dreaming that we are awake."[7] Likewise, if we want to discover what entertainment meant for Americans, then a good place to start is with those films that take it as their subject.

In Gene Kelly and Stanley Donen's *Singin' in the Rain* (1952), the issue of the relationship between popular artists and their audiences is raised in the very first scene. Movie star Don Lockwood (played by Gene Kelly) has just arrived with his co-star, Lina Lamont (in a great pastiche by Jean Hagen), at the opening night of their new film, *The Royal Rascal*, at the famous Grauman's Chinese Theatre in Los Angeles. As the couple steps out of the limousine onto the red carpet leading into the theater, gossip columnist Dora Bailey (played by Madge Blake) stops Lockwood and asks him to describe to the assembled audience how it all happened. "The story of your success is an inspiration to young people all over the world," she graciously declares, to which the crowd ecstatically agrees. After a moment of mock humility, in which he appears to have nothing especially interesting to say, Lockwood replies with not one, but rather two, parallel autobiographies. The first one follows what we might think of as a classic narrative of dedicated study and high-artistic achievement:

Well, any story of my career would have to include my lifelong friend, Cosmo Brown [played by Donald O'Connor]. We were kids together, grew up together, worked together. . . . I've had one motto I've always lived by: dignity, always dignity. This was instilled in me by Mom and Dad from the very beginning. They sent me to the finest schools, including dancing school—that's where I first met Cosmo—and with him I used

to perform for Mom and Dad's society friends. They used to make such a
fuss over me. Then, if I was very good, I was allowed to accompany Mom
and Dad to the theatre. They brought me up on Shaw, Molière, the finest
of the classics. To this was added rigorous musical training at the con-
servatory of fine arts. Then we rounded out apprenticeship at the most
exclusive dramatics academy. At all times, the motto remained: dignity,
always dignity. In a few years, Cosmo and I were ready to embark on a
dance concert tour. We played the finest symphonic halls in the country.
Audiences everywhere adored us. Finally we decided to come to sunny
California. We were stranded here. . . . I mean . . . staying here when the
offers from the movie studio started pouring in.[8]

The parallel story unfolds in visual and musical counterpoint to Lockwood's verbal account, and yet this second narrative is present only to us,
the movie's audience. For example, when the star proudly announces to the
crowd outside the theater that he and Cosmo attended the finest schools,
including dancing schools, what we (the movie audience) see is a cutaway
image of the two of them as kids, performing for money in a dingy pool hall.
His parents' "society friends" are in fact the other players around the pool
tables, who throw the boys some spare change for their efforts. Eventually,
we see Lockwood's father carting them out of the hall.

Accompanying Lockwood's comments about being exposed to Bernard
Shaw, Molière, and the classical theater is an image of the two boys sneak-
ing into a Nickelodeon to see B-grade monster movies. When he describes
his rigorous musical training to the adoring crowd, we see him on violin and
Cosmo on piano playing with a ragtime band in a beer hall. Their apprenticeship at "the most exclusive dramatics academy" is in reality time spent
at amateur nights in vaudeville, where they perform a comic dance routine
to the song "Fit as a Fiddle and Ready for Love" (only to be "gonged" off the
stage), while his description of touring the "finest symphonic halls" refers
not to Steinway Hall in New York, or Symphony Hall in Boston, but to the
vaudeville circuits, where they are regularly booed off stage by audiences.

The two performers finally get a job playing music for silent films and,
by chance, Lockwood offers to stand in for an injured stunt man. The director likes him, offers him some more stunt work, which he pursues with
a crazy single-mindedness that almost kills him. Eventually the head of
the studio spots him, tells Lockwood that "he's got something" (possibly a
death wish?), and so he lands a leading role. The two stories—one told by
voice-over, the other through a series of separate images—converge when
we return to the ever-smiling Lockwood, standing in front of the micro-

phone, reciting his motto once again, but this time for both audiences: "Dignity," he announces, "always dignity."⁹ From our perspective, the joke seems to be on that *other* audience, the one inside the film. Nonetheless, by the end it is clear that the joke might also be on us; for nothing we, or they, know about art, entertainment, singing, dancing, love, and life can be taken for granted.

By admitting from the start that when we go to the movies, or hear a song, or listen to someone speak, or go to a Broadway show, or fall in love, we are some way deceived by our senses, the scene raises a number of intersecting issues about our knowledge of the world, our place within it, and our relationships with those around us. Using the familiar conventions of the backstage musical, Kelly and Donen ask us to evaluate the powers of the medium, to consider the particular ways in which we experience its effects on us, and to assess our reasons for going to see a show in the first place (as audience members wanting to be entertained, but also as participants who believe in the particular world of song-and-dance routines that film musicals make possible). As with Lockwood's opening narrative, the film tells several stories simultaneously: the coming of sound to film, the story of Arthur Freed's famous production unit and its centrality to the MGM musical, the origins of popular entertainment and musical performance, the relationship between stage (Broadway) and screen (Hollywood), the rise and fall of popular entertainers (vaudeville stars, movie stars, popular singers, and dancers), and Gene Kelly's own success story (first as a performer in vaudeville and then as an actor as well as a director/choreographer). None of these stories can be seen to be in any way separate; each one relies on the other for the film to make sense to its various audiences. Coming to some sort of clear understanding of which of them is true, however, is by no means straightforward or immediately apparent, as both the film's audiences subsequently discover.

A later sequence amplifies this set of issues. With his new sound film, *The Dancing Cavalier*, ready for release, Lockwood describes the final scene to R. J. (played by Millard Mitchell), the head of the studio, in the projection room. "It's the story of a young hoofer who comes to New York," he begins. "First we set the stage with a song. It goes like this . . ." And then he launches into Arthur Freed's 1929 song, "Broadway Melody." "Bring a frown to old Broadway, Ah, you gotta clown, on Broadway, your troubles there, they're out of style, for Broadway always wears a smile." As the camera pulls back, we see that Lockwood is no longer in the projection room with his boss, but now on a stage-screen, with a spotlight on him. The interpolation of the songs "Broadway Melody" and "Broadway Rhythm" (both songs

that refer also to Freed's central role in the development of the film musical)
introduces one of Kelly's signature ballet sequences, which tells the story of
popular entertainment, from the street to the stage and back again.

It is the Jazz Age, and Harry the Hoofer (Kelly) steps into a crowded New
York street scene, awkward and garish; he's a country hick who betrays
his small-town origins with a suitcase in hand and thick-framed glasses
that cause him to peer intensely at everything around him. Like everybody
outside the city, he too is searching for its mythic center: Broadway. He
makes his way through the wonders of the great metropolis, surrounded by
many of the symbols, images, and figures of modernity, including conveyor
belts, flappers, skyscrapers, and the illuminated billboards of Times Square.
The accompanying overture combines the sharp, angular dissonances of
late expressionism, with motifs from jazz, folk music, and popular song,
and so echoes those attempts by George Antheil, Aaron Copland, George
Gershwin, and others in the 1920s, to forge an indigenous American ex-
pressionist sound. On Seventh Avenue, he auditions a jazz-tap routine—
"Gotta Dance"—for a series of agents, is rejected several times, but eventually finds one who will represent him. With a deal agreed, and his image
improved (no glasses, no suitcase, and a smooth city-slicker gait), the doors
into show business are thrown wide open to him.

After a chorus set piece, in which the theme "Gotta Dance" is used
to identify him with the community of popular entertainers, he falls in
love with the girlfriend of a gangster, realizes that she is only impressed by
wealth and fame, and so, in an effort to win her heart, sets to work to make
it in the big time. The next three shots record Harry's rise to the top as a
song-and-dance man: first burlesque, then vaudeville, and, finally, the Ziegfeld Follies, each one presenting a more refined version of the same chorus-
line routine than the one before it. Moreover, by the time he reaches the
Follies, he is barely dancing at all, hardly moving his lips when he sings, and
can just about manage a smile. Once he makes it to the top, however, Harry
realizes that he has lost those things that got him there in the first place; he
has forgotten what it means to be an entertainer and who his audience is. A
long ballet sequence then follows, in which the possibilities of modern art
appear to open up an abstract world of pure emotion, as if this might provide
a solution to his problems. However, these kinds of abstractions also prove
to be false. So Harry returns to the street for a large-scale Busby Berkeley–
style production finale, through which he rediscovers his passion for song-
and-dance, and learns once more the lessons to be had from a "Broadway
Melody" routine. And, then, suddenly we find ourselves back in the studio
projection room with Lockwood and R. J., who impatiently retorts: "Sounds

great. But I can't quite visualize it." So, for all the effort to make us believe in the make-believe, to celebrate the values of entertainment above all else, the film consistently raises doubts that we even know what those values mean, or even why they might matter to us in the first place.

These issues are also present in one of the greatest backstage musicals of them all, *The Band Wagon*, directed by Vincente Minnelli, and starring Fred Astaire and Cyd Charisse.[10] The film is about a washed up song-and-dance man, Tony Hunter (played by Astaire), who returns to New York in order to revive his waning career. In the third scene of the film, following a journey from Los Angeles during which his fellow passengers ridicule his fading celebrity, Astaire steps off the train at Penn Station and finds himself surrounded by reporters. Thinking they are waiting for him, he begins to make a statement about his forthcoming plans, only to realize that they are in fact waiting for Ava Gardner (in a cameo), who simultaneously steps off the same train, one door up from his carriage. This scene of mistaken identity, and Astaire's subsequent solo dance along the platform singing "All by Myself" to himself, absorbed in the thought of someone who suddenly comes to the realization that he is alone in the world, is enough to convey the film's reflexive structure, at once about loss of faith and renewal of belief in the artistic value of the musical.[11] Walking off the platform, he runs into his two friends and artistic collaborators, Lily and Lester Martin (played by Nanette Fabray and Oscar Levant), who are there to meet him. They are carrying the script for a show, written especially for his comeback, and are bursting with the news that the greatest producer and director in town, Jeffrey Cordova (played by the great British comic Jack Buchanan), has agreed to do the show.[12]

In *The Band Wagon*, the network of vaudeville theaters and cheap amusements, and the practices associated them, are the explicit context for Astaire's rediscovery of what it means to be an entertainer. While his friends go on ahead, he wanders down 42nd Street, wondering at the changes that have taken place there: theaters are now penny arcades or movie houses, while the refined audiences who once arrived only in carriages to see Noel Coward and Gertrude Lawrence in *Private Lives* have turned into surging crowds of people looking for cheap fun. He drifts into one of the arcades and starts to explore various amusement machines, including a mechanical fortuneteller, a life's-questions machine, a pinball poker machine, a love machine, and a distorting mirror. Confused by the messages these contraptions seem to be telling him, Astaire moves off in the other direction, only to trip over the outstretched legs of an African American shoe-shiner (played by Leroy Daniels) in the center of the arcade. He then launches into Arthur

Schwartz and Howard Dietz's 1932 song, "A Shine on Your Shoes," which is ostensibly about lifting yourself up when you know you're feeling low. The routine that unfolds between Astaire and Daniels, however, turns out to be a complicated meditation on the meaning of singing and dancing in American culture, in which Astaire rediscovers a sense of who he is, where he stands in relation to the traditions on which his art depends—especially his predecessors among African American singers and dancers—and the kinds of passions and moods his art is capable of expressing.[13] Once he has reconnected with his past and, in doing so, has found a way to live with the present, the process of renewal the film wants us to participate in gets properly underway.

Two versions of Schwartz and Dietz's showbiz anthem, "That's Entertainment," establish the film's central concerns. The first occasion of the song is a scene in an empty theater, where Hunter and the Martins have gone to meet the great Cordova in order to discuss their plans with him. Looking anxiously around the formal stage set, Hunter asks Cordova if he really wants to do a musical. "Musical, musical," replies Cordova, grandly and pompously. "I'm sick of these artificial barriers between the musical and the drama. In my mind there is no difference between the magic rhythms of Bill Shakespeare's immortal verse and the magic rhythms of Bill Robinson's immortal feet. I'll tell you, if it moves you, if it stimulates you, if it entertains you, it's theater."

A long and mannered exchange then follows between the characters on the relationship between art and entertainment, until Hunter reminds them, rather anxiously, that "whatever I am, whether it's a new me or an old me . . . I'm just an entertainer."

"What do you think the theater is?" Cordova responds, forcefully. "It's all entertainment." He then launches into another speech on what it means to entertain an audience, before starting to sing. "Everything that happens in life, can happen in a show. You can make 'em laugh, you can make 'em cry, anything, anything can go."

The others then join in. "The plot can be hot, simply teeming with sex," sings Lily.

"A gay divorcee who is after her ex," adds Lester.

"It could be Oedipus Rex?" queries Hunter, as he begins to get the idea of the song, even as he remains skeptical of its broader claims. However, one of the points the song is also making is that when people start to sing and dance, it is impossible not to want to get involved; Hunter can no more resist the claims of the song, or its infectious melody and rhythms, than can Cordova.[14]

The second occasion for the song is the finale, in which the film musical and stage musical that is taking place within it are brought together in
a powerful reiteration of the claim that within the world of the musical life
and art are continuous. All the cast participate here, collectively recognizing not just Hunter's earlier conversion, but also their own transformation
from a dispirited, unbelieving group of performers whose out-of-town premier has just bombed into a Broadway success story. In contrasting the emo-
tionally detached and formal qualities of Cordova's high art, with Hunter's
involved and spontaneous commitment to popular music and dance, and
then resolving the former into the later, *The Band Wagon* follows *Singin'
in the Rain* in claiming that it is the popular artist above all who is capable
of producing a new synthesis of the high and the low, the stage (New York)
and the screen (Los Angeles), jazz and classical music, rural and urban communities, and, ultimately, art and entertainment. Both films, however, rely
on a deeper claim about their origins: it was vaudeville that made this synthesis possible in the first place.

But what kind of entertainment was vaudeville? There are no simple
answers to this question. In *Voice of the City* Robert Snyder observes that
"vaudeville was a deeply contradictory form of theatre, its meanings as elusive as the patter of a doubletalk comedian."[15] It drew together a huge, heterogeneous urban audience that, outside the theater, was divided by class,
race, ethnicity, and gender, and yet it also enabled the consolidation of a
global entertainment industry that ruthlessly exploited its thousands of
workers, reduced popular entertainment and musical performance to highly
standardized routines and formats, and treated audiences as passive con-
sumers of theater in a package.[16] As Snyder goes on to say, although vaudeville was a fine way to escape from oppressive labor conditions, it still left
the structure of the working day intact. And while its philosophy of spontaneous expression and risqué humor displaced the older Puritan values of
self-discipline and self-improvement, its routines were also entirely consistent with the progressive ideology of the new corporate society.[17] He also
believes, however, that the twentieth-century retreat into private forms of
entertainment such as television and computers has left American culture
all the poorer:

> Going to vaudeville meant being part of the show. The dialogue between
> artist and audience reached people individually and collectively. . . . In
> small-time houses with boisterous gallery gods, and even in more polite
> houses like the [New York] Palace, vaudevillians learned to play to the
> crowd and the crowd learned to judge them. It could be a rough school,

but all were enriched by the experience. Performers learned to play to every kind of person, while audience members acquired a vocal and discerning temperament that encouraged them to insist on the best. It was a knowing and demanding audience, and not the artist's talent alone, that made vaudeville great theatre.[18]

I will come back to the relationship between artists and audiences in chapter 6. At present I want to focus on Snyder's broader theoretical claims. He develops his argument about vaudeville's artistic value and its significance for audiences in the context of those media that both emerged from it and, eventually, supplanted it: film, radio, the phonograph, television, and computers. What interests me most is the story he wants to tell. It is about the disappearance of shared popular culture that brought people together, however imperfectly, and its subsequent replacement by passive and privatized forms of entertainment that made the home into the basis for most people's experiences of the world. It is a well-known story, in which some kind of mass culture is either a symptom, or the cause, of a decline in what was once a vibrant public sphere.[19]

Because vaudeville involved a collective dialogue between artists and audiences in highly localized settings, and because its artists continually responded to the communities in which they performed, Snyder claims that going to see a show differed fundamentally from the experiences provided by most twentieth-century media. "As ludicrous as it might be for people to treat television characters as real people," he suggests, "in vaudeville at least they had the satisfaction of a real, live person performing before them."[20] By accommodating local preferences and customs, even as it remained national in scope, vaudeville offered audiences a living image of a democratic community "that was far more open, generous and egalitarian than most institutions people encountered."[21]

The larger issue here is what we think it means to be in an audience. Is it an active state? Or are we contained, immobile, passive, in our seats? "By the time sound invaded Hollywood," observes Rick Altman in his influential study of Hollywood film musicals, "Americans were thus thoroughly conditioned to a definition of 'entertainment' that was largely passive in nature. Whereas earlier generations thought of singing, dancing, and baseball as something entertaining *to do*, early twentieth-century Americans were already quite likely to think of those activities as spectator sports. More and more, it was necessary *to be entertained* in order to have a good time."[22] Altman's comments suggest that we need to think much more carefully about the kinds of terms we use to describe what happens when we go to a show. What if vaudeville did not simply mark the end of one era of democratic popular entertainment and the beginning of another, corporate-controlled one? What if the claim that audiences had become conditioned to entertainment that was largely passive is insufficient to account for what happens when we go to the theater, listen to a song, watch a film, or turn on the television?

In Altman's opinion, Hollywood musicals made the same kind of intimate appeal to a broad, heterogeneous audience as vaudeville had done before it; screenings of these films frequently occupied the same opulent palaces, along with the neighborhood dime-store theaters, that for over forty years had housed vaudeville performances. As we have already seen, musicals explored the possibilities opened up by the collapse of older cultural distinctions and changing ideas about artistic experience. Moreover, these films were in every sense about the relationship between new kinds of performers and new kinds of audiences; that was their meaning and significance. For even as they seemed to impose themselves on a passive audience, their songs told a different story. "The music of the musical differs from that of opera, *Lied*, and oratorio in that it is self-consciously written not to surpass the range and capabilities of average amateur music lovers," states Altman.

> Musical music is thus *engineered* not to be passive music. It is "hummable" music, the kind of music that most easily gets carried home, the kind of music whose life will not end with the intellectual experience of listening. In short, it is music whose major purpose is to counter the specialization engendered by the nineteenth-century aristocratic taste for "cultured" music. . . . Treating the process of listening to music as a beginning rather than an ending, as a tool rather than a finished product, American popular music consciously presents an alternative to the specialized model afforded . . . by classical music.[23]

The different emphasis in Altman's discussion is not just about sorting out the historical details, although this is certainly part of the problem. Rather, it involves us in some fundamental interpretive issues to do with our most basic understanding of musical forms of expression and how we have come to think about them, and to find value and meaning and purpose in the aesthetic experiences they create. Indeed, Snyder's and Altman's respective claims highlight the inadequacy of some of our most common assumptions about going to a show, a movie, or a concert. "Being a spectator is not some passive condition that we should transform into activity," Jacques Rancière suggests. "It is our normal situation. We also learn and teach, act and know, as spectators who all the time link what we see to what we have seen and said, done and dreamed. There is no more a privileged form than there is a privileged starting point. . . . Every spectator is already an actor in her story; every actor, every man [or woman] of action, is a spectator of the same story."[24]

In Rancière's account, the spectator occupies a wholly different position within the show than one usually assigned to her. We have become so used to condemning cultural institutions for creating passive audiences, and audiences for (either willingly or unwillingly) participating in this process, that we no longer recognize just how involved they already are in the performance. The many transformations and adjustments, shifts of tone and purpose, changes of key and timbre, the processes of refinement and displacement that words, tunes, dances, dialogues, gestures, and images go through as they move from the artist to her audience, from a family member to a neighbor, from a songwriter to a publisher, and then back again, involves us in a very different kind of social space. In this model of encounter and exchange, there is no way of knowing where the origins of the work, the event, the object, or the practice lie; there is no identity between cause and effect. We will return to these processes in more detail in later chapters, especially as it affected performers' understanding of the value of their acts. At this point, however, a brief sketch is sufficient to set out the basic issues.

The weekly "tryout" exemplified for many people what vaudeville was all about. Act after act paraded in front of the jeering crowd, hoping to persuade the assembled booking agents that their act or "turn" was worth a contract. "The toothy tenor and the one who lisped, the twitching blues shouter, and the lady hoofer who dressed as a Broadway Sioux, and the twin act, and the French soprano with the Gowanus accent, and the untonsured youth who danced acrobatically," wrote an anonymous reviewer. All "drew their mixed portion of applause and unruly criticism."[25] Creating continuity out of these discrete acts required a complicated understanding of show business on many different levels, from the songs and dialogue used by performers, to awareness of their particular booking schedule as they toured the circuits, to local knowledge of different audiences (which varied not just from neighborhood to neighborhood, but from night to night). Although there existed a set of conventions to guide performers, not to mention the specific expectations about making it in show business and what it promised artists, there was still the issue of unity.[26] George Gottlieb, who booked acts for the Palace Theatre in New York, summarized it in these terms:

Briefly, the whole problem is this—acts must be arranged not only in the order of their interest value but also according to their physical demands. . . . But there is still another problem the manager must solve. "Variety" is vaudeville's paternal name—vaudeville must present a *varied* bill and a show consisting of names that will have a box-office appeal. No two acts in a show should be alike. No two can be permitted to conflict. "Conflict" is a word that falls with ominous meaning on a vaudeville performer's or manager's ears, because it means death to one of the acts and injury to the show as a whole. . . . Part of the many sides to this delicate problem may be seen when you consider that no two "single" singing acts should be placed next each other—although they may not conflict if they are placed far apart on the bill. And no two "quiet" acts may be placed together. The tempo of the show must be maintained.[27]

Tempo, for Gottlieb, meant that there must be "no waits. Everything must run with unbroken stride. One act must follow another as though it were especially made for the position. And the entire show must be dovetailed to the split seconds of a stop-watch."[28] It was the relation between acts, the sequence in which they unfolded, and the technical procedures by which transitions between them were managed, that in his view distinguished a successful from an unsuccessful show.

These deeper structuring rhythms were then replicated at the level of each individual act, as performers defined themselves in relation to the other performers on the bill, as well as the thousands of other acts that might at any time be substituted in their place. They did this by constantly refining and testing their ideas, searching for a song or routine or visual trick that would tip the balance of the audience in their direction. Show by show they stripped their routines of anything superfluous, seeking the elusive word or image or gesture that would bring tears and laughter and, in the end, the thundering applause that signaled they had the house with them. If it failed, they took the act apart to find out what was wrong and worked on it until it was right. Such was their discipline that it was common to find performers in the theater early in the morning, rehearsing a routine that had gone wrong the night before. It might be that it had gone stale or that they had taken too much for granted. Either way, it was a precarious process in which timing was everything, especially when it came to the finale.

The finale was the crucial element that carried within it the show's underlying tempo while also highlighting the individual talents of the performers. As one artist noted, "start to tell a vaudevillian the idea of a new act and he will interrupt you to ask, 'What's the finish?'"[29] The "wow" finish at the end of an act thus became the catalyst by which performers were guaranteed a place on the next week's bill, a byline in the trade press, and, if they were lucky, a biography at the end of their career. More than that, however, the "wow" finish transformed the conditions under which performers arrived at sense of the legitimacy of their art, and managers developed a conception of an all-encompassing form of entertainment that spoke to audiences everywhere. Instead of relying on the claims of a specific class or community, or those attempts made by artists themselves, to secure aesthetic value, the drive to capture as wide an audience as possible through an ear- and eye-catching finale opened up this new kind of performance space within which different cultural practices interacted, jostled, and intermingled.

CHAPTER TWO

There's No Business Like Show Business

What could be more exciting than going on the road with a vaudeville act? So many plans of escape or dreams for a better life began and ended with the traveling shows. Year after year, for months on end, big-time and small-time performers alike covered thousands of miles, their journeys taking them back and forth between the cities and towns of the Great Plains, over the Rockies, and down onto the dry crust of the Pacific Rim, retracing the ancient paths of European conquest and trade, or moving south, through the old slave-holding states along the rivers of the Ohio Valley down into the Mississippi Delta. Traveling mostly at night, going from show to show, performers inhabited a multileveled world defined by railway timetables, telegraph offices, and prebooked schedules. Cheap boardinghouses were the rule, and comfort was an exception. They lived between the stage door and the railway terminus, relying on booking agents, press agents, programmers, tour managers, theater owners, and advance men to get them from one to the other.

In the previous chapter I made the case that vaudeville brought an entirely new set of relationships into being between the performers, managers, and audiences as they redefined the meaning of entertainment.[1] In this chapter I want to focus more closely on the forms these relationships took and consider some of the ways in which they were inseparable from the structure and realities of the theatrical circuits, which eventually came to dominate every aspect of the performing arts. To this end, I examine how the circuits affected performers' view of vaudeville and their place within it, especially insofar as they began to conceive of themselves and relate to each other as artists whose primary medium was the hit song or dance tune. This involved them identifying in show business a form of life unlike any other, with its own laws of existence and accompanying set of beliefs about the value of entertainment and the life of the entertainer. It also required that they recognize in themselves a particular attitude to their art, and a set of practices that distinguished their practices and ideals from other performers, especially those appearing on what was referred to in the press and by the performers themselves as "the legit" (the legitimate) stage, concert hall, or opera house.

This type of self-understanding relied on performers finding a way to feel at home on the circuits, to turn the experience that vaudeville chronicler Joe Laurie describes of "damp basement dressing rooms, layoffs, empty stomachs . . . terrible orchestras, [and] lousy boarding houses" into a rite of passage that was required of all artists. "When you finished serving your apprenticeship," Laurie recalled, "by playing every slab in all the whistle stops to all kinds of audiences from the ones you thought were painted onto the seats to the ones that applauded, laughed, stomped their feet and whistled, your diploma was a full route sheet, play-or-pay contracts, good orchestras, able stage hands, good hotels, decent food, comfortable rooms, riding in plush, and playing the Big Time."[2] Such ritual passages from one type of audience to another were essential to the ways in which performers came to recognize the meaning of their success as entertainers and their achievements as artists. In many cases, they justified the terrible working conditions on the small-time circuits with the claim that eventually, and with enough of an effort, they would make it in the big time. Moreover, the transition from one circuit to the other (in either direction) was called upon in support of a more general belief that there was no business like show business. To understand how vaudeville performers began to conceive of their lives in these terms, we must first explore the social contexts within which they developed their ideas about show business.

We begin, therefore, with two related changes in show business: the organization of groups of theaters into circuits, and the establishment of centralized booking offices. Beyond this basic descriptive problem lie some deeper questions, which will be set out in the rest of this chapter: how did the processes of cooperation and centralization affect the average performer signed to what were called pay-and-play contracts? If life on the circuits altered performers' consciousness of what theatrical success meant, how did this occur? Along with these questions, there are also some much larger ones relating to the structures of power and privilege in the United States. While I deal here with some of the initial attempts to organize show business within the broader principles of the emerging corporate culture, these questions will be addressed in more detail in the next few chapters.

The first circuits were developed in the 1870s and were essentially cooperatives, organized for the reciprocal advantage of each theater's manager.[3] "It was not my original intention to start a circuit," recalled B. F. Keith. "The houses accumulated and then it became necessary to join hands with others, in order to give the public the best kind of show. I purchased sites in Buffalo and Pittsburgh, but never built there. Acts could play a house three or four times a year. The circuit gradually grew from houses built or acquired."[4] Over the next three decades, it became increasingly common to group the theaters in a circuit under a common management structure, as owners sought to introduce greater certainty and consistency into the programming of acts, as well as controlling their production costs (particularly the performers' salaries).[5]

This process gained momentum at the same time as the stock system for theatrical production was being replaced by what became known as the combine system.[6] Whereas a stock company was a fairly permanent production unit, independent of other companies, and usually resident in a particular theater or opera house, the new combine or combination system was based on temporary groups of performers, without a permanent base, whom producers hired as part of a touring show. By the 1880s it was estimated that there were at least 250 of these combines performing in around 5,000 theaters in 3,500 cities throughout North America.[7] By 1900 *Billboard* reported that the promoter Charles Frohman alone had a controlling interest in thirty such companies, all traveling around 500 miles per week.[8]

According to the theater historian Alfred Bernheim, this breakdown of the stock system and the subsequent rise of the combine system was as comparable in its effect on the performing arts as the advent of power machinery and the evolution of the factory were on manufacturing. "We may, therefore, speak," he wrote, "of the 'industrial revolution in the theatre' since this term clearly connotes all that is implied by the movement we have outlined."[9] Bernheim attributes this revolution primarily to the emerging celebrity culture, which compelled theater managers to hire star performers, and the concentration of ownership in the hands of a few theatrical enterprises. As theater managers relied more and more on celebrity performers to fill their theaters, they became little more than "real estate operators, leasing their houses either for fixed rental or on sharing terms to the travelling combination."[10] At the same time, newly formed amusement enterprises were buying stakes in larger numbers of theaters, opera houses, musical halls, booking agencies, and pleasure gardens, consolidating their control over specific metropolitan, regional, or statewide circuits.

At the forefront of this shift in the overall organizational structure of theatrical production was an organization called the Syndicate, which was founded in 1896 by six New York–based entrepreneurs with extensive interests in theater ownership, booking agencies, artist management, and production. Represented by the agency of Marc Klaw and Abe Erlanger, the organization proceeded to buy up stakes in theaters throughout the United States, establishing a monopoly over both the booking process and theatrical production, and thereby compelling producers to stage their shows in Syndicate-run theaters and rely on the Syndicate booking agency for performers. By 1904 the organization had taken control of more than 500 major and minor theaters, including all but two or three in New York City.[11]

When Edward Albee first proposed a centralized booking system to his boss, B. F. Keith, it was the example of Syndicate he had in mind.[12] In March 1899, with Keith's support, Albee entered into negotiations with the owners of the big-time vaudeville circuits with the explicit purpose of incorporating their existing circuits and enterprises into a national organization that would manage and promote the interests of the major vaudeville entrepreneurs. Although he encountered substantial resistance, and there were some notable absences to begin with, eventually, in May 1900, eighteen of the big-time vaudeville managers gathered in Keith's Boston office with the express purpose of consolidating their business enterprises. As the *New York Times* reported:

> The plan to form an association of the vaudeville managers of the United States, which has been under discussion for the past ten days, first in Boston, then in Brooklyn, and more recently in the Hoffman House [in New York City], has finally assumed definite shape, and the articles of membership were signed by all interested yesterday. . . . Sixty leading vaudeville theatres, extending from Boston to San Francisco, are represented. Houses not yet affiliated will be invited to join later. . . . The association also aims to make possible the booking of a more compact route for the performer, and proposes to effect other reforms which will place the business upon a sounder commercial basis than has been the case during the past two or three years.[13]

The resulting organization—the Association of Vaudeville Managers—completely transformed the booking process, offering performers anywhere from several months to almost a year of engagements within a single route, while at the same time regulating salaries and establishing a 5 percent commission on bookings (along with a 5 percent agent's fee, which was also de-ducted by the managers). Their policy was to arrange performers' itineraries in advance, from the association's new offices in New York and Chicago, and so save time and money on what were called the "jumps" (travel time) between cities or towns, as well as facilitate the maximum number of bookings possible for every act on the circuits.[14] More controversially, individual managers within the organization regularly blacklisted those performers who did not use the association's booking services or who had signed on for tours on rival circuits (some well-known examples of blacklisting were the New Haven–based S. Z. Poli Circuit and the independent William Morris booking agency).

Compared with the leading nineteenth-century entertainment forms—the stock company, the minstrel show, the tent show, and the circus—the corporate restructuring of vaudeville exhibited some important structural innovations. Perhaps the most important of these was the creation in 1906 of the United Booking Offices (UBO) of America, which combined Keith's Theatres and Booking Circuit, those circuits managed or booked by his main eastern competitors—Mike Shea, F. F. Proctor, Percy Williams, and S. Z. Poli—and the more than sixty theaters booked by the Western Vaudeville Managers' Association (which included the Orpheum and other Midwestern owners), into a single integrated booking system. Here was a new kind of administrative apparatus designed to coordinate bookings throughout the big-time circuits, as well as evaluate acts on a weekly basis. "To the performer," notes vaudeville historian Bill Smith, "the advantage of a UBO booking was 'the route.' A route would take in theaters all over the country, arranged in time-saving geographical progression, to keep him [or her] busy working for three or more years, without repeating cities. Most of the bookings were in big time. If some small time was included, salaries and working conditions were equal to those in the big time, with UBO guaranteeing salaries."[15]

The momentum generated by the formation of national theatrical circuits, and the creation of integrated booking systems, meant that few managers or booking agents in the years between 1900 and 1910 were in a position to remain independent of a circuit or a centralized booking office. In the trade press for this period, we see frequent references to these newly formed combines, along with almost continual discussion of booking procedures. For example, on June 11, 1904, *Billboard* announced that "a combination of vaudeville houses in the Northwest will probably be effected for the purpose of arranging for the booking of attractions. Bookings will be made in Chicago and New York. A new [booking] system will be put into operation."[16] A month later, the same journal reported that on April 15, in Jonesboro, Arkansas, "an association known as the Cotton Belt Associa-

tion of Opera House Managers, was formed for the purpose of securing better shows, and providing for the theatrical managers a line of towns that
they could make without missing one night. The following towns are in
the association: Osceola, Batesville, Jonesboro, Newport, Forrest City, Mari-
anna, Clarendon, Stuttgart, and Pine Bluff; in Arkansas, and Caruthersville,
Popular Bluff, De Soto, New Madrid, St. Charles and Kennet in Missouri.
More towns in both states are to come into the organization."[17] This process
was so effective in reducing the jumps between theaters, as well as consolidating the different levels of vaudeville, that by 1905 theater critic Hartley
Davis observed that "from being a most uncertain business [vaudeville] has
become one of the most dependable."[18]

Central to this shift was a conception of entertainment that placed great
emphasis on industrial efficiency, technical mastery, and entrepreneur-
ial initiative as the basis for a national and, increasingly, transcontinental
touring and booking system. Stories abound in the trade journals of epic
struggles between the rival entertainment managers (dubbed the "vaudeville wars" by the press) for control of the circuits and the booking system,
along with the few (mostly unsuccessful) attempts by groups of performers
to challenge the power of the emerging entertainment oligarchy. Just as
important, however, was the extent to which the corporate reconstruction
of vaudeville redefined the everyday possibilities available to performing
artists. If, as Michael Leavitt claims, the leading vaudeville managers "had
things systematized in a manner not surpassed by a national bank," then
what were the consequences for performers once they became part of such
a system?[19] And what do their experiences of this system reveal about the
day-to-day realities of life on the circuits?

The issue was not so much the size of the circuits, but the principles of
corporate control and efficiency around which the new combines were organized. "To the actor," observes Royle, "vaudeville offers inducements not
altogether measured in dollars and cents. He is rid not only of financial obligation, but of a thousand cares and details that twist and strain a nervous
temperament." With one's times and terms arranged by the booking agents
and theater managers in advance, notes Royle,

> the rest is easy. The actor provides himself and assistants and his play
> or vehicle. His income and outcome are fixed, and he knows at the start
> whether he is to be a capitalist at the end of the year; for he runs almost
> no risk of not getting his salary in the well-known circuits. . . . It is then
> incumbent on him to forward property and scene-plots, photographs and
> cast to the theatre two weeks before he opens, and on arrival, he plays

twenty or thirty minutes in the afternoon and the same night. . . . The actor's only duty is to live up to the schedule made and provided.[20]

Royle's account is notable for the way in which he assesses the impact that vaudeville had on existing conceptions of the performing arts, from music to drama.

> It cannot be denied that the vaudeville "turn" is an experience for the actor. The intense activity everywhere, orderly and systematic though it is, is confusing. The proximity to the "educated donkey," and some not so educated; the variegated and motley samples of strange things in man and beast; the fact that the curtain never falls, and the huge machine never stops to take breath until 10:30 at night; the being associated after the style of criminals with a number, having your name or number shot into a slot in the proscenium arch to introduce you to your audience; the shortness of your reign, and the consequent necessity of capturing your audience on sight—all this, and some other things, make the first plunge unique in the actor's experience.[21]

And yet he also notes its significance for coming to terms with the changing social conditions and cultural values associated with the new mass market for goods and services. "The vaudeville theatre," he suggests, "belongs to the era of the department store and the short story. It may be a kind of lunch-counter art."[22]

In the context I have been developing, these comments reveal how the incorporation of show business was redefining performers' consciousness of themselves as artists, as well as transforming their awareness of the possibilities of their art within a new cultural context. The more particular issue, and the one that will be pursued in more detail for the rest of this part of the chapter, is the claim that the consolidation of the vaudeville system was responsible for shifting the responsibility for artistic production onto the circuits and the booking agents. A significant aspect of this claim concerns the degree to which popular entertainers were in a position to take control of, and thus define, the contents of their acts, and what they might have lost or given up in the process of transferring their managerial responsibilities to the vaudeville combines and the booking agencies. This problem has implications that reach far beyond popular entertainment into the study of mass cultural production and corporate reform more generally, and involves us in some basic questions of individual and collective agency in such circumstances.[23]

One way to get at this problem is to compare the performers' experiences on the vaudeville circuits with similar social practices and institutions. For example, by 1900, there were an estimated 350,000 traveling salesmen doing business throughout the United States, numerous fraternal organizations that supported them, and several influential trade journals that highlighted their particular needs and concerns.[24] They criss-crossed the continent on trains, or rode horses and stagecoaches into remote regions, "drumming" up business for their companies and, in the process, transforming patterns of distribution and consumption. These men (and a very few women), however, did not exist independently of the manufacturing or wholesaling firms that relied on them; rather, they formed the basis for the emerging model of corporate production, with its emphasis on developing new models of commercial success. "Don't forget," the sales employees of the Du Pont Corporation were told at their firm's annual banquet, "you are part of an organization just as much as the bass drum is part of the orchestra—likewise, don't forget that bass drum solos are rather monotonous."[25]

Moreover, the claims made about the commercial salesmen were remarkably similar to those that were made about vaudeville performers. As Timothy Spears has shown, the restructuring of manufacturing and business enterprises in the late nineteenth century had a profound effect on the commercial traveler's professional identity and his role in the market place.[26] As salesmen were integrated into, and became essential parts of, the selling practices of the new corporate enterprises, they began to think of themselves primarily as performers, whose job was to continually reshape and refine their sales pitch in response to their customers' differing needs and expectations. Relying on the latest jokes, songs, and dances, as well as on detailed knowledge of each region or town they visited, "the commercial traveller adjusts himself to the wishes, reactions, and replies of the buyer," argued psychologist Hugo Munsterberg in 1913.[27]

The development of integrated sales networks enabled manufacturing firms to consolidate national markets for their goods and services, to control their competition, to streamline and regulate production, and to increase their profit margins substantially. Their sales departments were increasingly divided into geographic districts and bureaus, which were serviced by a series of branch offices whose staff answered directly to the senior management at the company's central offices. Decisions were made by a complex hierarchy of sales managers, district managers, assistant managers, accountants, and right down to the salesmen themselves, who made up a large percentage of the workforce.[28] A good example of this is the Du Pont Corporation, which pioneered many of the sales techniques that eventually became the standard for large-scale corporate enterprises. For example, in 1917, Du Pont and its subsidiaries had fifty-one employees in sales reporting to the Chicago office. Thirty of them were responsible for territories covering two to five Midwestern states, while twenty-three of the salesmen who reported to Chicago lived outside the Midwestern metropolis. "The effect of this highly developed, highly diffuse hierarchical structure," in social historian Olivier Zunz's view, "was that it spread the new corporate culture through scores of employees, and through them to customers."[29]

Traveling salesmen were thus critical to the process of incorporating the cities and towns of North America, and their vast rural hinterlands, into the processes and institutions of large-scale industrial production. Moreover, their sales practices were inseparable from the kinds of claims that were being made about the new corporate culture, particularly the widespread argument that these corporate enterprises were the necessary, and only, solution to the unpredictable and contradictory features of capitalist exchange. The basis of these claims also had a powerful mythic dimension, as historian Jackson Lears demonstrates. According to Lears, the arrival of a traveling salesman in town was "the primal scene in drama of capitalist 'modernization': the rootless representative of cosmopolitan values penetrates the pristine organic community, tempting it with glittering wares, disrupting its rhythms of life, and transfixing its credulous inhabitants with his hypnotic powers."[30]

The cultural appeal of this primal scene only intensified as nineteenth-century itinerant peddlers or confidence men, who frequently invoked magic and deception to justify their sales pitches, were transformed into a class of professional salesmen, equipped with manuals dedicated to the "science of salesmanship" and committed to an ideology of service to the values of the corporation, and, beyond that, to a corporate vision of society.[31] In this context, traveling salesmen exemplified the social conflicts and anxieties that accompanied the corporate reconstruction of American culture. On one level, they asserted an authentic relationship to their customers, one founded on personal trust, a respect for the values of the community, and an acknowledgment of people's ordinary desires and needs. On another level, their presence in communities was made possible by the processes of economic progress, technocratic efficiency, standardized modes of production, and centralized control that characterized the modern corporation. In either case, the debate centered on who controlled whom, on the claims and counterclaims made by, and for, the subjects of this new corporate culture, and the implications these claims had for emerging conceptions of a corporate self and society.

I will address these claims at greater length as we move deeper into the unique world of the vaudevillian. In the present context, however, I want to emphasize some of the ways in which expansion of the vaudeville circuits and the centralization of the booking system opened up questions of artistic authority and legitimacy. Take the following account by the actor Bennet Musson in which he describes a week of one-night stands. From cold dressing rooms to missed train connections to sleepless nights because of rowdy hotel rooms, Musson's narrative concerns the many problems faced by performers on the circuits. In particular, though, he documents the tensions that existed between different groups of performers. He recounts,

> You have heard other actors refer to one-night standers as "jays" and "yaps" and say that "anything is good enough for them." You have seen these players slight their performances, and when the audience received them coldly, you have heard players say that the performance was "over their heads"—the most foolish of all theatrical ideas. But you don't hold to this opinion; you are a wise actor—that is why you are getting a good salary. Also, you know, incidentally, that if you are ever to be a star, you must have a following all over the country.[32]

There are two things worth noting about this passage: first, popular success was explained in terms of the national spread of the circuits ("to be a star, you must have a following all over the country"); and, second, a performer's position within the vaudeville system was based on how he conceived of his artistic value ("you are a wise actor—that is why you are getting a good salary"). Moreover, what Musson's account confirms above all (as Royle's also does) is that the relationship between performers and their audiences in vaudeville was not a straightforward one; recognition of one by the other involved both groups in complicated issues of judgment, status, artistic value, dependence and independence, self-knowledge and wisdom. And the relevance of these issues relied, for the most part, on a set of claims about the possibilities and constraints of corporate culture on people's lives.

The most important of these claims appeared in an editorial in *Billboard* on April 20, 1901: "It has been estimated," noted the editors, "that not less than from 7,000 to 10,000 vaudeville performers who work the theatres in the winter are engaged in parks and at fairs during the summer months. A good performer of this kind is employed nearly the year round." The paper then goes on to suggest that, above all, such continuous employment throughout the year was evidence that "the vaudeville performer owns himself."[33] For the editors of *Billboard*, it was the restructuring of vaudeville into national and international circuits, and the inclusion within those circuits of various off-season entertainments in parks and fairs, that made year-round employment feasible in the first place. Far from contradicting their claim about self-ownership, the new vaudeville combines made these claims of autonomy possible in the first place.

The transition from nineteenth- to twentieth-century forms of cultural production thus involved performers in a process of redefining and revaluing older concepts of artistic practice, but in terms consistent with the corporate realities that were reshaping Americans' day-to-day existence. By incorporating performers into a national system of circuits, and centralizing the booking procedures, the vaudeville managers opened up a social space for the development of a huge class of professional entertainers who were now in a position to achieve unprecedented wealth and fame as stars on the big-time circuits. At the same time, and as a consequence of this process, performers became acutely aware of the costs of such a system, especially the vast disparities between the various levels of show business and the many practices that the managers developed to maximize their profits from each act.

The Theatre Owners Booking Association (TOBA) was in many ways emblematic of these changes. In the first decades of the century, numerous theaters either owned or managed by African Americans were established to cater for the thousands of African American artists who were earning a living in vaudeville. In 1912 a vaudeville performer, Sherman Dudley, proposed that African American owners should set up their own circuit. One of Dudley's supporters, actress Emma Griffin, wrote that such a circuit would offer performers "adequate salaries and good dates rather than be at the mercy of white speculators, who will often take advantage of the helplessness of the colored performers and refuse to give either the opportunity or the money to which she or he is justly entitled. There is nothing to brag about in being on 'white time' unless there is a square deal for all concerned."[34] According Sylvester Russell in the *Freeman*, by 1918 Dudley had built a "successful and stable circuit" with shorter jumps that covered much of the Southeast and which provided performers with anything from a fourteen- to a twenty- week route.[35]

The following year Dudley joined with two other owners, Sam Reevin and Martin Klein, to form a new circuit, the United Vaudeville Circuit, so that he could provide his performers with a full forty-week route. The three owners also had a stake in the white-owned Southern Consolidated Vaudeville Circuit and, after a series of internal struggles for control of this business, they formed an even larger network of theaters. In 1921, however, Dudley's plans to take control of the so-called colored houses in the southern states, and thereby improve working conditions for African American performers, were disrupted by the formation of the TOBA.[36] According to the *Chicago Star*, this new enterprise "is a 'Lily White' syndicate of houses and managers whose patronage is Negro."[37] After a tense round of negotiations, Dudley's Southern Consolidated Vaudeville circuit joined the TOBA and he was appointed to run its Washington office. Although he continued to play a role in this enterprise, his ambition to create an organization that would "do its utmost for Negro performers" was effectively overturned. The new circuit became notorious for its treatment of African American performers and eventually gained full control of vaudeville routes in the South.[38]

The circuits were the most powerful means of enforcing and, in many cases, exacerbating the disparities between performers. This included edicts that banned artists appearing on one circuit from appearing on another, the censorship of those entertainers who signed with rival booking agencies, and well-documented cases of exploitation by many small-time managers on circuits such as the TOBA. A clear sense of this comes from those accounts by performers that describe in detail the challenges of touring.

Even though in her autobiography Sophie Tucker is highly critical of conditions on the circuits and complains at length about the many pressures and expectations she had to deal with, she never abandons her basic faith in show business as a distinctive way of life, and, more important, she frequently refers to it as a context for individual and collective transformation. Moreover, her narrative is primarily about the problem of recognition: what it takes to go from being "nobody" to being "somebody," and how that transition affects a person's sense of who she is and where she belongs. In Tucker's memoir, furthermore, popular songs are the critical medium for the transformations she undergoes, as well as forming the basis for her reflections on the meaning of theatrical success. She talks at length about how her way of performing, or what she calls "putting over," a song enables her to connects with an audience. *Some of These Days* is, in many ways, the archetypal show business story in that Tucker does not simply list the details of her career, but weaves her narrative of vaudeville success into the broader contours of American history. "I was born on the road," she begins. "Not on the Orpheum, the Pantages, Keith, or any other of the circuits I've travelled since. The road I mean is a long, rutted track that leads away from Russia across Poland to the Baltic."[39]

Tucker started out on the small-time Park Circuit during the summer of 1907, and it was during her first couple of seasons that she began to develop her theories of vaudeville performance:

The Park Circuit kept actors working from June until Labour Day. We played the smaller cities in New York, New Jersey, Pennsylvania, and Ohio, with one-week or three-day stands in each place. . . . In each place I played I would ask the manager for a return date before I left. "I promise to have new songs," I would tell him. And when I got a return engagement I kept my word. Something new, that was what counted with audiences. After a few months I found the managers were asking the office if I had any open time. Meanwhile, I learned that by playing return engagements quickly the audiences remembered me.[40]

Tucker then describes some of the other techniques she developed so as to establish her legitimacy as an artist, as well as opening up a creative space in which she could begin to take control of her act: "I started a practice of giving the stage crew a dollar every week to buy smokes," she says. "Another dollar went weekly to the orchestra leader, to 'buy a cigar.' Those two dollars bit into my thirty-five per cent, but they paid in the end. I found when I came back to play those houses again that I had good friends who were ready to help my put my act across."[41]

For Tucker, traveling the small-time circuits was a process of trial and error. It provided her with an education in the art of success, while at the same time it enabled her to learn how to entertain an audience. Initially, she modified her act in response to the suggestions of managers and agents, adopting a "blackface" persona and emphasizing her "coon song" style. As a result of her efforts to personalize relationships on the circuits, especially with the stagehands, publicists, and house managers, she eventually had enough support to unmask herself, to define her act on her own terms. There is more to be said about this moment of unmasking in the next chapter. For the moment, however, it is enough to reiterate the emphasis she places on the process of trouping and the practices she developed in order to feel at home on the circuits.

If we compare Tucker's experiences with those of Harpo Marx, the issues of artistic legitimacy and control are brought even more clearly into focus. "The vaudeville circuits that guaranteed an act thirty weeks of work for a season wanted no part of us," writes Marx. "We put up with whatever we could find for ourselves: one-night stands, conventions, picnics, benefits, anything that guaranteed a minimum of dinner and train fare."[42] Marx's narrative, too, is primarily instructional, emphasizing the distance he and his family traveled on their way to popular success, and confirming just how much the concepts and practices of these new forms of entertainment were derived from movement between the small-time and the big-time circuits.

We had no itinerary. We took the train until we came to a town. We got off the train, walked to the local theatre or "air-dome," made a deal for a percentage of the box-office take, plastered the town with posters announcing our show, opened, and prayed for the best. If we made more than train money, we stayed the night in the cheapest hotel or boardinghouse we would find and took the morning train out of town. If we couldn't afford this, we slept on the night-train coach. If we couldn't afford even the train, we walked. . . . We were completely at the mercy of local managers and booking agents. If they ran off with our share of receipts they had promised us, we had nobody to appeal to. There was nothing we could do except pick up our bags and start walking to the next town, before we got thrown in the jig as vagrants.[43]

In many respects, it is easy to focus almost exclusively on the big-time vaudeville and identify its links with theaters, booking agencies, publishing companies, songwriters, lyricist, publicists, banks, railways companies, and so on. Furthermore, the perspective we tend to assume in most cases is that of the cultural critic or manager or booking agent or successful artist, secure in her or his study, office, or hotel suite, in one of the major metropolitan centers (Howell's column for *Harper's Magazine*, the "Editor's Easy Chair," exemplified this perspective). And the entertainment industry encourages us to inhabit such perspectives, so as to reinforce its central claims and affirm its mythology. But it is clear from Marx's account that there was another, indistinct level of show business, often difficult to perceive, that existed below small-time circuits and encompassed the most marginal or invisible performers. In most cases, this shadowy world of chitlin circuits, tent shows, or medicine shows appears only as the negation of popular success, obscuring the connections between its origins and the big-time circuits. "Of all those rinky-dink dumps I played," wrote Ethel Waters, "nothing was worse than the Monogram Theatre in Chicago. It was close to the El [train], and the walls were so thin that you stopped singing—or telling a joke—every time a train passed. Then when the noise died down, you continued right where you left off."[44] In her autobiography, Waters repeatedly stresses that the more successful a performer was, the easier it became to forget where her ideas and practices had come from, and to recall why she was successful to begin with. In Waters's view, understanding the experiences of performers on the small-time or segregated circuits offers us a way of remaking those connections and rethinking out understanding of show business.

We can now begin to appreciate the extent to which the circuits were inseparable from the way performers were coming to understand the meaning of artistic success, and to measure their social worth as popular artists. As the jazz clarinetist Garvin Bushell noted, "Your social value was set according to your rating in show business. If you were a big-time act you came into contact with big-time people."[45] Moreover, the policies and managerial practices that had come to characterize life on the big-time circuits in the first decades of the twentieth century set the terms of debate about the impact of mass entertainment on American culture and the effects of the corporate control of show business on performers' sense of artistic worth.[46] The importance of these accounts is that they focus our attention on, first, the relationship between vaudeville's performers and its managers; second, how the qualities of "showmanship" identified with the vaudeville stage opened out onto broader questions about the meaning of success in the performing arts; and, third, the significance of the corporate reconstruction of entertainment for defining concepts of mass culture and mass entertainment.

The consolidation of the circuits throughout North America became the basis for the claim that vaudeville had a "wider appeal than any other form of stage entertainment."[47] Thus instituted, the circuits became indispensable to performers' conception of their art, the conviction they brought to their act, and their understanding of a mutual dependence on audiences and managers alike. We might say then that on the circuits a new form of life was invented by the vaudeville managers and the booking agents for American popular performers, and that it was the emergence of this form of life that explains many of the claims that were made about the significance of show business, as well as the position of musicians within it. In the next two chapters, we will consider the kinds of social practices and contexts that formed the basis for such claims.

CHAPTER THREE

Rites of Passage

If, as I want to suggest, the institutionalization of vaudeville invented a new form of life for popular performers, then we need to know a bit more about that life and why certain claims were made for it. To help us to get a better sense of these claims, I want to return to the problem of what it meant to entertain an audience on the vaudeville stage. This raises a number of issues relating to the way in which performers came to understand the value of their practices, and how they then explained their successes and failures not just to themselves as a community of performers, but to their audiences as well. One way to get a perspective on these issues is to examine the entertainment rituals that emerged as part of the corporate reform of the vaudeville system. Such entertainment rituals were essential to the continuous reproduction of vaudeville as an idealized space for achieving popular success, and their basis in everyday moments of exchange derived from the new conditions of the industrial city and the corporate institutions that were taking shape there.

As pointed out in the introduction, Albert McLean has gone the furthest of anyone with this kind of structural analysis. He argues that the vaudeville aesthetic answered to specific psychological needs of Americans as they adjusted to enormous social, political, cultural, and economic changes taking place in their day-to-day lives. "As ritual," he claimed, "vaudeville arose in an era of crisis to offer the American people a definitive rhythm, a series of gestures which put man back in the center of his world, a sense of human community, and an effective emotional release. In this respect, for all its similarity with European entertainments, vaudeville was a uniquely American achievement and fulfilled uniquely American needs."[1] Out of the flexibility of its form, the focus on the accelerated climax toward the headline act, the quick transitions in mood, tone, and tempo, the oscillation between high-cultural pretension and low-cultural parody, the huge bureaucratic and technical apparatus on which performers relied, and the relentless recycling of familiar routines, songs, and jokes, there emerged a fantasy world of infinite human possibility and unprecedented material fulfillment.[2] In McLean's view, it was the ritual structure of vaudeville through which Americans primarily encountered the myths of the new corporate culture and negotiated their place within it.

McLean's analysis raises a number of important interpretive issues around the meaning and practice of ritual in contemporary societies. In this chapter I want to explore some of his claims in more detail, especially those in which he relates vaudeville to new experiences of self and society.[3] More precisely, I want to concentrate on the ritual passages that performers took from being a nobody in the audience to becoming somebody on the stage. These passages were particularly important because they framed the larger issue of a performer's popularity and, in a more complex way, the kinds of relationships that developed between artists and audiences: Why were some performers more popular than others? How did they become so? What were audiences responding to in an act? Explanations by way of personal appeal or charisma or talent only get us so far; they were part of the way people within show business explained their success to each other and to their audiences. The structural account I am proposing here shifts our focus on to the problem of why certain values and practices became prevalent when they did, and the circumstances in which they did so.

I am using the terms *ritual* and *rite* in a very definite sense. In an influential study of Brazilian society, the anthropologist Roberto DaMatta suggests that rituals are those cultural practices through which people recognize the values in their lives that are permanent. At the same time, however, he also claims that rites are essential "not only in transmitting and reproducing values but also in simultaneously creating and constructing them." In DaMatta's analysis, moreover, the purpose of a ritual is to dramatize fundamental aspects of the social world, such as class distinctions, kinship relations, forms of power, or cultural ideals, in order to raise fundamental questions about our place in the world. They do this by condensing some aspect, element, or relationship in a culture that is spotlighted and set in relief, and which then comes to symbolize a common social identity. As complex sequences of symbolic actions, rituals thus rely on and reproduce a heightened sense of collective experience, even as they also open up the possibility of reflecting on the real world or envisioning an alternative to it.[4]

Like so many other success stories told by vaudeville performers, Sophie Tucker's autobiography begins with a series of intimate exchanges between parents, siblings, teachers, friends, and acquaintances concerning her aspirations to become a performer. "If I had a dollar for every greasy dish I've washed I'd be the richest woman in show business today," she begins. "Hell, you may say. What kind of a start-off is that for the story of the Last of the Red-hot Mamas? Where's the glamour? And the sex-appeal?" But this was precisely the issue at stake in vaudeville: her particular immigrant working-class background and the social experiences she describes were essential to the corporate reconstruction of the entertainment industry; her experiences enabled her to dramatize the passage from one kind of life to another as a possibility open to anyone; and yet her life was also unimaginable outside of show business. "There may be things in the story that you don't expect," she observes. "And maybe some of them you will wish had been left out. But that's life, isn't it?" Moreover, her narrative personalizes this process, linking performers and audiences within the larger set of claims about the recognition of talent and about the value of entertainment. "You can see," she declares, "that my story *has* to be the story of show business during the past thirty years."[5]

The surest way to understand what is happening in these early chapters of Tucker's text is to focus on the sequence of events that frames her decision to go into show business. It starts in her singing class at her school, where the teacher "usually called on me to lead the singing. And did that make me feel proud?"[6] She then discovered that she could make extra money in her parents' restaurant by performing popular songs for the customers.

> At the time the great popular hit was "Just Break the News to Mother." Everybody sang it, including me. At suppertime, when the restaurant tables were filled and the place steamy with the plates of hot food, I would stand up in that narrow space by the door and sing the tearjerker with all the drama I could put into it. At the end of the chorus, between me and onions, there wasn't a dry house in the house. . . . Later, when I went round to wait on the tables, a lot of customers would slip me an extra tip, "for the entertainment."[7]

Her ability to get over a song separated her from the group, changing her social position from one of anonymity and marginality within her community (as a child who was not celebrated for her looks, and was confined to waiting tables) to one in which she was recognized and called upon to provide the entertainment for that community.

The most significant shift occurred at school, however, when one of her teachers acknowledged her abilities. "Mr. Emerson, the music teacher at the Brown School, was talking to one of the grade teachers. As I passed by, I heard him say: 'Sophie Abuza has personality.'" The problem was that she had no idea what he was talking about. "What was personality?" she asked. And no one else she talked to had any idea either: "The word that was to make Dale Carnegie famous was beyond Mama. She had neither the English nor the patience to explain it. . . . 'Personality, is it? What next? You should get to dishwashing, and not fill your head with craziness.'"[8] Of the many issues Tucker identifies in these opening pages, it was this one (along with her mother's disavowal of it) that proved central to how, first, she came to understand what popular success meant and, second, how she ultimately came to achieve it.

As Tucker describes it, her personality was essential to her ability to take control of an audience, as well as being the crucial element in the kinds of relationships she had with those around her, both professional and personal. But first she had to discover what it meant to have a personality, and why it was even important for a performer to develop one in the first place. She did this in the first instance by attracting professional performers to her parents' restaurant by offering to entertain them with their meals, and then doing comic impersonations of their routines. They, in turn, started to acknowledge her ability to put over a song by paying her substantial tips, as well as writing down the lyrics to some of their own material for her to learn. She then spent some of the money she earned on going to shows with her friend Doris at Poli's Vaudeville Theatre and the Hartford Opera House, which became a ready source of new songs for the routines she was developing for the restaurant. And, finally, she started to frequent an amateur talent quest in Riverside Park in Hartford, where she began as the piano accompanist for her sister Anna.

At first Tucker was shy about going on stage, partly because of her weight, but then the audience began to call out for her to do her singing act: "That was what really started me thinking seriously about going into show business. I said to myself: suppose you could earn a living by singing and making people laugh, wouldn't that be better than spending your life drudging in a kitchen?" Each one of these moments forms part of a ritual sequence through which Tucker came to recognize herself as a popular performer. Only once she had arrived at a level of self-awareness about what it meant to appear in front of, to respond to, and to find an answering response in an audience was she then able to ask herself: "But how? How did a person get started in show business?"[9]

The principal point that DaMatta makes, and one I want to develop here, is that such ritual moments, and the questions that follow from them, have no substantive content. On the contrary, any gesture or image or sound or statement in a society can be ritualized. "Everything in the world," he explains, "can be personified, spotlighted, and ultimately reified. Ritual does not pose the problem of substance but rather the problem of contrasts and relationships. That is why, in studying the social world, it is absolutely necessary to take as our starting point the relationships between its most important moments: the daily round and the festival, waking life and dream, the real and the paradigmatic personage."[10] The ritual sequence is one in which the most banal and trivial actions and exchanges in the everyday world acquire exceptional meaning, and are then subjected to and transformed by the specific dynamics of the rite.

In the first instance this involves a process of displacement, when something like a handshake, for example, goes from being a greeting between two friends to becoming a symbol of universal brotherhood. "[The rite] individualizes some element given in the 'natural' infrastructure," DaMatta suggests, "which is appropriated and transformed by the collectivity into a social thing and then serves to frame an ideology and actually becomes an ideology."[11] In the case of vaudeville, this natural element was the performer's personality. Although in many ways intangible, and the source of much mystification, this conception of a public self both framed the ideology of entertainment—to succeed you must have "it"—and was the basis for the new modes of performance derived from it. In the performance of popular songs, for example, the singer had to inhabit the "I" of the song with her personality or, to put it another way, the singer's personality had to become the "I" of the song.[12]

Everything about Tucker's narrative conveys the importance of personality to the social identities of popular performers. By focusing primarily on those instances in which her talent for performing was isolated from the chaotic flow of everyday relationships, family problems, and social expectations, and then transferred to the highly artificial and reified world of the stage, she endowed personality with ideological significance. Having one was not simply a means to becoming somebody in vaudeville; instead, the performance of her personality opened up an idealized world in which artist and audience recognized in each other their own human potential to transcend their daily routines. This interdependence of self and other thus formed the condition of possibility for vaudeville's claim to be all things to all people, and was also vital to Tucker's belief that a life in show business was the only life she had ever wanted. To achieve this kind of mutual self-realization, however, she had to make two important discoveries: a stage name and her show business identity.

> I found a room for five dollars a week, which included breakfast, on Second Avenue near St. Mark's Place. I lived there for several weeks while I tried all the doors in Tin Pan Alley without success. Meanwhile my funds were running low. I knew I must save every fifty cents. I grudged every cent I had to spend on food. One evening it occurred to me perhaps I could sing in one of the restaurants in the neighborhood and earn a meal that way. Around Eighth Street was the Café Monopol. I went in and said to the proprietor: "I'm hungry, and I haven't got any money. I'm a singer. If I sing for your customers tonight will you give me my dinner?"
>
> He thought for a moment. "What kind of songs do you sing?" he demanded.
>
> "Popular songs," I told him. "I'll sing what the customers ask for. I used to do that in a restaurant in Hartford, my home town."
>
> "All right," he agreed. Then he asked me my name.
>
> I had my mail sent to Mrs. Louis Tuck, care of General Delivery, as of course that was my name. But "Mrs. Tuck" didn't sound right for a singer.
>
> "Sophie Tucker," I told him.
>
> Right like that a career was born.[13]

There are a number of important themes that emerge from this exchange. First, Tucker's rebirth as a popular singer enacts a fundamental moment within the ritual sequence of popular entertainment. In finding the right-sounding name for her career, she undergoes a transition from being a nobody, whose identity was derived from her social position as either a daughter or a wife, to being somebody, a personality, whose identity was derived from and spoke to the essential values of show business.[14] The critical point to take note of here is the association of theatrical success with taking on her new name. Although her name retains elements of and remains connected to her former identity, it is the act of naming that both expresses and produces the moment of self-realization. As Elsie Clews Parsons argued, around the same time that Tucker was becoming one of the leading stars in vaudeville, "the *new* woman means the woman not yet classified, perhaps not classifiable, the woman *new* not only to men, but to herself."[15]

Themes of self-production through naming were a major part of the way in which female performers redefined the theatrical space as one in which

they could experiment with their autonomy, as well as explore the limits of
their art. In an autobiographical sketch published in *Cosmopolitan Magazine* in 1922, Lillian Russell explained this process in detail:

> Then the question of a name occurred to me. I knew that if I used my
> own name, Helen Louise Leonard, my mother would be certain to see it.
> I told Mr. Pastor of my predicament without adding that I also felt that if
> I failed, I didn't want it to be under my own name. . . . When I went into
> his office the next day, I found Harry Sanderson, the house manager [of
> Pastor's Theatre], awaiting me with a huge square of heavy cardboard on
> which were printed many names. Together we went over them—then
> suddenly, in opposite corners, I saw two that I liked. I fitted them to-
> gether swiftly as I spoke them aloud. . . . "There," I said, "they stand out
> above all the names on that board. The L's in both of them make them
> musical. They're easy to say and to remember, LILLIAN RUSSELL—that's
> a lucky name. I'm going to choose it." . . . And thus I was rechristened
> as Lillian Russell—the name which I have always felt meant as much in
> my pursuit of success as all the hard work and the prayers and the faith
> I carried along with me.[16]

For Russell, the act of naming involved moving from her home—with all
the obligations and expectations identified with that particular place—into
the world of show business. However, it was only in retrospect that she
came to understand how finding the right stage name was the final, inte-
grative act in the passage from one social world to another. Moreover, in
undergoing this transformation, she had to experience something like a loss
of self, a realization that she was nobody, and that she knew nothing about
the world she was entering, "I had no self-consciousness the day my voice
was tried," she recalls in the article.[17] Although compressed into a single
idealized event, the ritual process Russell described was critical to the way
in which she established her claim to speak directly to, and for, her audience. Once she had a name, it could literally go up in lights, enabling her to
become both the object of her act—to perform in vaudeville was to acquire
and thus to make a name for oneself—and the medium through which she
was able to appeal to her audience.

Not only names, but faces, too, were an essential aspect of the rituals
of entertainment. In the passage from nobody to somebody, making a name
for oneself invariably required putting a face to the name, and so finding
out what it meant to be present to and for an audience. Once again, I want
to begin with a quote from Tucker's narrative, which foregrounds this issue

in a striking way. She began her career as a blackface performer, and in the first few years on the circuits, she was generally billed as "SOPHIE TUCKER WORLD-RENOWNED COON SHOUTER."[18] Following a rehearsal at the Howard Athenaeum Theatre in Boston, however, Tucker looked around for her stage trunk, which was nowhere to be found. It had been sent with a lot of other theatrical luggage to Lowell, Massachusetts, instead. When she inquired at the railway station, however, the baggage man assured her that she would get it back soon enough.

> "It'll come back all right, miss," he said comfortingly.
> "When?"
> "Sometime this afternoon. We'll get it right over to the theatre soon as it comes in. You'll have it in time to dress up pretty for the show tonight."
> "Tonight," I blared at him. "Hell! It's today's matinee I've got to think about. I'm a blackface comedienne and all my stuff is in that trunk."[19]

Faced with the prospect of going on the stage without any of her props, Tucker returned to the theater and spoke with the theater manager, who recommended going on without her black makeup. "Now," she reminded her readers,

> here's something funny. Remember, though, that I had never yet walked out on stage without some sort of disguise. It was the hardest thing in the world for me to step out of the wings in my tailored suit, white linen shirtwaist hastily pressed in the dressing room, with no covering on my blonde hair, and no make-up except lipstick, a dab of rouge, and a dusting of white powder. In tights and a G-string I wouldn't have felt more stripped. . . . The [orchestra] leader and the boys in the pit gaped at me. They expected blackface. So, of course, did the audience. I could see them consulting their programs. I'd have to explain . . . "You-all can see I'm a white girl. Well, I'll tell you something more: I'm not Southern. I grew up here in Boston, at 22 Salem Street. I'm a Jewish girl, and I just learned the Southern accent doing a blackface act for two years now. And, Mr. Leader, please play my song." . . . "That Lovin' Rag" got them started. They were right with me. All the time I was singing five numbers, six, seven, then eight, inwardly I was exulting: "I don't need blackface. I can hold an audience without it. I've got them eating right out of my hand. I'm through with blackface. I'll never black up again."[20]

Tucker's account in this passage raises a number of large and complicated issues about blackface minstrelsy in the context of vaudeville. Why was this practice of masking and unmasking so prevalent? And how did the process relate to the way in which performers came to understand the pathway to popular success? Most of the work that addresses Tucker's career focuses on the way in which immigrant Jewish blackface performers either undermined racist distinctions through a shared sense of mutual suffering, as Irving Howe does in *The World of Our Fathers*, or reinforced them by exploiting blackface in order to fully participate in the dominant white culture, as Michael Rogin argues in *Blackface, White Noise*.[21] Even though they reach very different conclusions, I want to connect their respective claims to the practices I have identified with the ritual passages that performers underwent as they entered show business.

Tucker's racial masquerade emerged in such a way as to raise deeply problematic and contradictory questions about the cultural origins of her act, as well as the claims she was making—especially through her choice of songs and gestures—about her ability to find a way to represent, and so physically embody, the specific desires and expectations of her audiences. There are two points that we need to keep in mind here. First, the decision to blacken up was not initially hers, but taken by a theater manager, Chris Brown, who had decided that this was the only suitable medium for someone of her physical size and looks. "This one's so big and ugly the crowd out front will razz her," he called to his assistant, as Tucker was getting ready to go on stage for Brown's weekly amateur tryout show. "Better get some cork and black her up." And, second, this was the moment of her big break into show business. "I felt sick and frightened inside," she recalled. "Then the pianist thumped out the opening chords and gave me a signal. That jolted me out of my stage fright. . . . What the hell? That crowd couldn't scare me now."

In spite of Brown's humiliating comments, Tucker was a hit with the audience and got herself signed with one of the best-known small-time booking agents, Joe Woods, who had been at her performance. "Joe Woods booked me on the small-time circuit at a salary of fifteen to twenty dollars a week in New York; twenty-five dollars a week when out of town. I'd been pulling down four or five times that at the [German] Village [the "high-class beer garden" in the Tenderloin District on Broadway, where she had a regular spot], but I didn't care," she wrote. "This, at last, was show business."[22]

Ultimately, her appearance on stage in blackface—and the fact that she devotes a chapter to it—highlights the importance of her passage from a threshold persona to her integration into the world of show business as a star. According to cultural anthropologist Victor Turner (whose analyses I am drawing on here), such threshold entities are "neither here nor there; they are betwixt and between the positions assigned and arrayed by law, custom, convention, and ceremonial. As such, their ambiguous and indeterminate attributes are expressed by a rich variety of symbols in the many societies that ritualize social and cultural transitions. Thus, liminality is frequently likened to death, to being in the womb, to invisibility, to darkness, to bisexuality, to wilderness, and to an eclipse of the sun or moon."[23]

The show business world Tucker describes in this passage is a largely unstable and shadowy one: basement dives, beer gardens, cheap boarding-houses, and other precarious areas of the city, including the Bowery and the midtown theater district. Although it reinforced the racism of American show business, blackface also provided Tucker with a set of familiar theatrical conventions, musical forms, and verbal materials—a type of theatrical currency—through which she was able to find a place for herself and explore the possibilities available to her within it.[24]

This same ritual sequence is also evident in accounts of other vaudeville performers. For example, Bert Williams's father recalled that as a young, aspiring performer he "studied just enough that he passed and his reports were good, but I am inclined to think that all the joy he ever got out of studying came from his own observations. Indeed he seemed delighted with each new achievement in mimicry and he developed this gift to a degree while he was only a child. We punished him for this at first, but soon discovered that the punishment was of no use."[25] Williams's family emigrated from the Bahamas to the United States about 1885, and it was not until after he completed high school that he discovered his interest in a career in show business. With some college friends, he undertook a small tour of the small coastal towns south of San Francisco, offering a range of "entertainments." Although the tour was a failure in just about every respect, he found he liked performing, and so he returned to San Francisco looking for further opportunities.

In her biography of Williams, Ann Charters describes how he

> spent hour after hour in the smoky, poorly lit "free and easies" of the Barbary Coast, the tough waterfront neighborhood [of San Francisco] where the damp, foggy streets were cluttered with ramshackle wooden taverns, shabby boarding houses, outfitters' shops, and cheap restaurants selling oyster loaf, one of the town's specialties. Under the gas lights of East Street or Steward Street, the taverns catered to the sailors on shore leave. Inside the crowded saloons waiters scurried to bring glasses of cheap lager

beer and whiskey to impatient customers, and the quiet, soft-spoken young singer had to shout his songs to be heard above the din.[26]

Having occupied the same sort of indeterminate space as Tucker had, the turning point for Williams, too, involved blacking up. "One day at Moore's Wonderland in Detroit," he recollected, "just for a lark, I blacked my face and tried the song, 'Oh, I Don't Know, You're Not So Warm.' Nobody was more surprised than I was when it went like a house on fire. Then I began to find myself. It was not until I was able to see myself as another person that my sense of humor developed."[27] Williams's comments underline how the connection between self-recognition and artistic success formed an integral part of this ritual process.

Another version of the sequence takes place in Ethel Waters's account of her growing awareness of her stage identity:

I had the most fun at Harrod Apartments on the days when I substituted for one of the chambermaids. I was allotted a half-hour to make up each room, but soon became so efficient I could finish the work in ten minutes. . . . Then I'd lock the door, stand in front of the full-length mirror, and transform myself in Ethel Waters, the great actress. I played all sorts of roles and also the audience, mugging and acting like mad. . . . First of all I'd applaud vociferously. When I played the "other woman" in the play I'd pretend she was some girl enemy of mine and hiss her shamelessly. Was *she* a terrible performer! . . . When I'd finished portraying all the roles I'd seen played by Negro stock companies I'd imitate the acts I'd seen at the Standard Theatre in Philadelphia. . . . The vaudeville half of the entertainment started with an announcement by the master of ceremonies: "And now, folks, the famous and spectacular Miss Ethel Waters will sing!" Again there was wild applause from the eager audience, followed by joyful cries: "Come on, Miss Waters! Please sing for us, Miss Waters!" . . . After a slight and dignified pause I'd persuade myself to bow graciously before the mirror. Sometimes I'd be so carried away by my own magnificent performance that I'd forget where I was or what I was doing. . . . In spite of all of this, my big ambition was not then show business. What I dreamed of was becoming the lady's maid and companion of some wealthy woman who was travelling around the world and would take me with her.[28]

This passage is rich in the kinds of symbolism that Turner refers to in his study. Waters's confusion about where she was or what she was doing prepares her passage from chambermaid to the star she imagines herself to be, even as she declares that she had no ambition to be in show business. Her situation was made even more complicated by the many physical, psychological, and institutional barriers that African American female performers had to overcome to even conceive a career in vaudeville (Waters's childhood experiences were marked by horrifying instances of domestic violence and neglect). More important, however, was the way in which she connected self-recognition to the moment of recognition by others. In this period, as she began to assume the manner of a performer, people frequently mistook her for one. "I was always pleased," she notes, "when they asked, 'Are you a show person?' But I'd tell them, 'No, I work as a scullion in the Harrod Apartments.'"[29] As I have already argued above, the movement from one sort of life to another, and the values and practices associated with this transition, were essential to performers' sense of legitimacy as popular artists. Not only did Waters's imaginary performances—both in private and in public—open up a space of self-recognition, but they also managed to dramatize the existential transformation from anonymity to stardom that was implied in the very structure of the circuits.

On and off the stage, vaudeville performers developed their acts in response to the new culture of consumption that was reshaping the city. They did this by extending their shows into the restaurants, the bars, the after-hours clubs, society parties, and onto the streets of the emerging entertainment districts. They explored the ritual power of words, phrases, rhythms, sounds, images, gestures to engage with people's everyday experiences. Their routines were based on the changing tempos of the city, connecting their art to the work rhythms of the factories and offices, the new media of mass communication, and changing ideas about human potential and social identity.[30] According to Charters, Williams and his stage partner, George Walker, used to

> stroll through the Tenderloin [District], talking in the crowded bars with friends under the large, slowly moving fans that vainly attempted to cool New York during the summer heat. Williams would tell stories in his lazy drawl, and he and Walker would soon be surrounded by listeners, until Walker would get tired of the place, settle the bill, take his straw hat from the rack, and move Williams along to the next café. They usually finished the evening at Marshall's Restaurant on Fifty-third Street, where a number of theatrical performers congregated. According to legend, Lillian Russell, Diamond Jim Brady, Anna Held, Florenz

Ziegfeld, and Weber and Fields sat and talked for hours at Marshall's, encouraged by the restaurant management to take "unlimited extended leisure."[31]

As they strolled, Williams and Walker underwent a series of transformations, from their on-stage personas as blackface performers, to nobodies on the street corner, and then back into blackface for the night's show. Their journey typified the ritual process I have described above, as the two men moved from the faceless anonymity of the crowded streets to the heightened visibility of the big-time theaters. Williams's well-known ballad, "Nobody," speaks to this ritual passage like no other vaudeville song I know. He combines within in it humility, sophistication, awkwardness, aloofness, and naivety to create a finely nuanced portrayal of the contradictions of city life.[32] The song's pathetic character, along with the hesitant way that Williams shuffled on and off the stage, embodied the dichotomies of success and failure, wealth and poverty, social acceptance and loneliness, turning Bunyan's Pilgrim into a Hapless Nobody looking for a break. Backed by a funereal brass accompaniment, Williams sang, mournfully, sliding from word to word, "I ain't never done nothin' to nobody, I ain't never got nothin' from nobody, no time. Until I get something from somebody, some time, I'll never do nothin' for nobody, no time."[33]

As with several of Williams's other songs, such as "I Thought I Was a Winner" and "Fortune-Telling Man," "Nobody" gave poignant expression to the contingency of the urban world, yet affirmed the city as a privileged context for social transformation as well. Even as he challenged the illusion of the theatrical space, by crossing into the public domain of the audience in order to become more like those he entertained, his character was forever seeking a way to escape from the confusion of the world, to find purpose and meaning in a context where none seemed to exist. This series of reversals, from street-corner "nobody" to blackface "somebody" and back again, formed the basis of Williams's act of unmasking, as he entered into, and came to exemplify, the mythologies of the entertainment industry.[34] The ritual sequences that framed these narratives thus simultaneously realized and reinforced the cultural and social hierarchies that characterized the vaudeville system, from the economic and aesthetic divisions between the various circuits, to the racialized, gendered, class-based, and ethnic distinctions that formed the contents of most popular acts on the circuits. In the next chapter I want to focus on the configuration of social relationships identified with vaudeville performance, and consider to what extent these transformed the social lives of performers and audiences alike.

CHAPTER FOUR

Elementary Structures

Whereas the last chapter examined the ritual processes through which vaudeville performers came to understand what it meant to be a popular artist, in this chapter we will concentrate on how they accounted for their relationships with each other. The pages of *Billboard*, *Variety*, the *New York Clipper*, and the other trade magazines are full of news items about rivalries and feuds between vaudeville performers, reports of well-known acts breaking apart, followed by announcements of little-known acts coming together. Stories of celebrity gossip, social club news, fund-raising efforts, and performer obituaries fill in the remaining print space between the lists of performances, feature articles, show reviews, and pages of advertising. Likewise, interviews with or autobiographies by performers are frequently preoccupied with backstage friendships, partnerships, love affairs, and (in some cases, life-long) feuds with other performers.[1] If, as Albert McLean suggests, vaudeville was raising questions about the mythic identity of "the people," especially the forms of community and the collective values that were possible within the emerging corporate culture of the United States, then these backstage relationships were as essential to its meaning as those that were formed, and came to define, what performers did when they took the stage.

There are two important points to make about this idea. First, the claim that there is no business like show business is in large part a claim for and about a specific kind of community and a set of values deriving from it. And, second, the claim speaks to a widely accepted view among show-business people that however difficult it is, whatever the price you might pay personally, a career in show business is preferable to any other. "Show business has been my life," declared Sophie Tucker. "I wouldn't have had any other. It is the life I always wanted."[2] I want to spend some time in this chapter setting out what such a claim might have involved for performers, especially why it became so important for them to identify show business with a life unlike any other. This discussion entails questions about how performers made sense of their successes and their failures. But it also raises a number of quite complicated issues to do with the way in which the circuits affected the commitments they made to each other as family-members, business partners, artistic collaborators and friends.

"There are too many grifters and grafters among them [show business people]," declared Tucker's mother. "They have no real homes; no sense of responsibility. That kind don't care what they do on the road." So far as she was concerned, "marriage, having babies, and helping her husband get ahead were career enough for any woman." However much she tried, though, Tucker was unable to convince her mother that "it wasn't a career I was after. It was just that I wanted a life that didn't mean spending most of it at the cookstove and the kitchen sink."[3]

This brief exchange between mother and daughter highlights a number of important issues for understanding the way in which vaudeville both appealed to its audiences and legitimated its artistic and institutional practices. Above all, the theaters opened up an imaginative space within which both performers and their audiences redefined their understanding of the relationship between their day-to-day existence and the experience of going to a show. Tucker's determination to change her life also underlines the extent to which vaudeville presented significant opportunities for young women from immigrant backgrounds to "make it" in American culture. In addition, she sets up an opposition that shapes the whole narrative: between show business and her home life.

This passage suggests that issues of kinship, friendship, and other intimate relationships were far more important to performers' self-understanding than we might expect. "In every show I have been in, as the star, or headlining the bill," writes Tucker, "I have known every single person in the cast. I've made it like one big family."[4] Likewise, the comedian George Jessel recalled in an interview that vaudeville "gave us great camaraderie. There were circuits where you played twenty, thirty weeks with the same bill and you became like one whole big family. It was warm and comfortable."[5] But what kind of family was it?

In a recent study of kinship, anthropologist Marshall Sahlins argues that family relations rely on what he calls the "mutuality of being," which, he explains, covers "people who are intrinsic to one another's existence": that is, the concept refers to "persons who belong to one another, who are parts of one another, who are co-present in each other, whose lives are joined and interdependent."[6] This seems to offer an effective way of understanding why so many performers claimed that the "vaudeville family" formed the basis for their day-to-day interactions with each other, with the theatrical managers, and with their audiences. Moreover, "mutuality of being" also suggests an approach to the more complicated issue of how family acts, or two-acts involving a parent and a child, or those made up of two siblings (such as Adele and Fred Astaire), became integral to show business.[7]

The clearest example of this can be found in George M. Cohan's auto-biography, *Twenty Years on Broadway*, which charts his coming of age on the vaudeville circuits in the last decades of the nineteenth century, along with his subsequent triumph as a playwright, actor, and producer on Broad-way.[8] The problem that Cohan's book raises is how to succeed as a popular performer. But rather than focus solely on presenting a practical guide to success, or simply celebrating his artistic output, instead his narrative takes his readers inside the world of the popular vaudevillian in order to show how them just how much his prodigious talent was dependent on his twenty-year apprenticeship as a child performer with his family's act—the Four Cohans—as well as the many opportunities that were opened up for him as a result of their network of friends and business partners. At least three-quarters of the text describes in great detail the day-to-day exchanges that took place between the members of his family—his parents, Jerry and Nellie Cohan, and his sister, Josie Cohan—as they endeavor to make it in big-time vaudeville. The rest of Cohan's book covers his various attempts to fashion his own career, as well as documenting his (at-times turbulent) relationships with booking agents, stagehands, managers, and the group of performers who formed his immediate circle of colleagues and friends.

Twenty Years on Broadway is structured more broadly around the mul-titude of (often unexpected) successes, as well as the significant number of failures, that Cohan experienced in an effort to establish himself as an en-tertainer on *his own terms*, even as he acknowledged the extent to which his career was dependent on those closest to him. While he spends con-siderable time on his family, he also foregrounds the enormous influence that B. F. Keith had on their careers. To a large extent their lives were so thoroughly entwined that he and his family's careers were in many ways inseparable from Keith's increasingly dominant position within the vaude-ville system. Cohan recalls,

My father had just disbanded his "road show," and he and my mother were appearing in a little store on Washington Street in Boston. This

store space had been converted into a theatre by a man named B. F. Keith.
My sister, Josephine, who had also been taken out of school, was already
in Boston when I arrived. We had a real family reunion that night. Mr.
Keith attended the affair and presented Josie with a rag doll, and slipped
me a toy balloon. . . . I learned afterward that B. F. [Keith] was trying to
jolly my dad into believing that "hard work hurt no man" and that "six
performances a day was little enough for any ambitious actor to do."[9]

According to Cohan, whenever the family found themselves at the close of
a tour, or without a regular booking, for several years they invariably ended
up booked at one of Keith's theaters.[10]

At each critical juncture in Cohan's life, opportunities were either
opened up or closed off depending on how each family member responded
to the demands made upon them, whether by other members of the family,
other performers, or the different managers and booking agents they relied
on. And he often referred to the consequences that a decision or a performance involving one member of the family had for them all. Following the
closure of "Jerry Cohan's Irish Hibernia" in 1888, for example, the family
returned to Keith's theater for a six-month run. It was during this run that
Cohan first appeared on stage as a violinist. "It came about in a peculiar
way," he wrote.

> An act disappointed one Monday morning, and Josie, who had been prac-
> ticing grotesque dancing for some time, now was rushed in to "fill the
> gap." Josie made a hit. In fact, a big enough hit to be retained the second
> week. She was billed as 'LITTLE JOSIE COHAN: America's youngest and
> most graceful skirt dancer." . . . I wasn't exactly envious of my sister's
> success, but I must admit that my nose was a bit disjointed and I was
> bound not to be outdone.[11]

Without telling his family what he was up to, Cohan had been secretly
rehearsing a trick violin act, and as soon as he heard of Josie's booking,
he immediately went to Keith's newly appointed manager, E. F. Albee, and
convinced him to take him on as well, starting on the same Monday bill as
his sister. According to Cohan, he suggested to Albee that he pay him what
he thought the act was worth once he had appeared for a full week; Albee
responded by putting $6 in an envelope for the young performer following
his last show on the Saturday night.

Cohan here places great emphasis on his attempts to achieve autonomy
as a young performer, which often turned on his ability to compete success-

fully with his equally talented sister or, alternatively, his frustration with and attempts to alter his father's decisions. However, on closer inspection, the passage also suggests the extent to which his theatrical persona was ultimately an expression of the deep affinity that existed between his parents, his sister, and himself, as well as his life-long connection to those other performers on whom he depended for support. Two examples are sufficient to make this point clear. In 1892 the Cohans were in Buffalo, New York, playing a series of variety dates at Robinson's Theatre. Initially engaged for a week, the family ended up putting on sketches, specialties, dancing acts, farces, pantomimes, melodramas, and any other form of entertainment that the management demanded from them (which demonstrates how versatile a vaudeville act had to be), well into the following summer. "During this engagement," Cohan recalled, "I played everything from Boucicault's Irish heroes to black-faced comedy parts. One week I played my own mother's father, mother being cast for the old General's daughter, and I for the General."[12]

The other example occurred a year later, in 1893, when the family performed for the first time at Keith's Union Square Theatre. As they entered the stage door of the theater, the house manager passed them news from B. F. Keith instructing the family to reorganize their act. "Tell Cohan family not to do four act," ran the telegram. "Mr. and Mrs. Cohan in sketch and two children in single turns better for New York audience."[13]

While the family reluctantly acquiesced to this demand, when Cohan discovered that he had been given the opening spot on the program, his whole world fell apart. "They can't do this to me," he hollered. "I won't be disgraced by these guys. I'd rather be a tramp in the gutter than stand for this." Having waited for so long to perform in New York City, Cohan found now himself relegated to the most difficult spot on a vaudeville program. "For several minutes I ranted and raved," he continues, "and finally threw myself on top of a trunk and wept bitter tears."[14]

Rather than urging their son to set aside his concerns for the sake of the family, however, both parents demonstrated remarkable empathy with the youngest member of the family (his mother "was having a little cry herself"), while his sister made an even stronger declaration of solidarity. "If Georgie feels this way about it," she announced, "let's not play the engagement at all. Let's all quit and be done with it."[15] And his parents immediately agreed with her; this is what they *all* should do.

These examples exemplify what Sahlins means when he refers to people's sense of kinship as a form of belonging to one another.[16] The Cohans' discussion about canceling their New York premier (in the end they decided to go on anyway) was mediated by the feelings of mutuality they had developed for each other as a family act. How they defined themselves as performers, along with their approach to the opportunities that were afforded them, was bound up in the specific claims that were made about family acts on the circuits: that such acts exhibited a shared sense of existence that was derived from, but also reproduced, the larger claims of show business as a unique world, with its own set of laws and values, that existed beyond either the conventional models of work or family.

This sense of mutuality was brought into even sharper focus several weeks later when another telegram appeared, this time offering Josie a single spot at another of the big-time theaters in New York, Koster and Bial's on West 23rd Street. Cohan's parents decided to accept the offer, even though it clearly undermined their trademark identity, as well as dividing the family into individual acts. Only Cohan believed they should refuse the offer. "It's an insult," he retorted, "that's what I think of it."[17] After a "peppery" family meeting, however, he too eventually conceded. Such was her success on opening night (Cohan described his sister as a "heavenly dancer") that she was subsequently booked at the theater indefinitely, along with a series of other high-profile engagements.[18]

It is clear from this example that the Cohans' identity as a family act also empowered the two children to intervene at important moments in the family's career. Even though both siblings were beginning to consolidate their own artistic identities, the future of their family act was their principal concern. "Georgie, I don't think we're managing ourselves very well," remarked Josie Cohan, "and it's up to you and me to have a chat with mother and dad and decide just what our future is going to be. . . . We've got to look to the future and make up our minds pretty soon whether we're going to stick together or not. . . . I think we should."[19]

Ruth Finnegan's influential study of amateur music making in the English town of Milton Keynes suggests how we might begin to interpret this decision by the Cohans to stick together. Instead of interpreting texts, scores, and recordings, she focuses more on how people make music together. Of most interest to her are what she describes as the "pathways" individuals take in order to participate in a range of musical activities, and the terms that performers use to articulate their musical experiences to themselves and to others. Ultimately, Finnegan wants to understand the specific social contexts within which people come to learn what music is: what it means to play an instrument, how to engage with other musicians, and how find a specific musical group, club, band, or society to join. Although Finnegan concentrates on amateur or part-time musicians; nonetheless, her emphasis on the way in which different musical traditions overlap and intersect demonstrates a broader set of interpretive challenges for understanding music more generally.[20]

What is evident from her discussion is the significance of kinship to the pathways that people take to and from music. She notes that one of the most striking characteristics of local musicians was the high proportion who had grown up in families that were in some way or another already musical. She then suggests that "this hereditary feature could be perhaps explained by saying that there was a lot of music around, so some family connections were only to be expected. But I suspect there was more to it than that, not least because of the mechanisms by which this hereditary pattern was implemented. Given the way many kinds of music are currently practiced it is difficult to see how music-making could emerge generation after generation *without* family influence."[21] Family influence and, in particular, the parents' existing musical interests and expertise, including their involvement in different kinds of ensembles, proved decisive for understanding more about which children participated in what kinds of musical activities, beyond the basic requirements of their schooling, and what kinds of musical choices they made. She concludes,

> With the only partial exception of rock, one of the most striking characteristics of musical transmission—of how people tended to enter onto musical pathways—was its hereditary basis. Of course there were exceptions, and people were not programmed into pre-selected pathways: but essentially the tendency was for people from musical families to themselves enter on musical pathways of some kind, often ones similar to those followed by one or both parents or grandparents, by siblings or by other relatives. This was evident through all the local musical pathways.[22]

Of the many things that Finnegan stresses in her study, there is one, especially, that is relevant for understanding the elementary structures of vaudeville. The presence of multiple and intersecting musical pathways within a family, let alone within the wider community, underlines how critical an expanded concept of kinship was to the artistic possibilities that were available to performers. For the Cohans, the issue of sticking together had to take into account those years during which they toured together (Judy Garland's performance of "Born in a Trunk" in *A Star Is Born* conveys this claim very effectively as well), the quasi-apprenticeship the children undertook as fledgling members of their parents' act, the members of their larger "show biz family" (from B. F. Keith to Isidore Whitmark), and their stage identity as a family act. "My father thanks you, my mother thanks you, my sister thanks you, and I thank you . . ." was the line that finished every one of their thousands of shows, and became inseparable from Cohan's later reputation as "The Man Who Owned Broadway." Vaudeville family acts, and the even larger touring shows that often encompassed them, thus reconfigured popular entertainment through a metamorphosis of personal and social relationships. This deep investment in an expanded vision of the family derived from the claim that there is no business like show business, an issue I will return to in the final section of this chapter.[23] This sort of account raises a number of theoretical problems. First, what are we talking about when we extend discussions of kinship to the diverse bonds it creates within, and between, show business families and their stage partners (George Walker and Bert Williams, for example)? Second, what implications does focusing on kinship have for our understanding of artistic forms? And, finally, what happens when those family ties intersect with and affect larger issues of power, wealth, ownership, and cultural value within popular entertainment?

Although he does not focus on popular culture as such, Paul DiMaggio's study of cultural entrepreneurship in nineteenth-century Boston provides a useful model for addressing these problems. In his view, the founding of the Boston Symphony Orchestra in 1881 was made possible by the intricate network of familial connections that its founder, Henry Lee Higginson, relied on for support and, ultimately, patronage. "It is likely that Higginson's keen instinct for brokerage—and the obligations he accrued as principal in one of Boston's two major houses—served him well in his efforts to establish the Orchestra," DiMaggio argues.

> At first glance, Higginson's achievement in creating America's first elite-governed permanent symphony orchestra in Boston appears to be the work of a rugged individualist. On closer inspection, we see that it was precisely Higginson's centrality to the Brahmin social structure [of Boston] that enabled him to succeed. . . . His career illustrates the importance of kinship, commerce, clubs and philanthropy in Boston elite life. Ties in each of these areas reinforced those in the others; each facilitated the success of the Orchestra, and each brought him into close connection with the cultural capitalists active in the MFA [Museum of Fine Art] and led, eventually, to his selection as a Museum trustee.[24]

While I will have more to say about DiMaggio's study in the final chapter, all we need to note at this stage is his claim that family relationships and hereditary structures should be an integral, rather than a marginal, element in the study of music. Furthermore, other accounts of the founding of American symphony orchestras, opera companies, music schools, and music societies indicate that Boston was not an isolated case. In his history of the American middle class in late nineteenth-century New York City, Sven Beckert shows us that because "the focus of the typical firm [in the 1850s] was still to an important degree the family, as it had been for centuries, it was not surprising that merchants and bankers, together with their wives, expended extraordinary effort to maintain and strengthen these relationships, both among relatives and among large social networks." This effort culminated in a "class segmented public sphere" framed by an integrated set of cultural institutions, including the Metropolitan Museum of Art, the New York Philharmonic Society, and the Metropolitan Opera.[25] These institutions placed the fine arts (in the broadest sense of that phrase) at the center of a highly complex system of kinship relations. This system came to characterize the city's new corporate-managerial class, while at the same time providing a substantial basis for the development of its collective identity beyond the family.

When it comes to understanding these cultural dynamics within vaudeville, it is important to recognize that the effort to secure its cultural legitimacy as an art form in its own right was based on a similarly complex system of kinship. In Marian Spitzer's account of the Palace Theatre in New York, for instance, there are frequent references to these family connections and their bearing on the kinds of acts that appeared there. "The Marx Brothers," she recalls, "were the nephews of Al Shean, of Gallagher-and-Shean fame; their mother was Shean's sister. Together on and off since early burlesque days, Gallagher and Shean struck it rich with the song that became their trademark, 'Oh Mr. Gallagher, Oh Mr. Shean.' That endless and endlessly imitated number was written for them by Bryan Foy, motion-picture producer and one of Eddie Foy's seven children."[26] The proliferation of connections between different acts, the frequent reconfiguration of acts, the collective process of creating an act and a show, which relied on songwriters, bandleaders, stage hands, and so on, thus underlined performers' shared sense of self-identity and their dependence on each other. This is evident in Spitzer's description of Eddie Cantor and George Jessel's relationship, which mediated between their on-stage personalities and their off-stage lives.

Few things are more fun than tracing the separate careers of Cantor and Jessel, but that would take too long. . . . Remarkably, in view of the end-

less contradictions in all show business biographies, the Jessel and Cantor accounts agree pretty well. They both became singles [single acts],
they sometimes worked together, they each played the Palace on and
off over the years; Eddie had one marriage and five daughters, George
had four marriages—if you count two with his first wife, Florence
Courtney—and may well by the time this appears in print have added
a fifth. . . . Through it all, though the two men could hardly have been
basically more different, they remained close friends. More than friends,
George says, they were brothers.[27]

It is evident from these examples that the ritual structure of vaudeville intensified the shared sense of the social interaction and mutual dependency
among performers, even as the uniqueness of each performer's individual
talent was the basis on which he or she appealed to the audience.

This extended to the children of performers as well. "A show kid seemed
to grow older faster than regular kids," Joe Laurie observed.

The kids got tired of waiting in the wings, and eventually Pop and Mom
would take them on for a bow, not that they wanted to commercialize
the kid (although I know many times the baby taking a bow saved the
act . . .). But the parents wanted to show off to the town people that they
too were "family" people and had a kid. Of course a "traveling kid" sort
of itched to get on stage. So it was a short step from just taking a bow to
letting the kid do a bit. They usually knew everybody's act word for word
and could imitate anybody (fresh memories).[28]

Laurie then goes on to document the great family acts, which amounted to
a huge number and variation of and within groups, from two acts to sister
acts to large combinations, before concluding that "what I am trying to tell
you . . . is that vaude people were no different than anybody else. They had
pops, moms, brothers, and sisters, and most of all, they had talent."[29] It was
this talent, however, and how it was perceived within the show, that made
all the difference to the structure, meaning and purpose of these relationships; conversely, the structure, meaning and purpose of those relationships
profoundly affected how a performer came to recognize their artistic potential in the first place.

The issue Laurie highlights is how the specific affinity between family,
relatives, friends, and artistic and business partners was integral to the ideological claims that were made about vaudeville as a unique cultural form.
Because daily life on the circuits was so constant and demanding, and per-

formers' successes and failures so bound up in the successes and failures of their partners, many of whom were also family members, or relatives, or "like brothers," the sense of participating in and being dependent on one another's lives was paramount. For Sahlins, "the extensional aspects of kin relationships, the transpersonal practices of coexistence from sharing to mourning, are better motivated by sociocentric considerations of mutuality. . . . 'Intrinsic' to each other . . . kinsmen are people who live each other's lives and die each other's deaths. To the extent that they lead common lives, they partake of each other's suffering and joys, sharing one another's experiences even as they take responsibility for and feel the effects of each other's acts."[30] The common claim that a life in show business is a life unlike any other involves performers in the reconfiguration of procreation and performance within the larger narrative of entertainment *as* the embodiment of the national culture. "'Great actors are born,'" announces Cohan, at the beginning of his book. "There are many who still doubt the truth of this old saying. But it's a fact. I know because I was born. Not just ordinarily born, but born on the Fourth of July."[31]

Susan Glenn quotes a review of the comedians Cissie Loftus and Gertrude Hoffmann at Keith and Proctor's 125th Street Theatre in Harlem in 1908, in which the critic Alan Dale asks his readers: "Isn't it exquisite, to be occasionally somebody else?"[32] Glenn's study explores the ways in which female comics such as Loftus and Hoffmann used vaudeville to question conventional ideas about individual and collective agency by mimicking other vaudeville performers. "The comedy of personality," she argues, "not only posed the question of what happened to the individual personality when someone else 'became' you. It also raised issues of what happened to the mimic's individuality when they 'became' someone else."[33] The claim that show business was a unique world relied upon this endless play of the self, which in turn implied a metamorphosis in the values and practices of kinship. Let me explain what I mean.

We know that on the circuits, performers were as caught up in love affairs, multiple marriages, complicated business relationships, changes of name, and looking after their theatrical progeny as they were in putting across a song. As Sophie Tucker so eloquently revealed, one was the condition of the other. It was common for onstage routines, songs, or plots (such as Cohan's "Song and Dance Man") to include references to, or intersect with, performers' lives offstage, and for them to use this ambiguity between the real and the imaginary in order to question the distinction between the stage and the backstage world. "It is that feeling of good-fellowship," Caffin observes, "that makes the audience love to be on confidential terms with the performer, to be treated as an intimate. It loves to have the actor step out of his part and speak of his dressing room, or hint at his salary, or flourish a make-up towel. There are no secrets, no reserves between them."[34]

This intimacy between artist and audience relied on the claim that popular entertainers by definition presented a truer image of the world than their counterparts in other art forms. As Marian Spitzer suggested, "there seems to be very little in common between a regular actor and a vaudeville actor. . . . So many regular actors and actresses are inclined to act just about as much off the stage as on it. They are always aware of themselves, watching to see if they are making the right effect. Not the vaudevillian, though. His philosophy is 'Be yourself.' He is above all things natural and forthright. You can take him the way he is or leave him alone. He hates affectation and cannot bear ritzy, upstage people."[35] In this way, performers asserted a vision of popular entertainment in which it was more than just an escape from the exigencies of everyday life. It was a new community capable of transforming the boundary between life and art

This claim is made in Busby Berkeley's 1939 film *Babes in Arms*, with Judy Garland and Mickey Rooney (one of a series of films about vaudeville in which they starred).[36] Set in 1921, the film opens with the camera following the crowd as it enters the front doors of New York's Palace Theatre ("the pulsating heart of vaudeville"). It pauses briefly in front of a series of pictures of the great Palace stars, pans across them, and then continues with the crowd into the space of the theater where a single song-and-dance act is already taking place on the stage. The performer, Joe Moran (played by Charles Winninger), suddenly rushes off stage to discover that his son has been born in the dressing room of the theater. Returning to the stage for his encore, he takes off his wig, stops the music and the applause, and addresses the audience directly. "Thanks folks. It's been five years since you first said hello to me and Florie [his wife, played by Grace Hayes]. But this time she asks to be excused." Knowing laughter all round, and then another performer shouts from the wings that it's a boy, and Moran returns to the stage and cries, "Well, it looks like I got a son. Born in the Palace Theatre!" The orchestra then breaks into 'Rock-a-Bye-Baby,' as Moran and his audience cheer and clap the new arrival. Moran then rushes off stage, and Berkeley cuts to a bar where the new father and his colleagues are celebrating with another round of the song (". . . bye baby and all," they sing). "Here's a toast to vaudeville," Moran declares. "The greatest entertainment in the world. After all, it made me what I am today, a papa!" After a brief (and apocryphal) exchange about a dark shadow approaching that might threaten their livelihoods (the movies), everyone in the bar raises their glass to "40 weeks. May it last forever!"

As with most of Berkeley's musicals, *Babes in Arms* shows a group of performers discovering what really counts as entertainment in the United States and what it means to be an entertainer.[37] The film combines a coming-of-age story about Joe's son, Mickey (played by Rooney), who is learning to be a great song-and-dance man, with a narrative about the decline of vaudeville in the late 1920s (as a result of the movies), and a story about young love between Mickey and Patsy Barton (played by Garland). Faced with the collapse of the vaudeville system, Mickey, Patsy, and the other "show biz" children who were "born in a trunk" put on a show in order to pay a fine (incurred by Mickey, who fights a local boy for criticizing his father), to save themselves from having to go to school, and to save their parents from having to give up their careers as vaudeville troupers (and all the dreams that go along with such a life). In spite of many barriers that conspire against them—the law, the military, wealth, the adults, and even nature—the kids eventually manage to put on their self-created show . . . on Broadway. Needless to say, it turns out to be a huge hit.

While many things can be said about this film, not the least its complex perspective on the relationship between making a film and putting on a live show, in the context of this chapter the important issue is its claim about the relationship between the show biz kids, their parents and friends, and the significance of the theatrical community for popular entertainers.[38] What I take the film to be trying to show us here is that the kids' conviction in their parents' way of life, and their sense of entitlement to its inheritance as a living tradition, frees them to experiment with who they are and to discover what they are capable of achieving, as performers and as young people coming of age. The cooperative effort that goes into putting on a successful show thus requires them to reconcile the backstage world, and all its various challenges and complexities, with their onstage characters—to recognize that only by reconciling one with the other will they ever discover the true meaning of entertainment and, ultimately, of life.

CHAPTER FIVE

Show Me the Money

Up until now, I have been arguing that the organization of vaudeville theaters into national circuits, along with the centralization of the booking system, consolidated a new system of corporate entertainment in American culture. I then set out an account of the kinds of changes in artistic self-consciousness that, in my view, resulted from this process. This account is by no means complete without some further discussion of the ways in which the new class of vaudeville managers set out their plans for structural reform of show business, especially the specific claims they made for their managerial practices, and the principles on which they based those practices. Although contemporary critics have often treated the problems the managers set out to resolve as primarily strategic and self-serving (and there is no doubt that they were), I want to position their plans to transform vaudeville within the broader social struggle over the corporate reconstruction of American culture. The term *reconstruction*, as I use it here, refers to far-reaching and interrelated changes transpiring in the political, political, cultural, social, and economic spheres.[1] The outcome of this social struggle was the triumph of a new form of capitalism in which the dominant institutions in the United States were vast industrial-administrative corporations, whether privately owned, publicly traded, or state controlled.

In chapter 2 I argued that the reorganization of show business into large-scale, transcontinental vaudeville combines was, in many ways, an original contribution to this process of corporate reconstruction. The claims discussed in this chapter further address these principles that the vaudeville owners developed in their efforts to systematize the amusement business. A large part of this chapter will focus on the managers' claims that they were involved in a necessary reform of the amusement business. Their use of the term *reform* in this context meant corporate reform, and connected their policies with similar processes taking place in other industries, including oil, steel, banking, and transportation. We have already seen in chapter 2 how effectively this concept was applied to the integration of the theatrical circuits and the centralization of the booking system. I want to extend this discussion to the basic administrative practices and values that were developed by the managers, including their theories about the programming of artists, the publicizing of shows and performers, the relationship with the music publishing companies, and the integration of the performing and dramatic arts into a single structure.

Throughout this chapter (and the rest of this book) *progressive society* and *progressivism* designate the ideological claims made for and about corporate society; in other words, they refer to the theories of progress that came to define and justify the claims of the emerging social and political culture. *Corporate reform* as I use it is best understood as a *process* by which this new social order, and the political institutions that supported it, became the dominant social reality for Americans in the three decades following the Civil War. "Progressivism," suggests Gabriel Kolko, "was initially a movement for the political rationalisation of business and industrial conditions, a movement that operated on the assumption that the general welfare of the community could be best served by satisfying the concrete needs of business. . . . It is business control over politics . . . rather than political regulation of the economy that is the significant phenomenon of the Progressive Era."[2]

As I pointed out in the last chapter, in Hollywood musicals such as Berkeley's *Babes in Arms*, the success of a show usually turns on the performers being able to reconcile the many tensions and conflicts of the backstage world with the one they finally bring to life on stage. A central theme of backstage musicals is that the narrow (and usually elitist) interests of the producer, or those of a self-absorbed star, or sometimes both, must be overcome in order for the show to go on and for it to succeed with the largest possible audience.[3]

While I have already discussed several of these films in detail, it is worth emphasizing here just how important this theme is for thinking about the kinds of relationships that took shape within vaudeville. The division of labor between managers and performers was inseparable from the dynamics of corporate consolidation taking place throughout the United States, but it was also essential to the specific ideological claims that were made about the emerging system of popular entertainment. Central to these claims was the mythology of the "Great American Showman," which brought together

a number of cultural themes relating to individual success, talent, organizational ability, and self-recognition, into a general theory of show business
production.

More than any other nineteenth-century public figure, it was P. T. Barnum who played a critical part in this process and in the course of his lifetime came to personify this mythology.[4] As British traveler John Delware
Lewis wrote in his account of the American theater in 1850, "Barnum is not
an ordinary showman. He is not one who will be handed down to posterity
only on the strength of the objects which he has exhibited. . . . He stands
alone. Adopting Mr. Emerson's idea, I should say that Barnum is a representative man. He represents the enterprise and energy of his countrymen in
the 19th century, as Washington represented their resistance to oppression
in the century preceding."[5] From his earliest experiments with freaks and
oddities in the 1830s, to the huge traveling circuses of the 1880s, Barnum's
desire to produce the "Greatest Show on Earth" kept him at the forefront
of every important change in nineteenth-century entertainment. According to Leo Braudy, Barnum's many triumphs confirmed for Americans that
the stage was "the proper display for the democratic, the unique, and the
natural, rather than the hierarchic and the artificial."[6]

Such convictions were especially significant for the first generation of
big-time vaudeville managers. Keith, Albee, Pastor, and Proctor each spent
some of their early show business careers with one of Barnum's many enterprises, and many of the entertainment practices and principles they adopted,
and the values they espoused, were derived from those early experiences of
"joining out" with the traveling shows. "I claim," wrote Keith in 1912, "that
the circus, with its vast field of opportunity for one who has his eyes open
and is willing to improve his chances, offers more practical education for a
limited period than the better average of other fields of labor, recreation and
enjoyment combined." For Keith, a job in the circus was like reaching "the
Elysium Fields where there could be no more sorrow or care . . . for there
were really no days that I did not enjoy." He then goes on to describe how
his circus days had "naturally imbued" him with an understanding of show
business, recalling that when Barnum paid the occasional visit, "he never
failed to make his appearance in the ring with a few remarks of an educational and instructive character."[7]

Albee, too, recalled that when he first saw Barnum's circus, it proved
an opportunity to study "human conditions in all its phases. There was
plenty to observe, plenty to learn. Every phase of nature is experienced."
After first joining a wagon show in 1873 when he was sixteen, Albee was
then employed by several major circuses, including the Van Amburgh, Burr

Robbins, Sells Brothers, and the Batcheller and Doris shows (where he first met Keith). He then worked with Barnum's "Greatest Show on Earth" for three years, from 1879 to 1881, as a ticket seller, advance man, and fixer (or troubleshooter), and eventually Keith hired him in 1885 as a fixer and "blower" for his newly established Dime Museum in Boston.[8] As with Keith's account of his early years, Albee identified his youthful circus days with the best available education in the practicalities of showmanship. "In my opinion," he told a reporter, "the advantages gained which fit a man for later years in business cannot be found in any other calling; the diverse experience which one encounters in traveling with a circus—the novelty, the contact with all classes, the knowledge of the conditions of the country, its finances, its industry, its farming."[9]

This focus on self-improvement proved an essential part of Keith's and Albee's appeal to audiences throughout their respective careers, along with a continual emphasis on respectability, temperance, thrift, self-reliance, and hard work as fundamental conditions of business success. The process of securing vaudeville's cultural legitimacy, therefore, by attracting a middle-class, family-oriented audience, became inseparable from the ideology of progressive reform that underpinned the process of corporate reconstruction.[10] A feature article on the two managers, published in *McClure's Magazine* in 1923, made this connection explicit. "This story of two young men," began its author, Walter Eaton, "who, thirty years ago, dreamed of making the despised 'varieties' respectable, who invented 'refined' vaudeville in a Boston dime museum and struggled up to a realization of their vision in a chain of palatial theatres, is an extraordinary romance of big business seasoned with the glamour of the theatrical world." Such was their ambition, he claimed, that they revolutionized "an entire branch of the amusement industry in America."[11]

Not only did they set out to transform the contents of the show and the way in which artists were booked, but they wanted to reshape the whole theatrical experience as well. When you enter one of Keith and Albee's "neighborhood houses," Eaton observed, you

> step into a roomy lobby behind the seats, decorated in an Adam style much less ornate and much more dignified than the old Keith house in Boston, with stairs of real marble rising at each end to the balconies. On each of the balcony floors, as well as the orchestra floor, are retiring rooms, with matrons in attendance for the women, and the second-balcony rooms are just as fine as those on the ground. The women's rooms are furnished with richly framed mirrors and rare mezzotints in

keeping with the beautiful furnishings; the men's rooms are paneled in English walnut. On the tables are vases of fresh flowers. There is not a speck of dirt anywhere, nor any noise during a performance.[12]

Conditions were just as comfortable for the performers as well. "Behind the scenes," he noted, "[the theater] is equally clean, equally quiet, and equally comfortable. Each dressing room has a tiled bath with tub and shower. There is an elevator to reach them by, and corridors are carpeted."[13]

The language of progressivism supplied Eaton with a basic terminology, as well as the principal concepts, for making sense of the managers' innovations. Consider the attention to detail in the interior design of their theaters, which Eaton identified with a process of cleaning up American vaudeville. "In the task of theatre building," he wrote, "Mr. Albee was always the leading spirit. He likes to build them. He picks out all the material, all the colors, all the hangings and furniture and pictures and decorations himself. . . . And, as his resources have increased, he has put more and more money into these new houses, on both sides of the footlights, planning both for the enjoyment of his patrons and the comfort of his artists."[14] Albee repeatedly confirmed this claim. "The whole credo upon which we founded our beloved and respected 'Business,'" he declared, "began with the mutual and deep-rooted determination to maintain cleanliness, comfort, and courtesy in our theatres."[15]

Keith and Albee were not, however, alone in their campaign. In 1872 a young Frederick Proctor embarked on his first tour of Europe. Following appearances in all the major music halls and concert-cafés, he began to conceive of a theory of vaudeville production based on his experiences. "Variety in America," he commented, "is like a house that is good in design but is composed of cheap material. I'll build the house of variety with the best material to be had."[16] When Proctor eventually returned after three years abroad, he spent another year touring the United States, returned to Europe in 1876 for a further series of engagements with his partner, Dan Bushnell, and then settled in Albany, New York. For another three years, he performed on small-circuit tours in and around Albany, as far south as New York and Brooklyn, and east into New England, until he had saved the money to purchase his first theater on Green Street in downtown Albany. Dubbed "The Great Little Man" by Jerry Cohan, George Cohan's father, Proctor eventually established a formidable group of theaters in cities such as New York, Brooklyn, Hartford, Boston, Rochester, and Wilmington.

Although most studies focus on Keith and Albee as the central figures in the corporate consolidation of entertainment, most contemporary accounts suggest that Proctor played an equally significant role in putting in place the kinds of systems required to guarantee the financial success in show business. For example, in June 1888, the *Brooklyn Times* claimed that

> there are few managers better known in the United States than Mr. F. F. Proctor. . . . Mr. Proctor is without a doubt one of the most progressive men in a profession which commands genius and talents of a high order, and he has reached his present enviable position by his splendid executive abilities, wide powers of discernment and thorough appreciation of what the public demands. . . . Although not in the prime of life, he has inaugurated reforms, provided innocent amusement to hundreds of thousands of persons in their hour of recreation and placed the prices of admission to good attractions on a popular basis.[17]

Two decades later, in his overview of the amusement business, Robert Grau made a similar claim: "There may be some question as to the priority of the individual efforts of such magnates of to-day as B. F. Keith, but on balance, when it is all summed up, Mr. Proctor may well lay claim to being 'a' father of the great expansion from the 'variety' of the 60's to the vaudeville of to-day."[18]

It is evident from these few examples that the managerial reforms undertaken by Keith, Albee, Proctor, and other big-time managers were conceived of as continuous with the politics of Progressivism. They, along with their various biographers, frequently appealed to their "executive abilities, wide powers of discernment and thorough appreciation of what the public demands" in order to support their claim to be merging efficiency and uplift, science and morality, art and entertainment, within a highly integrated, bureaucratic structure.[19] At the same time, as Kathryn Oberdeck demonstrates in her study of the New Haven theater owner Sylvester Poli, this process was neither unified nor straightforward; many of the cultural conflicts over the practices of reform were highly localized and contradictory, often taking unpredictable turns, and usually involved continuously shifting alliances of social groups, from show business entrepreneurs to preachers to workers' unions, each one aiming to speak for, and take control of, the dominant forms of popular entertainment in a particular city, town, region, or theatrical circuit.[20] For Oberdeck, moreover, the efforts at centralized corporate control of show business generated numerous counter-movements within the vaudeville system that consistently challenged, and sometimes even undermined, the progressive claims of the managers.[21] I will discuss some of these in the next chapter, when I deal with the vaudeville aesthetic.

Vaudeville provided the context for the emergence of a new conception of entertainment as continuous performance, in which the audience was the primary object of the show. To get the right perspective on this change, we need to go backstage for a while, in order to appreciate what the managers were trying to achieve. We can start with B. F. Keith. In an article he published in the *National Magazine* in November 1898, Keith reflects on its origins:

> I do not think that the old saw, "Necessity is the mother of invention," ever had clearer application than in the case of my origination of the continuous performance idea of entertainment. Replying to the query of a friend, not long since, "What first induced you to establish the continuous performance?" I truthfully replied: "Because I had to do something." . . . A mental retrospection of the years prior to this particular period of "having to do something" discloses the fact that shadowy gleamings of the success that would follow the institution of the new form of amusement were constantly flitting across my mental vision, with the result that I pondered over the problem betwixt waking and sleeping many a restless night. . . . All at once the full formed idea was made plain, and I never hesitated in putting it into execution. It was clear that the majority of people would stay through an entertainment so long as they could, even sitting out acts that had to be repeated. The old form necessitated a final curtain at a specified time, and the emptying of the house. As a result the succeeding audience gathered slowly, the theatre was necessarily dreary as they came into it, and there was nothing going on. Did you ever notice the hesitancy on the part of early comers to a playhouse to assume their seats in the auditorium, how they hang back until reassured by numbers? Well, that is one of the continuous performance does away with. It matters not at what hour of the day or evening you visit, the theatre is always occupied by more or less people, the show is in full swing, everything is bright, cheerful, and inviting.[22]

It wasn't enough to reform the show, however. He had to find new ways of publicizing it. "I was always maneuvering," he recalled, "to keep patrons moving up and down the stairs in view of passersby on the sidewalk for the specific purpose of impressing them with the idea that business was immense."[23]

According to McLean, Keith had understood that entertainment "for the city-dweller had ceased to be merely the evening pastime of the leisure class and had long outgrown the older traditions of the holiday gathering for circus of carnival. No single time schedule could accommodate the many different routines of city folk and only round-the-clock amusement, available for whatever duration of leisure one might have, could hope to draw the mass audience."[24] The same point was made by Joe Laurie in his account:

Keith found that many persons would ask at the box office when the next show started, and, on being told that there would be a wait of half an hour, would turn away, unwilling to spend the waiting time in the dreary curio hall [of Keith's dime museum]. One Sunday morning he took space in the Boston papers to advertise the continuous performance. "Come when you please; stay as long as you like." The idea was so revolutionary that even his stage manager and lecturer, Sam K. Hodgdon, could not grasp the idea. . . . Hodgdon opened the show with a brief lecture. . . . When the first show was over, Keith told Hodgdon to go on again without clearing the house. Hodgdon protested that most of the people who had just seen him would walk out. "I hope they do," was Keith's reply, and Hodgdon got the idea. This made Sam Hodgdon the first "chaser" act in the business.[25]

Following Keith's success in Boston, Proctor, too, initiated continuous performance at his theater on 23rd Street in New York. In 1892 his "Ladies Club Theatre" opened with a list of twenty acts, running from 11 a.m. to 11 p.m. Cards reading "After Breakfast Go to Proctor's and Hear Campanini" (the great operatic tenor) were distributed throughout New York and placed in every shop window, trolley car, hotel, newsstand, and elevated train.[26] With the advertising jingle, "After Breakfast Go to Proctor's, After Proctor's Go to Bed," Proctor demonstrated that, like Keith, he was actively responding to the changing social experiences of the rapidly expanding urban population. Indeed, for Proctor, the connection between the new forms of urban existence and vaudeville was explicit. "See," he observed, "when people are shopping or relaxing, they are ready for the theatre."[27] We can see from the above examples that continuous vaudeville was more than simply a technical fix for Keith's or Proctor's profits. It was part of a much wider set of changes that were taking place in Americans' lives, from the length of the working day to the kinds of aesthetic experiences available to them.

When he was asked by a reporter to describe its impact on popular entertainment, Proctor announced that "Vaudeville is King." Proctor's confidence in his business was matched only by his conviction that "vaudeville's reign is in its infancy . . . it will eventually and perpetually dominate all other forms of amusement, not only in the number of people it delights but also in the number it helps and profits. It is, I sometime think, like an auriferous mine whose surface has barely been scratched." In another interview in 1912 for the *New York Morning Telegraph*, Proctor connected his vision of vaudeville to the emergent consumer capitalism. "We deal in amusements these days," he claimed, "as our great merchants deal in their wares. We must study the markets of the world, so that we may supply our customers—the public—with just what they want, and just when they want it. If they tire of a pattern we must change it to suit their capricious taste."[28]

Similarly, in a series of articles he published in trade magazines in the 1920s, Albee claimed that

> the diversified, contrasted and all-embracing character of a vaudeville program gives it in whole or part, an appeal to all classes of people and all kinds of tastes. For its patrons it draws upon all of the artistic resources of every branch of the theater—grand opera, the drama, pantomime, choreography, concert, symphony, farce and all of the kindred fields of stage entertainment. . . . In addition to this wide diversity of its attractions, the personnel of its army of artists is as cosmopolitan as the population of the cities and towns of the United States. Not only are all the arts represented in vaudeville, but all of the nations and races of the civilized world are also represented by and through some characteristic form of expression. . . . Thus, in the arrangement of the ideal modern vaudeville program, there is one or more sources of complete satisfaction for everybody present, no matter how "mixed" the audience may be.[29]

What effect did these claims about vaudeville have on popular entertainment, the values associated with it, and the managerial practices that were developed to support it? Albee's model of show business that was diversified, contrasting, and all embracing provided the managers with their principal formula for incorporating all the major nineteenth-century art forms into what would eventually become a global entertainment industry. An essential part of this process was the integration of formerly separate activities and functions into a single managerial system.

To clarify how this integration was achieved, the kinds of changes identified with it, and the progressive values assigned to those changes, I want to focus on two accounts by the booking agent Robert Grau, who documented the backstage world in great detail from the 1880s until around 1909. Before turning to Grau's accounts, however, it is worth citing a January 1904 editorial from *Billboard* that reflected on the changes in vaudeville's cultural significance over the fifteen-year period that Keith, Proctor, and the other managers worked to establish continuous vaudeville as the principal model for show business. To make their case, the editors cite an article from the *New York Morning Post*:

> Vaudeville, as it is now known, has been lifted to a far higher plane than was dreamed of fifteen years ago, or, for that matter, even ten years ago. It is today *a little amusement world of its own*, and is daily growing larger and stronger and better in every way. The day of the rough act has passed. The day of vulgarity and commonness has gone with it. The men and women who make their living in the vaudeville field today are of a higher intellectual order and the "thrown-together" act of some years ago is conspicuous by its absence. This change is mainly due to the managers, and partially due to the performers themselves. In the early days of the business, there was a lack of system, a lack of organization, a semblance of hand-to-mouth method of securing time, and a general feeling of uncertainty about results that was exceedingly harmful to *the business as a business*. It was but a case of business conducted on anything but business principles [emphasis added].[30]

Grau's two books explore this transition in detail. He concentrates on documenting the movement from a largely uneven and fragmented set of managerial practices, that promoted insecurity and uncertainty, in which the opportunities for business "advancement" were limited to a few individuals, to "an amusement world of its own," based on systematic organization and business principles, and open to, and in fact dependent on, an increasingly large and highly trained workforce. "As a field for progressive and enterprising young men," proclaims Grau, "modern amusement catering offers opportunities unexcelled by few, if any, lines of endeavor. Organization and capital have reduced the dangerous nature of amusement enterprises, as they stood some 25 or 30 years ago, to what can really be a termed a 'Legitimate Business,' with not half as much danger to the cautious and ordinary operator as an ordinary speculation in stocks or real estate."[31]

Grau's story is about the increasingly legitimate status of vaudeville, in which the effective organization of popular amusements based on scientific business principles resolved problems that earlier entrepreneurs had failed to address. As vaudeville became recognized as a secure means of capital accumulation, the managers, too, gained in reputation and influence. They dispensed with those "harmful" practices that had undermined "the business as a business," especially those of unreliable performer-managers, and

in the process opened up untold opportunities for "progressive and enterprising" young men (there were very few women managers). But, and perhaps more important, these changes aligned vaudeville with the general
principles of corporate reform to such an extent that it eventually surpassed
speculation in stock and real estate.

In this account the efficiency and effectiveness of backstage management, especially on issues of organization and system, was directly related
to the kinds and quality of the acts on stage. The key reform in this regard
was to the booking process, as Grau points out in the introduction to *The
Businessman in the Amusement World*. "It is the desire and purpose of
this writer," he begins, "and an effort is made throughout this volume, to
emphasize this—to impress the reader with the fact that the men who have
become wealthy and powerful, and are in control of the balance of power
in the dramatic and vaudeville portions of the general amusement scheme,
have reached their position far less through any great efforts as managers
and producers, than by their foresight and ingenuity in creating efficient
methods for the 'booking' of theatres and attractions."[32] The rationalization of the booking process, especially the formation in 1900 of the United
Booking Offices by the first generation of vaudeville managers, reinforced
the processes of intensification and differentiation in artistic value that continuous vaudeville set in motion. The demand that performers appear anywhere from twice to six times a day, depending on whether they were on a
big-time or small-time circuit, radically altered the value of individual acts,
even as it enabled managers to begin monitoring and thus to measure this
value with much greater precision (primarily in terms of audience response).

On another level, the centralization of the booking process compelled
managers to adopt new communications technologies, accounting procedures, and bureaucratic processes so as to facilitate the movement of acts
through the system. This is evident from Grau's description of the Chicago
offices of the Western Vaudeville Managers' Association. The WVMA office,
he writes,

> is among the most luxurious in Chicago, a city famed for its magnificent
> buildings and offices. Occupying two floors in the Majestic Building, Mr.
> C. E. Bray, the executive head, has fitted them with every convenience
> and aid known to the modern business world. Files containing inexhaus-
> tive reports on all acts from every city in which they have played; private
> telegraph wires and telephone service to all departments; an attorney
> who passes upon all legal questions; travelling representatives both in

this country and abroad on the alert for new ideas and acts, and a general office staff of more than fifty persons employed year round.[33]

As with most other areas involving large-scale production, managerial reform in vaudeville was focused primarily on solving problems of processing information and centralized control. In his study of scientific management and its impact on twentieth-century work practices, Harry Braverman explains that "when a production line has reached this continuous and automatic state, it is close to the point when it becomes a single machine, instead of a system of connected machinery. Thus the machine which prints, folds, gathers, covers, and binds the sheets of a paperback book would hardly be recognizable to an outsider as a combination of the several machines it has brought together in such a process of evolution. For this to take place, all that needs be done is for the production system of linked machines to be conceived and redesigned as a single, massive, integrated whole."[34] The task of managing such an integrated whole required a new kind of administrative apparatus, a radically altered technical base, new scientific concepts, different types of machinery, and profound shifts in social relations. Corporate reconstruction in one part of the society (say, the communications industry) invariably (but not inevitably) transformed every other branch of industry as well.

Braverman's analysis can help us better understand the ways in which entertainment was being reorganized in the last decades of the nineteenth century as an entire production process.[35] Rather than rely on discrete units of production in the form of a touring stock companies or traveling shows, the vaudeville entrepreneurs were quick to adopt the principles and practices associated with the large-scale combine in order to incorporate every aspect of production, distribution, and consumption into a single entity: the amusement corporation. They achieved this by instituting the practice of continuous vaudeville, connecting theatrical programming to a centralized booking process and consolidating national (and then international) circuits. This required major artistic, technical, and administrative changes at every level of show business, including organizational structures, theater design, and performance practices. At the same time, the meaning and the position of the performers were also altered. She or he was no longer the object of the performance—which explains the nostalgic tone of those accounts that lament the passing of older forms of variety, in which the performer was "king"—but merely part of the global production process. The outcome was that performers were reduced to interchangeable "acts," while the structure of the show was reshaped to fit within and respond to a large, heterogeneous, and increasingly mobile urban audience.

I want to finish this chapter with a comment from one of the principal architects of these changes: booking agent Michael Leavitt. "The finest and most thorough kind of training," writes Leavitt, "travelling with the business end of a circus—developed in E. F. Albee early in life a keenness for values in real show features and a capacity for ceaseless industry. While he has never lacked in the realization of the adage that in competition lies the life of trade, at the same time he has shown a foresight and an acumen in grasping the fact that in combination and amalgamation of interests lay the best results. . . . Apart from the keen instinct he displays in the manipulation of the commercial details of theatricals, Mr. Albee possesses the ideals of the artist."[36] There is perhaps no better example of the shift in perspective I have been describing. As Leavitt's account reveals, the managers brought art and commerce into a new kind of dynamic relationship, in which the art of vaudeville was the business of art.

CHAPTER SIX

On with the Show

Early on in *Can't Help Singin'*, his study of the American musical, Gerald Mast observes that George Cohan's shows were not "truly integrated pieces of musical theatre but melodramatic plays with vaudeville songs and jokes stitched in. Cohan . . . never quite left vaudeville behind."[1] In a 1957 essay the jazz critic Whitney Balliett wrote that Louis Armstrong "has recently begun offering in his public appearances little more than a round of vaudeville antics—clowning, bad jokes—and a steadily narrowing repertory."[2] And more recently, the film theorist Pascal Bonitzer dismissed the "excrement of vaudeville" in a discussion of film modernism.[3] For each of these critics, the specific practices identified with vaudeville performances were clearly incompatible with and, in some instances, detrimental to the values and principles of modern art. I will have more to say about these sorts of criticisms in chapter 10. In this chapter and the next, however, I want to set out the basic principles of the show: the types of acts that appeared on the vaudeville stage, their relationships to one another, the kinds of aesthetic claims that performers made about them, and the broader dynamics that existed between performers and their audiences.

In the previous chapter, I made the case that the consolidation of vaudeville fundamentally altered the experience of entertaining an audience in all areas of popular performance, and I suggested that this transformation was integral to the corporate reconstruction of American culture. The implementation of continuous programming, the emergence of the star system, and the integration of the national circuits contributed to a new set of artistic practices and conventions for producing a show. "In spite of the differences of personality or of the character they represent for the moment," commented vaudeville critic Caroline Caffin, "there are certain technical accomplishments which, consciously or instinctively, are used by every successful [vaudeville] artist."[4]

But what were those technical accomplishments? And what demands did they place on performers? In order to answer these questions, I want to reconstruct something like a performance history of vaudeville and identify some of the basic issues involved in developing a successful act. In the first section I focus on the changes that took place in popular entertainment, as various nineteenth-century forms were incorporated into, and modified within, the vaudeville system. In the next section, I concentrate on how performers accounted for those changes in published articles, interviews, and autobiographies. Finally, I want to examine two early and influential studies of vaudeville for what they can tell us about the broader context for these changes and the kinds of claims that were made to justify them. This will then help us to clarify the process by which vaudeville became the primary context for the dissemination and reproduction of popular music.[5]

The idea of a show based on a succession of unrelated songs, dances, comic routines, acrobatics, dramatic sketches, lectures, and burlesques had become an established principle of American popular entertainment by the middle of the nineteenth century. For example, the middle or "olio" section of a three-part blackface minstrel show generally featured "miscellaneous varieties," including ethnic material, topical burlesques, novelty acts, animal acts, Shakespearean excerpts, and operatic and musical parodies.[5] The circus, too, was increasingly organized around a spectacle of diversity, mixing scenes and sequences of physical prowess, wonder, monstrosity, and curiosity, along with comic routines, bands, orchestras, parades, lectures, panoramas, and pantomime.[6] The term *variety* also referred to a type of theatrical production involved a disparate group of specialty acts that toured provincial playhouses, appeared on riverboats, in medicine shows, store theaters, and box houses. Performers worked together to develop a program that would last all evening, based on varying the sequence of acts, and they seldom repeated an act. Theaters profited from the sale of drinks, not admission, so the performers' job was to keep the audience in the theatre for as long as possible.[7]

Aside from the minstrel show, the other major cultural institution to feature variety acts prominently was the concert saloon (or "dive"), which first appeared in frontier towns—think of its importance to the plot in many Hollywood westerns—and was then expanded to urban centers in the decade before the Civil War.[8] There is some evidence that the first concert saloon opened in New York in 1848 or 1849, using the label "variety show" because, according to the venue's owner, "I'm going to have a variety of things in my entertainment."[9] These shows, as with the variety segment in minstrel shows, combined singing, dancing, and instrumental music of various kinds, along with the usual comic sketches, romantic verse, minstrel show routines, operatic excerpts, musical parodies, and lectures on topical issues. There were also ethnic routines, mostly German and Dutch impersonators, gymnastic acts, and one-act farces. For example, the acts that appeared in a typical line-up at Levy's Concert Room in 1883 were listed as follows: "Piano and bones playing by two male performers. Song by a male performer, piano accompaniment. Piano and bones playing by two male performers. Song by a male performer, piano accompaniment, known as Dan Weaver. Comic song by a performer known as Charles Ladendorfer, piano accompaniment. Piano and bones playing by two male performers. Another song by Charles Ladendorfer, piano accompaniment."[10] Audiences in these venues were initially male and working class, although this began to change in the post–Civil War period, as managers began to shift their programs toward family entertainment.

Other related and equally influential contexts for the development of variety practices and conventions were the honky-tonks, free-and-easies, and dime museums that clustered in entertainment and gambling districts in most cities and towns. "In these places they [the talent] played to all types of audiences," Joe Laurie recalled,

> sometimes doing fifteen shows a day. As long as there was a customer buying, he had to be entertained. The comedians wrote their own stuff, the song-and-dance men wrote ditties and created new dance steps. The show usually followed set pattern: Opening chorus by the "ladies" (the start of chorus girls), then came the song-and-dance men, musical mokes, two-men acts, quartettes, contortionists, etc. Nearly everybody knew how to plunk a banjo. The show would finish with an afterpiece in which the entire company took part.[11]

For example, he describes how at Big Bertha's Casino and Comique in Spokane, the show "would start at 7 P.M. and finish at 2 A.M., when the men in the afterpiece would take positions on the stage and ad-lib for an hour about topics of the day. This gave the gals [who danced and served the drinks] another hour to collect commissions. At 3 A.M. everybody lined up and sang 'Auld Lang Syne' after eight straight hours of entertainment."[12]

The process by which these multiple practices of variety were incorporated into and systematized as vaudeville signaled important changes in the structure of entertainment. As performers became aware of these changes, they began to alter the form and contents of their acts accordingly. This process was particularly marked in the 1880s when variety was undergoing what Lawrence Senelick sees as a radical transition, particularly in its relationship to the minstrel show.[13] As the number of theaters was expanded, along with the frequency of shows and length of tours, performers required more and more material, engaging in what Senelick describes as a ruthless search for usable songs, stories, and skits. His example is the blackface comic J. C. Murphy, whose joke book was made up of "Negro spirituals, parodies of hymns, drinking songs, Irish ballads, limericks, riddles, cross-talk, parlour poetry, one-liners, and even chemical formulae for various kinds of stage fire. The routines ranged from blackface and rube doubles acts to a traditional minstrel trio to Tambo, Bones and Middlemen to 'The Irishmen's First Game of Baseball' to elaborate documentation of a classic act between clown and ringmaster."[14]

Because he was an all-round variety performer, Murphy had to know, and be able to produce on demand, an enormous amount of material, which he continually adapted and reworked in response to the shifting interests and tastes of his mostly working-class, male audiences. At the same time, he continually evoked the claims and values of older forms of entertainment, especially with his imitations of well-known performers, such as the blackface minstrel Dan Rice. "But," continues Senelick, "little of this material is original; it is cut out of newspapers, copied down from other performers, scribbled on the back of hotel stationery, fresh from the barroom. . . . When Murphy does set about creating, it is to add verses to songs or embroider an anecdote; these efforts are marked by a need to outdo his original, in an awareness that his audiences will appreciate a shout more than a hint."[15]

By comparison, the material contained in Jerry Cohan's (George Cohan's father) "gagbook" demonstrates how in the 1890s there were dramatic changes in the artistic conception of variety and how it was realized in performance. "[Cohan's] gagbook presents a vivid contrast to Murphy's," claims Senelick. "Instead of an omnium gatherum . . . Cohan's square quarto contains elaborated monologues, duologues, playlets and even a five-act melodrama set in the gold camps of California. . . . It would be misleading to overemphasis the originality of Cohan's work, for each of these pieces is a variant on a conventional, already established genre, using stock characters and situations. But Cohan attempted to tailor these clichés to fit the talents of himself and his family and to honour the new decorum of the age."[16]

Whereas Murphy's act maintained a tense and frequently ironic dialogue with his audience, and drew much of its material and conception from the social and political turmoil of the two decades after the great crash of 1873, especially the nativist crisis and the populist uprising, Cohan's approach conveyed a new confidence in and self-consciousness about the possibilities of show business. His act derived its legitimacy from the belief that he was the creative source for his material, and that its appeal to audiences was based on his unique personality. As the producer Sam Harris pointed out, "The aristocracy of vaudeville consists of the Jerry Cohans, the Helen Cohans and the old timers like them. They are the ones who wrote every line they spoke or sang, invented their dances, composed their own music, arranged their acts, wrote their own sketches and staged and managed and acted them."[17] Even though he relied on stock themes and characters, Cohan also recognized that within the new system, which placed such a high premium on the claim of novelty (if not the actual fact), success relied on transforming those conventions in some way. Even when he borrowed from other performers, whether songs or playlets or jokes, he still rewrote the material to suit the needs of his own act.[18]

In the course of this transition, perhaps the most significant change was the demand that performers dispense with any element that might in some way discourage women and children from attending their shows. Great importance was attached to notions of respectability, and in most big-time theaters the managers actively censored those acts that might be offensive to public manners and morality. As Keith pointed out in an article he published in 1911, "I made it a rule at the beginning, when I first opened my Washington Street [Boston] museum [in 1883], that I must know exactly what every performer on my stage would say or do. If there was one coarse or vulgar, or suggestive line or piece of stage business in the act, I cut it out. And this rule is followed in every Keith theatre in the United States today."[19]

Senelick suggests that what was lost in this process of refinement was any direct connection to the social and realities of American culture that had informed the routines of comics such as Murphy. "The interests that impel Murphy's comedy—," he writes, "food, sex, fear of poverty, race hatred—are absent from Cohan's material or present only in a very sublimated way."[20] In cleaning up their acts in response to management policy, and thereby seeking to appeal to the new corporate values on which the vaudeville system was increasingly based, performers such as the Cohans substituted the rough and tumble of the old variety, minstrel, and concert saloon stages for an anodyne form of mass-produced entertainment ("theater in a package," as it was often called) that promised release from, rather than any significant engagement with, the outside world. Or as theater critic George Nathan wrote in 1918, "As vaudeville has acquired this air of elegance, there has coincidentally departed from it its old bounce and gusto."[21] At the same time, however, the consolidation of vaudeville as an entertainment system that was focused on appealing to the largest possible audience also opened up a space in which variety entertainers were for the first time able to conceive of themselves as popular artists.

As they began to see themselves as popular artists, performers also began to reflect on their practices in ways that went beyond the kind of ad hoc notebooks studied by Senelick. They published articles in magazines and trade journals in which they set out in detail their theories of vaudeville production, as well as trying to understand the cultural significance of their shows. The reasons that performers gave for what they did on the stage, their explanations of how they did it, and their justifications for why they did it in the first place were all essential to the claims made for and against vaudeville's artistic significance. Following a line of analysis developed by philosopher Robert Pippin in his studies of modern subjectivity and collective experience, I want to suggest that such claims convey, and are dependent on, the complex and contradictory historical processes by which groups of people come to an understanding of themselves as a community and come to recognize themselves as subjects of that community.[22]

Royle's essay, "The Vaudeville Theatre," which he published in *Scribner's Magazine* in 1899, was one of the first attempts by a performer to make these claims explicit. Royle was a well-known actor, playwright, and author who moved into vaudeville production from the "legit" (the legitimate) stage. His account raises all kinds of questions relating to artistic subjectivity, as well as highlighting the many paradoxes involved in vaudeville production. In particular, he noted the tension inherent in the principle of variety itself. "The character of the entertainment is always the same," he observed. "There is a sameness even about its infinite variety."[23] Yet at the same time he understood that its famous "open door" policy—"Whatever or whoever can interest an audience for thirty minutes or less, and has passed quarantine, is welcome"—offered far better conditions than the regular theaters or concert halls, whose doors remained "shut and locked" to all but a very few privileged artists (those who could afford the minimum $10,000 required to produce a play or launch a star or mount a concert).[24]

Royle's study began with an assertion that vaudeville was an American invention, derived from the mutual or collective experiences of artists and audiences. Although he recognized its close connections with the British music hall, the French café concerts, and the German beer garden, the explicit appeal to what he described as "the royal American family"—his euphemism for the American people—sets vaudeville apart from those other forms of popular entertainment. In practice, this meant that once inside the theater, everyone's taste was consulted, and no one was offended. To achieve this, weekly programs were increasingly standardized across all the circuits to include various sentimental or comic songs, some kind of graceful or grotesque dancing, a one-act farce (this became Royle's specialty) or melodrama, a musical act of some kind, a dumb act of either trained animals or acrobatics, legerdemain, ethnic or class-based impersonations, perhaps a bit of clay modeling or human statues, a topical lecture, a novelty act of one sort or another, and the jokes or stories of a comic monologist. And the only serious aspect of the show was the fear of seriousness itself, which "hung like a solemn and awful obligation over everything."[25]

Even as it promised to open up a different kind of artistic space, however, Royle argued that the "unique and original world [of vaudeville has] its conventions, too, quite as hard and fast as elsewhere."[26] His description of those conventions is worth repeating in full:

> The vaudeville dude always bears an enormous cane with a spike at the end of it, even though the style in canes may be a bamboo switch. The comedian will black his face, though he never makes the slightest pretence to negro characterisation. The vaudeville "artist" and his partner will "slang" each other and indulge in brutal personalities under the theory that they are guilty of repartee; and with a few brilliant exceptions, they all steal from each other jokes and gags and songs and "business," absolutely without conscience. So that if the comedian has originated a funny story that makes a hit in New York, by the time he reaches Philadelphia, he finds that another comedian has filched it and told it in Philadelphia, and the originator finds himself a dealer in secondhand goods.[27]

Several things are happening in this passage that require further comment. Most obviously, Royle saw vaudeville as a world in and of itself, defined by its own set of laws. In his view, everything about the vaudeville performer was at odds with, frequently dismissive of, and only superficially related to existing practices or cultural forms. At the same time, there was nothing natural or self-evident about vaudeville's conventions; they appeared to exaggerate or distort or undermine, and so increasingly brought into question, any such claims. Modes of acceptable behavior, ways of perceiving the world, forms of communication, even the categories of artistic understanding and evaluation were all placed in doubt. However unintelligible it was to those outside it, Royle claimed, vaudeville did not just reinforce those doubts by cynically capitalizing on and exploiting the circumstances and needs of its audience. Rather, the performances were about those doubts, about the artist's ability to recognize and overcome them, and about the conditions that had given rise to them in the first place. Which is why he concludes with the claim quoted in chapter 2. Vaudeville theatre, he writes, "belongs to the era of the department store and the short story. It may be a kind of lunch-counter art, but then art is so vague and lunch is so real."[28]

With its appeal to the specific conditions of the industrial metropolis, and the sensibilities and practices that were taking shape there, vaudeville had opened up a different kind of social space for the production of art and offered a new medium for making sense of the social realities of its audiences. To succeed, therefore, performers had to respond to those realities in some way by producing routines that mediated between the older practices and the new techniques of vaudeville production. How did they do this?

Royle's references to the short story and the department store extended beyond simple analogy to the specific forms that were developed within vaudeville. Given the time limit for each act, the expectation that performers had to repeat it anywhere from between two to eight times a day (and sometimes more) and up to seven days a week, the small amount of physical space within which they were required to appear, and the intense competition between each act for a position on a bill (leading up to the headline spot), there was constant pressure to reduce performances to their most essential elements, while at the same time they had to "get" the audience within minutes of taking the stage. As the journalist Hartley Davis observed in 1905, "Broad sweeping effects without too much detail are wanted. The artistic 'legitimate' actor wastes too much time in working up to his points, but the skilled vaudevillist strikes them with a single blow and scores. A successful vaudeville sketch concentrates as many laughs in one act and as much action as are usually distributed over a three-act comedy."[29] Likewise, when the theater critic Brooks Atkinson was asked by the editors of *Billboard* to participate in a panel on the theme "What's wrong with Vaudeville?," he replied: "Vaudeville is a specialized technique that cannot be trifled with . . . it requires performers magnetic enough to dominate an inclosed area on a stage. They must be so exuberant or skillful that they can capture an audience's attention instantly and hold it until the act is over. Vaudeville is a form of free, bold, crisp and dynamic showmanship."[30]

When performers reflected on their acts, they, too, frequently compared themselves to artists on the legitimate stage. "What makes the vaudeville artist more competent than his legitimate brother?" asked the song-and-dance performer William Gould. "The 'legit' has his part handed to him. He is rehearsed by a competent stage manager. He does what he is told to do and no more. Everything is left in the hands of his manager." Vaudeville performers, however, were necessarily creative; they had to produce their own acts, either by buying material or writing their own, manage their own acts, find their own props, and double as their own press agent. "No stage manager gives [the vaudeville artist] personality or individuality," Gould remarked. "It simply grows."[31] This resourcefulness enabled performers to constantly "originate," in Gould's terms, to find new ways of presenting existing material, whether songs, dances, or jokes, and get them across to an audience as quickly and effectively as possible.

Increasingly, performers began to develop authoritative accounts of their performance practices. As already noted several times throughout this study, one of the most important of these was Sophie Tucker's autobiography. As with the chapters on the circuits, show business rituals, and the elementary structures of entertainment, Tucker reflected in great detail on her stage business, from many different perspectives and at various points in her career. While there is certainly an element of self-promotion in her narrative, and while its structure and many of its themes rely on the formulas for star biographies, nonetheless, it can also be read as a thoroughly modern account of artistic agency and collective life. I single out a couple of passages at this point to quote at length:

> On the road I used to watch the box office all the time. I would go out in front of the house to hear what the customers said when they bought their tickets. After the show I would go out into the lobby to catch the comments. When I heard them say: "Sophie Tucker with the man who pushes his piano out on stage while she's singing is awfully funny," I knew we were all right. We hadn't lost touch, as the Boss [her manager, William Morris] called it. Of course we had to keep the act alive with new ideas, new tricks all the time. You can't let yourself get stale in this business. And each new piece of business we added had to be put to the same test—did it have human appeal? Was it the kind of thing everybody was going to laugh at? . . . "What gives an act its great entertainment value," the Boss used to say, "is its spontaneity. It's the way an actor seizes on something that happens unexpectedly and turns it into a laugh. The public loves that."[32]

This is the definitive statement of the principles of vaudeville practice. The central concept here is "great entertainment value," which only emerges from the performer's ability to reflect on, and decide if, her act has some kind of "human appeal." What counted as human appeal, however, was discovered from an ongoing dialogue between the artist, her audience, and her manager, about what worked and what didn't work on stage:

> When I started singing, I was terribly clumsy with my hands. I didn't know what to do with them, and I was conscious of their size long after I had eliminated the red dishwashing look. I used to stand in front of the mirror every day and make gestures, learning how to use my hands gracefully. Today, when I see a singer standing in front of a "mike" hanging on for dear life while she sings into it, instead of to the audience, I feel like yelling at her: "Let go, sister. If only you knew how terrible you look like that, you'd lower the mike and stand clear of it and use your hands as a part of your act, the way an entertainer should."[33]

Both passages showed the complex process of developing her stagecraft. This was not a skill that came to her naturally and nor was it guaranteed to last. The only guarantee, in Tucker's view, was that the show had to go on. But what kind of show was it?

"Watch the audience trooping into a New York Vaudeville house," advises Caroline Caffin. "There is no more democratic crowd to be seen anywhere." Once inside what she described as the magical space of the theater, she invites her readers to both reflect on, and make sense of, what they experienced there: "Let us watch some of them [the performers], as they do it [cast a spell over their audience], and try to catch a hint of their methods, and possibly analyze the reason of our response. The show is about to begin. The orchestra leader is in his place, tapping with his baton the call to attention. The music starts, the curtain raises. 'The actors are at hand and by their show you shall know all that you are like to know.'"[34] The great value of Caffin's account turns on her sensitive and detailed descriptions of individual acts, even as she folds those descriptions into a larger set of questions about the social meaning of vaudeville.

The above quote from Shakespeare's *A Midsummer Night's Dream* was meant to convey vaudeville's historic connection to the centuries-old theatrical traditions of premodern Europe, as well as underlining its relevance to the cultural concerns of modern Americans. In chapter after chapter, Caffin urges her readers to consider the ways in which a successful vaudeville act offered profound insights into the most fundamental questions of human being. Moreover, she also asks them to reflect on how a great act transformed their view of themselves and their society. "More or less truly," she claims, "it throws upon its screen the current sentiment of the day. We cannot escape its influence. The echoes of its songs are in our streets, our homes, our ballrooms, we hear them at our parades and public ceremonies. . . . We have put our entertainers behind the frame of a proscenium arch and let down a curtain to mark the division between actor and audience. But the actor is still the reflection of his audience."[35]

Explaining vaudeville's appeal, however, posed considerable challenges for the critic. "For at first glance," she notes, "the special favor for this or that artist may seem to be a mystery. Here is one whose voice is meagre and whose dancing is negligible. Yet her appearance is greeted with salvos of applause; while another, with pretty face, graceful dancing and sweet singing voice, attracts languid approval." For Caffin, this requires a deeper understanding of the methods and appeal of different artists. It is "the strong personality and the ability to get it across the footlights and impress it upon the audience that distinguishes the popular performer . . . quite as much as the ability to sing or dance."[36] On one level, then, her book is an exhaustive guide to the whole world of vaudeville. On another level, though, it is an attempt to come to terms with specific artistic achievements of the great performers and the reasons for their success.

Crucially, her study opens with a discussion of the relationship between the performers and their audiences. An act, she claims, had no chance of success independently of the audience's response to it. Performers are compelled to constantly seek "the chord which shall evoke an answering vibration in [their] audience and to attune [their] offering in a key which, in spite of modulations and varying harmonies, shall strike constantly on that string." Unlike the "highbrow" genius, the "genius" of vaudevillians resided in their ability to recognize this "answering vibration" and, in the process, create an individual technique that accentuates "the key in which they pitch their appeal." Moreover, because they are actually on the stage for so little time, their appeal must necessarily be "vivid, instantaneous, and unmistakable."[37]

These claims are developed at length in Caffin's discussion of Eva Tanguay, whose stage presence seemed to defy the conventional categories of artistic explanation. She describes Tanguay as a "very puzzling enigma," who contradicted every preconceived notion of a successful entertainer. "A Song and Dance Artist who does not dance, cannot sing, is not beautiful, witty or graceful, but who dominates her audience more entirely than anyone on the Vaudeville stage," writes Caffin. "How can we account for the almost breathless intensity with which the audience awaits her entrance?"

They sit up, eagerly awaiting her entrance; the orchestra plays with renewed exuberance, their instruments sharper and louder; and even the lights in the auditorium seem to burn brighter. And then Tanguay appears on the stage: "The voice has no music in it . . . the steps make no attempt at rhythmic movement. . . . And naively, childishly, self-conscious are her songs—if one can call them songs. Mere recitation of her own eccentricities, her extra-vangances, her defiance of all conventions, with the refrain, 'I don't care,' phrased in one way or another, forms the topic. . . . And the audience likes it. . . . Why?"[38]

Although she leaves the question unanswered, Caffin urges her readers to think very carefully about the kind of illusion Tanguay created on stage and to reflect on its social origins. "I wonder if the secret [of Tanguay's success]," she muses,

> is that she is the epitome of that strong force of modern civilization—advertising. It is more than the press-agent's work, though that has been very well done. We have come [to the show], already impressed by the amount of her salary, her continual engagements, her popularity. But she herself tells us and keeps on telling us how extraordinary she is, how successful, how unassailable by criticism and how popular. Again and again we are reminded that money is flowing in on her. Again and again we are informed that she is unique. And this reiteration, so forcibly and believingly uttered, with an assurance that we really are interested, hypnotizes us into belief that we are.[39]

While the endless variety of acts, the relentless demand for novelty, and the commitment to weekly public tryouts were central to vaudeville's appeal, for Caffin, they also highlighted its internal contradictions. "For of necessity the most distinguishing feature of Vaudeville is its variety. Anything that will amuse, interest or satisfy the curiosity is welcome. But," she continues, "the welcome is easily outworn and, if the only claim to interest is that of novelty, it cannot expect to have more than a brief day. But novelty is one of the essentials, so that even acts, having interest beyond that of curiosity, must be constantly refurbished to make them appear new."[40] Performers had to reconcile vaudeville's relentless demand for novelty without undermining or disrupting the show's claim to continuous entertainment. Each time they took the stage, they mediated between the demands of their individual acts and the larger demands that were made of the medium as a whole.

A year after Caffin's book appeared, Brett Page published an influential home study guide for aspiring vaudeville sketch writers, dramatists, or lyricists in which he describes in detail the principles and demands of vaudeville's stage practices. *Writing for Vaudeville* contains extensive instruction on every aspect of vaudeville production, from the technical issues of stage management and lighting, to advice on how to write the kind of popular song that "the boy on the street will whistle and the hand organs grind out until you nearly go mad with the repetition of its rhythm." He urges would-be writers to develop an intimate knowledge of the distinctive structure of the vaudeville stage, an intuitive awareness of how words sound when spoken or sung (rather than as they appear on the page), and a deep understanding of the role of gestures and glances in vaudeville performances. "It is only by acquiring *special* knowledge of one of the most difficult of arts," he advises his readers, "that anyone may hope to achieve success."[41]

Beginning with a discussion of the specific space of the vaudeville theater, and then moving through each of type of act, from the single monologue to the multiperformer playlet, Page explores the philosophical as well as the practical problems of putting on a show. Citing both Aristotle and Freud in support of his claims, he proposes a general theory of plot and lyric, event and action, sound and image, that supported what he calls vaudeville's "tabloid" effects. "Today," he suggests, "a vaudeville performance is the best thought of the world condensed to fit the flying hour." Working in such an environment, the sketch-, joke-, or song- writer had to dispense with unnecessary words, gestures, phrases, and sounds in order to keep an act in motion. "There must be action in the idea—in the thought," Page argues, "even though the performers stand perfectly still."[42]

Several preliminary things can be said about these claims. First, the reference to the flying hour recalls Royle's insight that vaudeville was part of the same social reality that had produced the short story, the department store, and the lunchcounter.[43] Second, writers could not expect to rely upon prior dramatic conventions to tell their stories; to succeed, they had to adapt their narratives to the peculiar requirements of vaudeville. The point of a vaudeville sketch, he observed, "is not to leave a single impression of a single story. It points to no moral, draws no conclusion, and sometimes it might end quite as effectively anywhere before the place in the action in which it does terminate. It is built for entertainment purposes only, and furthermore, for entertainment purposes that end the moment the sketch ends. When you see a sketch you carry away no definite impression, save that of entertainment, and usually you cannot remember what it was that entertained you."[44] And, third, Page connected vaudeville to the emergence of new conceptions of behavior and consciousness.[45] "A playlet," he writes, "is nothing if it is not action, so a comedy playlet is nothing if the comedy does not develop from situations. . . . It is in the inventions of new situations and new business to fit these situations that the playlet writer finds his reward in production and profit."[46]

This was a highly reflexive process. Developing a successful act, Page argues, is only possible in the course of performing it: "A dramatic entertainment is not written on paper. There is an inexplicable something which playing before an audience develops. Both the audience and the actors on the stage are affected. A play—a monologue and every musical form as well—is one thing in a manuscript, another thing in rehearsal, and quite a different thing before an audience. Playing before an audience alone shows what a play [or a song or a dance routine] truly is. Therefore, a play [or a song or a dance routine] can only be made—after it is produced."[47] This link, between playing before an audience and producing a successful act, became the principal claim made by performers in support of their distinctive performance methods. And as we shall see, it was an audience's approval that above all confirmed their feelings of artistic self-worth.

CHAPTER SEVEN

In Search of an Audience

On October 12, 1909, the *New York Times* published the following review of an act at the Colonial Theatre:

> Yvette Guilbert, an artiste who is known and appreciated all over the world, and who has appeared with great success in this city on several occasions, had an experience with an American vaudeville audience . . . yesterday afternoon which she will not soon forget. When it is said that Mme. Guilbert was almost forced to leave the stage during her second number, and that only the persistent applause of a few appreciative persons in the orchestra chairs encouraged her to continue, it may readily be understood that Mme. Guilbert's experience was not a pleasant one. . . . The disturbance during the singing was largely confined to the upper part of the house, but even down stairs there was loud talking and disorder during the artiste's best numbers. To those who observed the paroxysms of delight with which the audience received the troupe of vulgar vaudevillians who preceded her on the bill it was perhaps not surprising. . . . She made her entrance as usual wearing the early Victorian costume of many wide flounces, and with her auburn curls dangling about her neck and shoulders, and the quaint, old-fashioned costumes, suggestive of an ivory miniature done in the days of grandmothers. This was the cue for the first noisy outburst from the gallery. . . . Mme. Guilbert announced that she would begin with "Seventeen Come Sunday," a quaint old English number, which she sings inimitably. She had not gone further than the first verse before the noise in the gallery increased, and there was an interruption of loud laughter. The singer looked surprised, hesitated slightly, then went on bravely, and the noise gradually subsided. Her next song, "Les Cloches Des Nantes," a most dramatic

and impressive little number under ordinary conditions, in which the singer's bell-like tones convey a suggestion of growing terror, was altogether too much for the intellectuals in the upper circle. To begin with it was in a tongue which they did not understand, in itself an offense not to be overlooked. Added to this, the fact that the singer was trying to be serious was too much for them. And so they roared, continuing the disorder throughout the next song, "Mary Was a Housemaid," the humor of which might have appealed if they had been able to hear it. Finally, amid more noise, Mme. Guilbert sang "The Keys of Heaven," one of the best-known numbers in her repertoire, and was then allowed to retire.[1]

According to the *Times* reviewer, there were no problems with Guilbert's performance—to the contrary, in fact. Her singing was just as "delicate and beautiful as it has ever been." The "boorish treatment" she received was due to the "bad taste" and "ill-breeding" of the American vaudeville audience, whose pretensions and prejudices prevented them from collectively recognizing the singer's artistic greatness.[2] The critic then notes that Guilbert had been respectfully and enthusiastically received only months earlier at the Palace Music Hall in London, which in the reviewer's opinion only served to further highlight the audience's lack of refinement. Thus, the refusal of Guilbert was not simply about her choice of songs or her manner of delivering them, but about the very question of whether Americans were collectively able to recognize, and so respond to, great artistry when it appeared before them.

Guilbert's experience highlights just how important the artist's relationship with the audience was. As many writers have pointed out, perhaps more than any other form of late nineteenth- and early twentieth-century popular entertainment, vaudeville performers consistently reached out to make their audience feel like part of the show, appealing to them beyond the footlights with every technique they had at their disposal.[3] The explicit tensions cited in the review above—between those seated in the Colonial Theatre's upper gallery, the less demonstrative though just as restless audience members who occupied the stalls, the "appreciative few" in the orchestra seats, the reformist newspaper critic, and the performer herself—convey how complicated this relationship was. At every moment, and no matter who they were, performers were continually being tested, as audiences challenged them to reveal themselves. As Ethel Waters recalled about her early days on the circuits: "Even the applause didn't convince me I was all right. After each performance I'd take off my make-up . . . and rush out to the lobby to hear what the people were saying about me as they came out."[4]

Or as comedian George Burns once noted, "All you've got is delivery and an attitude and the audience will either defeat you or you will be a sensation."[5] For vaudeville performers, knowing what it meant to "wow" an audience was inseparable from their artistic identity

In the last two chapters, I have spoken at length about the cultural practices developed by vaudeville managers and performers within the process of corporate reconstruction, and tried to set out the basic principles around which their different kinds of business on and off the stage were organized. Moreover, I have also suggested that the managers' ambition to appeal to a national, family-oriented, respectable audience altered the contents of variety acts in significant ways, just as it changed the experience of what going to see a show was all about. Not only did performers have to adjust their material to the new classes of people who were attending shows at the expanding numbers of theaters, but they also had to refigure their practices to account for the demands of continuous production. "A comedian in vaudeville," Eddie Cantor, "is like a salesman who has only fifteen minutes in which to make a sale. You go on stage, knowing that every minute counts. You've got to get your audience the instant you appear."[6]

One consequence of this situation was that performers frequently identified the problem of developing a genuine or sustained relationship to their audience with the problems of their art more generally. As Cantor also noted,

> It's almost impossible to describe the theatre's heights and depths to any non-performer. The heights, perhaps, an outsider can begin to understand—because the audience participates in each success with its applause. But those agonies *without* an audience! The sudden knowledge—with opening night a night or two away—that the lines are stale, the songs all stink, the scenes don't "play." . . . You don't eat, you can't sleep, your stomach churns, your head throbs, and you're seven kinds of psychosomatically sick. This is your life—and you haven't long to live. At least you hope not. And then they haul the curtain up, and suddenly it's all right. All right? It's all you ever want in life! . . . But the livin' ain't easy.[7]

In the days, hours, minutes, before the curtain went up, there seemed to be no way for Cantor to know whether the routine he performed on stage would be accepted as a legitimate act or ridiculed. As he saw it, only the presence of the audience guaranteed the success of an act, and only once they had acknowledged him positively did he feel secure in his abilities as an entertainer.

Cantor's autobiography—*My Life Is in Your Hands*—makes this claim explicit. "Drifting as I did into every conceivable type of crowd," he writes, "I trained myself to the fact that 'the audience is never wrong,' and if a performance failed to go across it was either the fault of the material or the manner of presentation. By carefully correcting the one or the other or both with an eye to the peculiarities of the audience I could never fail a second time."[8] There are two issues to take note of here. First, Cantor conceptualized his material, and what he refers to as his stage manner, in relation to and not independently of his audiences. Artistic legitimacy in these circumstances was derived from a performer's understanding that, ultimately, his act depended on the audience's approval. It was not something achieved separately or even gained from rejecting or ignoring the audience's response. Moreover, Cantor had to train himself to believe in, and to accept, the role of each different audience as authoritative. He had to reach a point where he recognized that their powers of judgment were final, which explains the title of his book.

Second, the structure of continuous vaudeville produced a highly self-consciousness and self-critical relationship between artist and audience, in which the success of an act was never fixed or given in advance, but emerged through constant revision. Thus, even the most successful of acts was always under review. Or to put it another way, an act was always to some degree incomplete or unfinished, because no performance was ever definitive.[9] Cantor even ascribed cosmic significance to this process: "I feel that no man's life is sufficiently interesting in itself unless it is in some way a pattern or design created out of the times and reflecting in it bits of other personalities. I have always felt like a part of other people and that other people were a part of me."[10]

Cantor underlined some of the central problems of vaudeville performance, especially those relating to a performer's ability to respond to the changing tastes and expectations of his audience. Equally, they raised the issue of the audience's ability to find their way into an act, to find something within a performance that offered them a space within it. Philosopher Stanley Cavell refers to the artist's capacity for improvising, his or her willingness for taking and seizing chances, and the audience's readiness to accept such improvisations or risk-taking as an essential part of what they experience.[11] For although an act might well be fully scripted and tested on countless other audiences, the songs already composed, the dance sequences choreographed down to the most minute of specifications, the jokes rehearsed and re-rehearsed so that their timing is impeccable, and the musical accompaniment tightly cued in order to concentrate its impact, the question still remained each time a performer went on stage. Would their abilities as a performer—their talent—be recognized by the audience as such? "Talent can be developed," proclaimed Ethel Waters, "but no one in show business discovers it. Only the public can do that."[12]

Because audiences were encouraged to identify with specific acts as their own, to actively respond by judging one a success (now that's entertainment) and another a failure, performers had to be able to anticipate, adjust, and reorient their acts without undermining the broader shape of the show. For instance, in a review of the singer Blanche Ring, *The Standard and Vanity Fair's* vaudeville critic observed that "she seems to be able to make a hit out of a song that other performers would not even sing if they were on a salary to sing anything handed to them. Just as soon as she begins to warble the chorus and to reach out her arms as though to draw all fear away from them, the audience—not only in the gallery, either—becomes courageous and begins to whistle or hum, and even break into song, and the song is made."[13] Ring's performance incorporated the audience into the musical space as the subject of her song, and she did this by reaching out and appealing to them on an existential level. By whistling, humming, or breaking into song the audience was no longer an abstract presence. They were in the theater only for her; and they recognized in her act some part of themselves.

According to Caffin, the vaudeville performer's ability to overcome the limits of the stage by projecting her personality into the audience was what separated her from artists in other traditions. "As we become better acquainted with the methods and appeal of the different artists," she noted,

we find it is ever the strong personality and the ability to get it across the footlights and impress it upon the audience that distinguished the popular performer. And the ability to do this, quite as much as the ability to sing and dance, is a matter of special study and watchful experience. Of course it looks easy and natural, as if it were no effort; but when you see the same turn given by the same artist two or three times you become aware of how little that is effective is left to chance, even in what seem like impromptu effects. The genial familiarity, that confident smile which seems to break out so spontaneously, the casual entrance and glance around the audience—all have been nicely calculated and their effect registered, but with the artist's sympathy which informs each with the spirit of the occasion and robs it of mechanical artifice.[14]

How did performers overcome the perception that what they did was mechanical or formulaic? And why was their search for an audience essential to this process? Sophie Tucker offers a number of important insights into these issues and the kinds of solutions that were available to performers. "Success in show business depends on your ability to make and keep friends. You'll notice that the entertainers who last are the ones who aren't standoffish and high-hat. To hold your audience you've got to give something of yourself across the footlights," she writes. "And that something has to be genuine, sincere. You can fake it for a season or two maybe. Then the public gets wise and gives you the razzberry. And you're done. Washed up!"[15] Note how she moves seamlessly from the comment about the making and keeping of friends into a discussion of her audience. In Tucker's view, the kind of relationships she formed on stage with her audience were inseparable from and to a large extent determined by those that she developed backstage, particularly with the members of the stage crew, the orchestra leader, and the publicity people in each venue she appeared in.

The singer began to think about her act in this way when she was booked on the New England circuit of the Hathaway theaters, which included performances in Malden, Brockton, Lynn, Lowell, Worcester, New Bedford, Fall River, and Providence, along with several small-time houses in Boston. She recalls that it was the comedian George Le Maire who first advised her on how to build up her program. "First the bright number ('to get the audience to like you'); second, the dramatic song ('to rouse their interest'); third, the novelty ('that's to start them laughing'); fourth, the fast ragtime number ('by this time they'll be ready to applaud and keep time with you.') . . . 'Don't overfeed the audience,' George Le Maire was always preaching to me. 'Leave them hungry. Make 'em yell for more.'" Over time, such catchphrases or show business clichés became part of the structure of her performance, preparing her a sense of a routine's possibilities, but also eliciting the audience's response as well. "My act was allowed ten to twelve minutes," she notes. "If the house kept applauding and wanted an encore, I would come off the wings and ask the stage manager what to do. If George Le Maire was standing there, he would yell, 'Go out. Ask them what they want. If you've got it, if you know it, sing it.'"[16]

Taking her cue from Le Maire, who, like Tucker, was a blackface performer, she began to experiment with the possibilities of presentation and the techniques required to achieve such effects. "All the songs I used were straight singing songs. No tricks, no fancy arrangements, no talking songs such as I do now. I made it my job to learn all the new popular numbers as they came out and to have these with me. Then it is easy to ask the orchestra leader to turn to whatever song the audience asked for." She positioned herself between the orchestra and the audiences and turned her act into a constant reflection on how a song or routine came to sound the way it did. "If the music went wrong," she noted, "I would keep right on. If the music was so bad I had to stop, I would tell the audience, 'Sorry. That's my fault. Let me try again.' Or, 'I didn't learn that one right.' Or, 'I tried something new and it didn't work out.' Taking the blame to myself—and not laying it onto the leader—laughing my way out of the difficulties, made the audience more friendly. They liked me better because I didn't grouch. After a while I caught onto the trick of starting the song myself and letting the orchestra come in after two or three measures."[17] As she became more confident about which effects worked best with different kinds of audiences, and why and how they worked in such a way, she opened up more and more room for the audience within her act, inviting dialogue and commentary from different parts of the house, as well as involving the orchestra as an active participant. In this context, songs were the medium for bringing the audience to understand the meaning of her performance, but they were also a way of transforming relationships within the theater as a whole.

She was, however, also conscious of another problem.

> From the first bill I played I noticed something. An act would go on and something would go wrong. The light cues would be wrong or something would happen to the music. The act would come off ready to tear everybody's hair, cursing, fuming. Between the ravings he would run out to smile and bow and wave to the audience. Maybe he thought he could smooth it over that way. Now what I noticed was that the acts that did this invariably lost the audience before they were through. The energy they put into being mad backstage took something out of their work. Besides this, they got the crew and the musicians down on them. Even a headliner can't afford to make enemies of the stage crew and the orchestra.[18]

Tucker's attention to the possibility of losing an audience was as important to her self-worth as her many examples of successfully gaining and then keeping their attention. This led her to frame her career as the search for an audience, and to characterize this search as a process that took place on and off the stage simultaneously.

As I already explained in chapter 2, Tucker's effort to build a network of friends in the many different theaters and boardinghouses she visited was primarily about finding a way to feel at home in the impersonal world of the circuits. She was also conscious of how important these people were to maintaining her profile. "I found out how important the publicity man of the theatre is," she noted. "I kept the names of the publicity men in all the houses I played. I would write them from time to time, sending them new photographs and the names of my new songs. The photographs were another heavy expense, but I knew I had to have them. The public got tired of the same old poses. Something new. That rule governs every department of show business."[19]

These practices were vastly complicated by the fact that, in nearly every venue in which an act appeared, audiences were distinguishably different from almost every house on any given circuit. According to the critic Walter De Leon, "The Palace, Chicago, will howl at a wisecrack, a nifty, that Duluth audiences won't even flag as it flies over their heads. Boston and Lowell, perhaps an hour apart, might be on different continents so far as their vaudeville tastes are concerned. Before the war, Washington D.C. was one of the best audiences in the country for a classy, clean, clever act." Such conditions presented enormous challenges to performers, especially given the pressure to appeal to audiences without exception. "The location of a theatre in any city," notes De Leon,

> the nature of the city's principal industry—steel-ribbed Pittsburgh could not expect to enjoy things in a similar fashion with rose-grown Portland, Oregon—the personality of the house manager and staff, these and fifty other elements contribute to determine the quality of an audience There are certain well-known good audiences and certain rough ones. Detroit is soft for comedy acts, either classy or hokum, but tough for highbrow musical turns. Youngstown—try to make 'em laugh there, that's all! A comedian playing Baltimore will sometimes insert a suggestion of the risqué when he would not think of pulling the line in Minneapolis.[20]

Other performers were equally conscious of creating an experience within which audiences might eventually feel at home. "Before each performance I tell myself the same thing," Ethel Waters observed. "'They don't have to like me, those people out there. They are not my friends. My job is to make them like me. I have to make these strangers my friends.'"[21] Along similar lines, George Whiting described how he personalized his audience, pursuing techniques much like those developed by Tucker. "I begin by regarding everybody within earshot as my friend; it works out that way. I try to understand my songs and let my understanding be known to audiences," he said.

"I study every song I sing, I do not mean that I merely study the words, but I endeavor to discover the various shades of meaning in the 'ditty' giving my idea of the words in the manner I sing. It is a real benefit to me to do this and I think the public in turn is delighted."[22] Songs in this instance were conceived of as unfolding within a space of intimacy that allowed audiences to understand the possibilities of the show, and artists to discover through performance the identity of their audiences.

"Playing vaudeville from 1912 to 1916 was an education," recalled Mae West in her autobiography. "I played every big city. Chicago, Detroit, Philadelphia, Baltimore—name them. I learned the subtle difference in audiences in different cities, not only from their loud reaction to my own act, but from the varied reactions of the audience to the other acts on the bill. I could attune myself to the faintest shuffle or cough." She also

discovered that a good musical act would always go well in any large city, although the act would sometimes have to change one of its musical numbers in certain cities because some cities liked ragtime songs, some popular ballads. If the act was closing its routine with a big hit song of the day, one that the audience was familiar with, and it was the Number One hit song, the act would finish with great applause. But if the same act with that same song were playing another city, and it did not go over too well, it was only because that particular audience had not yet become familiar with the hit song. It hadn't been "plugged" enough in that city.[23]

West also relied heavily on the local stage managers to tell her which song was popular with the audiences in their theaters, so she could always end her act with "a smash finish."[24] Her observations in the following passage underline the complex set of negotiations that invariably took place between vaudeville performers and audiences each time they encountered each other in the theater and often for the first time.

Each city and every town set its own standard for entertainment. . . . I would look out at my audience, standing in my tiger skin, before the show would start, when the house lights were up before the overture was played. I would try to figure out what the audience looked like, what they did, what problems of life they faced. I would ask a lot of questions of the stage manager. . . . I learned to adjust the mood, tempo and material of my act. I did whatever seemed necessary to get the best response from each type of audience. I gave it to them fast or slow, or low or mean or sultry. I changed a song, I adapted myself to the way they liked it best. . . . The audience did the rest—in imagination, of course.[25]

West's continual striving to be as simple, as direct, and as genuine was designed to eradicate the distance between an artist and her audience. Her talent lay in knowing herself as if she was one of them, suspending their disbelief in her as she did in them. By all accounts, the effect of her performances was mesmerizing. Nora Bayes, who spent many years reflecting on this same problem, noted that in seeking to hold an audience, "the artist forgets the immediate pressure of real things and makes the unreal situation on the stage an incident that is true."[26] Bayes's claim is that in vaudeville there is the possibility of reaching some kind of aesthetic truth, which helps to explain why audiences kept going back so many times to see her act, and why she herself continued to perform the same songs and routines for so many years.

As I have already suggested, the larger effect was to transfer the issue of artistic success and failure onto the audience, whose role it was to distinguish between the fraudulent and the true performer, to decide who had successfully put over their act and who was merely putting it on. The vaudeville artist was thus compelled to seek and continually renew the belief and response of the audience every time she stepped onto the stage. This meant that a performer's capacity to make her presence felt to an audience was paramount. According to Bayes, it was her obligation and thus essential to her artistic claims to create a stage personality so definite, rounded, unique, and so entirely her own that she would be understood wherever she went and acclaimed whenever she appeared on stage.[27] The all-embracing form of the vaudeville show, with its vast technical and imaginative range, was requisite for producing just such conviction. Through the constant repetition of her act, in thousands of theaters and over many weeks and years, vaudeville enabled the popular singer to arrive at an awareness of herself as an artist and, at the same time, to bring her audience to an awareness of itself as the object of her art. No wonder Mae West finished her act with the line, "It isn't what you do, it's how you do it." And no wonder the gallery went wild.[28]

The kinds of claims that performers such as Bayes and West made about their art, and the terms they used to appeal to a certain feeling for their audience, implied a specific understanding of artistic presence. What seems clear from the above examples is that the search for an audience in vaudeville involved a set of techniques for incorporating the audience within a performer's act, and that these techniques were contingent upon both parties claiming the space of the theater as their own. An elaborate statement of this idea appeared in an article that Bayes wrote for *Theatre Magazine* in 1917. As we saw above, Bayes was an influential figure in terms of articulating the changing relationship between performers and their audiences—especially female performers—and her article is notable for the way in which she invoked concepts of friendship and intimacy as primary conditions of hold connecting with an audience.[29] I want to quote several sections in full, so as to capture the full complexity of her argument.

"It is not my intention to tell you how I hold my audience," she began, 'because the situation is quite reverse—they hold me. They represent the most comfortable and valuable friendship. They are my friends. It is therefore with the intimate safety of friendship, that I go out upon the stage and shake hands with them. My performances are exactly like an intimate chat with one or two close friends." She then explained the principles for deciding what counted as a genuine act in vaudeville. "But I do know," she declares,

> that in holding an audience the most important factor is to be sincere towards them in your work. . . . One must have heart, mind, faith, and love for one's audience. These are the elements of friendship. . . . The artist who really has something to say, something to give to others, really confides a secret. That is to say the ideas of artistic value, are in themselves the outcome of inner feeling or thought. It is quite necessary always to have to something to *say* . . . . The vaudeville audience is the most sensitive, because it is there to meet old friends, to spend an hour of two in pleasant company, and has no objection to tears if they start from the hearts of their friends on the stage. They are just as ready to cry with you in the theatre as they would be in their own homes, but they must be real tears, not stage tears.[30]

Bayes's claims provided further evidence of the ways in which vaudeville performers were coming to conceive of themselves as popular artists, as well as their growing sense of speaking directly to and for their audience. Her comments also testified to the importance that performers attached to having something to sing about that connected with their audience's most intimate experiences. In Bayes's view, this was achieved by reimagining the space of the theater not simply as a medium for public display, but one in which the distinctions between home and work, public and private passions and desires, inner thoughts and outer ideas, were continually tested, explored, and redefined. In other words, it was a space in which artists and audiences found their way to each other, meeting there "as old friends," and so continually discovered the meaning of entertainment together.

Any fears about losing the audience or doubts about the failure of an act were dispelled by the capacity for performers to believe in their art and to invoke an answering response from their audience. In an interview in *Actorviews*, Bayes recalled "[the singer] Florence Nash coming to me in fear and trembling at the Palace. They'd changed her time from four to three [her position in the running order], and she was afraid the second week's opening audience would crucify her."[31] To Nash's anxieties about facing an audience with a different set of expectations, and the possibility of being "crucified," Bayes replied: "'See here,' I says to Florence . . . 'Why, you're trembling and sighing like the North wind—how do you expect the public to love you when you go out to them like that? That's what's the matter, Florence—you aren't letting the public love you enough.'"[32] For Bayes, vaudeville was defined by the audience, and, like a jury in a court of law, its members sat in judgment upon the artistic truths to which she aspired.[33]

These claims can be usefully compared to various strands of twentieth-century modernism, in which the refusal or rejection of the audience by the artist was essential to the cultural legitimacy its participants wanted to achieve. "The loss of a public is in fact the artist's withdrawal from his [or her] public, as a consequence of his [or her] faithfulness to his [or her] art," writes Stanley Cavell, in an influential study of film.[34] Whereas vaudeville performers were searching for an audience for whom the show meant everything, modernist artists were confronting the issue of what it meant to have an audience at all. Hence their concern with the uncertainty or instability of point of view, an insistence on the inaccessibility of the work of art, and a deep suspicion about any well-meaning, sympathetic audience.[35] That such a crisis began to occur around the same time that vaudeville was coming to dominate popular entertainment suggests that in their common focus on the audience as the primary issue for artists, the participants in both forms were addressing similar problems and raising doubts about the meaning of art in modern societies. In both cases, practitioners were questioning if it was possible, and even whether it was desirable to form a genuine relationship with an audience.

I will have more to say on this matter in chapters 9 and 10. For the moment, I want to return to Keith's description of his early vision for vaudeville. "Two things I determined at the outset should prevail in the new scheme," he wrote. "One was my fixed policy of cleanliness and order should be continued, and the other that the stage show must be free from vulgarisms and coarseness of any kind, so that the house and entertainment would directly appeal to the support of ladies and children—in fact my playhouse must be as 'homelike' an amusement resort as it was possible to make it."[36] The idea is that vaudeville would come to resemble the home; to its patrons, it would feel like a home away from home and, as such, dispel the sense of emptiness or loneliness associated with walking into an empty theater. The power of this vision is unmistakable. It conveys the wonderment and mysteries of the great metropolis; it carries with it answers to some of the most challenging cultural problems of the 1890s; and it proved to be a blueprint for the many of forms entertainment that followed. Moreover, in answer to the sense of alienation and loss, the collective crisis, that Americans were experiencing because of the immense changes taking place in their social world, Keith's conception of vaudeville promised a place of intimacy and identification, of unparalleled activity and excitement, of joy and pleasure, in which both performers and audiences dreamt of finally coming home together. I now want to turn to the vaudeville melodies that proved so crucial in shaping and supporting this vision of a collective homecoming and consider the performer's claims that through their songs and tunes they spoke directly to and for the hopes and desires, the passions and aspirations, of their new audiences.

CHAPTER EIGHT

Vaudeville Melodies

//**A**t one time," explained the singer and actor Bert Williams, "it seemed to me that almost everybody in the United States was writing a song 'just like 'Nobody.' It never occurred to any of them that to be 'just like 'Nobody' a song would need to have the same human appeal as 'Nobody,' mixed with its humor, the human appeal of the friendless man. Most of these imitations were called 'Somebody,' and that was the only single solitary idea they had, just a feeble paraphrase of 'Nobody,' with the refrain switched around to 'Somebody.' The majority of writers apparently think that one idea spread over three or four verses and the refrain is enough to carry the song. A really good song must be fairly packed with ideas."[1] Williams' description leads us into the central issue I want to focus on in the last three chapters. This primarily concerns what Williams refers to here as popular music's "human appeal," the ideas and practices embodied in such an appeal, and the problem of how artists came to understand the value of their songs. None of these issues will make much sense, however, unless we know a bit more about the processes of popular song production. Although I concentrate on several examples of what we might think of as "vaudeville melodies," I am not proposing an exhaustive interpretation of a specific genre or composer here—more like a clarification of how music was made and how it circulated within the vaudeville system.

To begin with, I want to consider the social practices of creativity, imitation, repetition, transcription, and performance that developed among vaudeville artists. These topics cannot be properly understood without first examining some of the most notable ways in which performers conceived of the value of their music. A large part of this chapter will therefore involve setting out these practices and exploring their relevance to theories of popular music performance. Beyond that, I want to focus on vaudeville's

part in bringing about fundamental changes in the American musical land-
scape, and particularly its influence on the respective histories of the blues,
jazz, the Tin Pan Alley pop ballad, the musical comedy and revue, and
syncopated dance music.[2] From there, the final two chapters return to the
broader theme of popular success as a measure of artistic value and the
kinds of problems this theme raises for a critical account of popular music
in American culture.

Let me begin by summarizing several existing studies that I think are most
relevant to this chapter. The point of this exercise is to establish in a broad
sense what counts as popular music for these authors, but also, and perhaps
more important, to acknowledge the influence their work has had on my
own thinking. From there, I want to sketch the basic outline of musical
production on the vaudeville stage, before turning to a more detailed discussion of specific instances of vaudeville music-making. In each case, my
aim is to describe, first, the processes by which these melodies were incorporated into vaudeville acts and, second, what happened once they began
to circulate through the system as objects of consumption. The standpoint
I take here emphasizes the shifting contexts in which vaudeville melodies
appeared, whether as instrumental or vocal arrangements, solo or ensemble
pieces, accompaniments to a song and dance routine or dumb act, supporting a performer's "wow" finish (drum roll please!), or as incidental music
for a playlet. To begin with, I want to consider the social practices that developed among vaudeville artists. These practices cannot be effectively discussed, however, without reference to a number of important debates about
the relationship between folk, popular, and classical musical traditions.

The concept I want to introduce, by way of defining these practices and
the values derived from them, is creative fragmentation, which comes from
Peter Van Der Merwe's study of pre-twentieth-century popular music, *The
Origins of the Popular Style*. "One of the great forces in American music . . .
is what one could call creative fragmentation," Van Der Merwe argues. "A
tune is broken down into simpler and simpler elements, while, in com-
pensation, these elements may develop a new complexity of their own."[3]
Although Van Der Merwe is skeptical of attempts to explain music in historical and social terms—at one point he describes *any* such attempts as
futile—nonetheless, his own evidence points in the opposite direction.
Creative fragmentation became a practice that was essential to the new
forms of popular music that took shape on the vaudeville stage.[4]

In order to get a better understanding of the issues involved here, I
want to turn to two key texts that argue for closer study of the relationship

between historical processes, cultural circumstances, and musical contents. The first is an influential study of the songwriter Stephen Foster by the musicologist William Austin. Austin proposed that we analyze the ways in which such well-known songs such as "Jeanie," "Susanna," and "The Old Folks at Home" circulated on a global scale, from the 1840s until the present, generating new and ever-expanding meanings, across a diversity of historical contexts and, in the process, transforming their significance in relation to each other and their respective audiences. In other words, songs were forms of value in motion; they were processes, rather than fixed objects. The capacity for Foster's songs to unify the most diverse, and often deeply divided, audiences established him as a representative American artist, but one who was already working within and understood himself as speaking to an international popular song tradition. Moreover, Austin argues that mere musical description or analysis alone cannot account for the phenomenal commercial success of Foster's songs or for their cultural significance. Only by exploring the cultural contrasts and connections between them, the social contexts in which they were produced, and their historical and poetic dimensions does he think we can explain why they have come to mean so many things to so many people.[5]

What interests me most about Austin's account is the connection he makes between the structure of Foster's songs, especially their tunes, and their reception and use by an extremely mobile, usually immigrant, and mostly working-class population. Here is how he describes the situation in the mid-1850s: "The tune [of "Oh Susanna"] was shared far more widely than the words Foster had given it, more widely than any one meaning. It served all sorts of groups, enhancing their internal unity, but among the groups, in relation to each other, the tune established no unity of will or understanding. The tune was adaptable to the functions of many separate 'folks.' What it meant to each of them depended on them more than on the music."[6] Austin's point is that the commercial value of Foster's popular songs or tunes, which on the surface appears to be self-evident—the songs were hugely successful commercial products—frames a much more complicated issue of how different groups of people create, use, and ultimately experience popular tunes, and how we account for those creative practices and the experiences identified with them. Rather than simply following a path from the songwriter to the public performance to the mass market for sheet music, Foster's songs crossed the lines between commercial and functional music, popular and art music, and popular music and "folksong" many times, and not always in the same direction.[7]

My second example is a study of Irving Berlin's early years as a songwriter—from 1907 until 1914—by Charles Hamm. Irving Berlin is central to the story I have been trying to tell for a number of reasons. First, his initial successes coincided with the consolidation of vaudeville as the primary entertainment medium for popularizing songs and new musical genres. Second, Berlin's songs and melodies frequently rivaled Foster's in terms of their widespread popularity and the varied contexts in which they appeared. And, third, his approach to songwriting exemplified in many ways the working methods developed by performers and composers who operated within the vaudeville system. As one early collaborator of Berlin's wrote, " The real basis of Berlin's success is industry—ceaseless, cruel, torturing industry. There is scarcely a waking minute when he is not engaged either in teaching his songs to a vaudeville player or composing new ones. His regular working hours are from noon until daybreak. All night long he usually keeps himself a prisoner in his apartment, bent on evolving a new melody which shall set the whole world beating time."[8] I will discuss the significance of this specific model of song production below and then in the following two chapters evaluate its relevance to the myths of popular entertainment.

Like Austin, Hamm's theory foregrounds the many and varied settings for performing popular songs, focusing extensively on vaudeville, Broadway theater, and the home as the most common contexts for encountering and learning Berlin's songs. Furthermore, he argues that "the contemporary perception of the genre of a song, and hence its meaning, was shaped most importantly by its performance and by the venue in which this performance took place."[9] Berlin's songs were thus notable for belonging to two or more genres, or occupying a space between several of them. More important, their compositional style and structure were always framed in terms of who the audience for each of his songs was, and the specific venue or setting in which it they were meant to be performed. In Hamm's view Berlin's songs were part of the same popular song tradition within which Foster had worked. This broadly international tradition relied on and, in fact, encouraged flexibility in the composition, circulation, and performance of a song or tune. It was essentially a corporate process involving multiple persons in the production of the song. The songwriters were generally responsive to, and derived their artistic relevance and value from, the specific concerns and identities of their audiences. And the songwriters' larger ambition was to achieve popular acceptance and therefore the sale of as many of their songs as possible.

I set out Berlin's conception of songwriting and song form in the context of vaudeville in more detail in the next section. For the moment I simply want to want note that the majority of Berlin's earliest songs were written for vaudeville and that the practices he developed in this period were in response to as well as being critical to the development of what in earlier chapters I called the vaudeville aesthetic.[10] Broadly speaking, this aesthetic encompassed and transformed not just particular songs or tunes, or the work of a particular composer, but the whole practice and conception of musical production, from creation to dissemination to reception. Two studies have been especially important in helping me to understand this process: Joseph Horowitz's authoritative study of the twentieth-century classical music industry, *Understanding Toscanini*, and Derek Scott's more recent, but no less impressive, study of nineteenth-century popular musical transformation, *Sounds of the Metropolis*.[11] Significantly, neither author confines himself to a single genre or style, but rather sets out to understand the ways in which the social, political, and cultural upheavals of the late nineteenth century affect our understanding of twentieth-century musical practices, forms, values, and experiences.

To begin with Horowitz: what he demonstrates is just how difficult it is to separate the concept of creative fragmentation, which formed the basis of musical production in vaudeville, from the high cultural claims of artistic autonomy that characterized European symphonic and operatic traditions. Furthermore, his study suggests that the processes of popularizing classical music in American culture, from the Boston Symphony Hall to the New York Metropolitan Opera, were in every sense a part of, as much as they were opposed to, the extensive corporate reforms undertaken by the vaudeville managers. The artists, entrepreneurs, and audiences in one sphere were simultaneously reaching toward, and pushing away from, the values and practices identified with the other. Moreover, understanding Toscanini's dominance of classical music in twentieth-century American culture, in Horowitz's view, means knowing more about Barnum's dominance of nineteenth-century popular entertainment. Explaining the rise of one relies on us making sense of the triumph of the other. And their respective successes and failures highlight the larger problem of what it means to be an artist in contemporary American culture. Most important, however, his book demonstrates that only if we are prepared to historicize the relationship between these different musical cultures and recognize their interdependence, as much as their independence from one another, will we be able to make sense of the particular claims, forms, or values characteristic of each.

Scott's book is somewhat different in tone and presents the reader with extended cases studies of relevant musical examples. He develops this perspective through a comparative study of the four great nineteenth-century metropolitan centers for the production of Western culture: Vienna, London, Paris, and New York. The musical culture within each city in its own way defined, but also empowered, a transcontinental revolution in the style of popular music, much along the lines set out by William Austin in his work on Stephen Foster. For Scott, however, the central question is how to account for the processes by which the polarization of music into two distinct spheres took place, and the subsequent development of new musical conventions, new techniques, new organizations, and new networks of distribution.[12] In the later chapters on the Viennese waltz, the American blackface minstrel song, the British music-hall voice, and the French cabaret style, he sets out in great detail how these variable contexts gave rise to distinctive practices that were, at the same time, continually integrated into a broader, global conception of popular musical practices and the values identified with them. What concerns us immediately, though, is the linking of musical phrases and forms to issues of reproduction, originality, imitation, purity, and mixture. All these issues were intensified in the context of vaudeville, partly because of the worldwide scale of the industry, but also because the structure of the shows were based on the relentless search among artists and managers for ever newer, and more remarkable, instances of musical novelty.

How did creative fragmentation become a principle of vaudeville musical production? Before we can answer this question, we need to understand the musical practices that were most commonly featured in vaudeville, as well as their relationship to the vaudeville aesthetic. Given its origins in the concert-saloons that were established in many nineteenth-century American cities during the 1850s, there was already a significant focus in vaudeville on musical variety or novelty, much of it derived from the older practices of blackface minstrelsy, especially its olio or variety section.[13] The emergence of variety, and then vaudeville, from the saloons—themselves undergoing a transformation into venues for burlesque and drag—involved a series of gradual changes in the role of music, particularly the accompaniment provided for comic sketches and monologues, dance acts, so-called dumb acts, and melodramas. The increasingly prominent place of "vaude" orchestras, for example, opened up a space that provided regular employment for thousands of performers, and frequently intersected with the hundreds of onstage bands and orchestras that appeared as small-time and big-time acts in their own right.

The process was the subject of a series of detailed sketches in comedian
Joe Laurie's memoirs, which provided a vivid introduction to life on the circuits. "For many years," he observed,

> the variety shows had the old "three-piece orchestra," piano, stool and
> cover! . . . The orchestras in vaude were built up gradually. First a drum-
> mer was added. Then some guy who liked music added a catgut scaper
> [a violinist]; we called them "Yeh, yeh men" because they usually led
> orchestras and while playing the fiddle they had to beat out time for
> the other guys, which they did with their heads, making it look like
> they were saying "yes" all the time. Little by little they added cornet,
> trombone, and when they got real swell they added the "one-in-a-bar" or
> "live-forever" guy (which is the nice bass player).[14]

Laurie's description of the shift from the "pit boys" or the house pianists
to fully fledged orchestras underlines the kinds of transformations in musical practices I am interested in exploring here. By focusing on the large
numbers of musicians who worked as house pianists, staffed the theater
orchestras, provided relief in between acts, supported the stars on stage, or
toured the circuits as part of larger ensembles, his account highlights how
little we actually know about these performers. At one point he cited a
touring singer who said to a small-town violinist at rehearsal, "You are not
a musician? What is your regular job?" The violinist replied, "No. I'm the
town undertaker, but I play to have fun!"[15] Having fun is notable mostly for
its absence from scholarly discussions of musical experience, especially if
the person playing is a full-time undertaker. Likewise, the generic gestures
of the bandleaders, nicknamed the "Yeh, yeh men" for the way they nod in
time to the beat, or the "thousands of singing acts" touring the circuits, are
frequently neglected in historical accounts of popular music.

Laurie also noted the way in which the most trivial of phrases or actions
often became the source for a great song-and-dance routine. His example is
Bill "Bojangles" Robinson's famous stair dance. "It all came about by acci-
dent, like most successes," he recalled. "At the Palace there are four steps
on each side of the stage for the use of the actor when he has to go down to
the audience or for a committee who are asked to come up on stage. One
matinee Bill came down to the audience to greet some friends (ad lib), and
when he came back to the stage he ad-libbed a dance up the steps, which
got a big laugh and plenty of applause. Need I tell you more?"[16] Robinson's
routine took the most conventional of gesture, walking down a set of stairs
to greet some friends, and transformed it into a model of human perfection.

He showed his audience that their desire for unpredictable and remarkable experiences was intimately connected to their most ordinary actions and feelings.

Laurie also provided us with an indispensable account of the development of music within vaudeville. He began with the house pianists, whose skills often competed with and, in some cases, surpassed the acts they were accompanying. The performers were mythic figures, whose talent lay in their ability to respond creatively to any request for a song or tune. "There were many great ivory-beaters," he claims, "most of them nonreaders but great fakers. I would say about 80 per cent of all old-time piano players could fake anything you could sing, hum or whistle."[17] The reference to "nonreaders" or "corroborated" confirmed his belief that vaudeville was primarily a medium for identifying real talent, and that it was the audience who ultimately judged them.

He then traced the emergence of the "vaude orchestras," which came to feature a mix of strings, brass, a rhythm section, and, most important for the comic acts on stage, a drummer with a multitude of accessories such as cowbells, ratchets, horns, and so on, who was as much part of an act as she or he was also the accompaniment for it. The crucial transition came when the manager of the western Orpheum circuit, Martin Beck, put fifteen-piece orchestras on his circuit and compelled them to play the last person out of the theater with the exit march. "The was a really big idea of Beck's," writes Laurie, "because nearly all musicians would stop playing a few minutes after the stereopticon slide, picturing a little child with a candle in her hand saying 'Good Night,' was thrown on the curtain. It left a void and was a letdown for the audience walking out of the silent theatre. With the orchestra 'playing 'em out,' the customers carried out the joy of the show with them and even hummed a hit tune heard during the performance."[18] For Laurie, the music that audience members heard as they arrived at and departed the theater was as much a part of the show as the hit songs featured by the headline acts. From his perspective, what counted as music in vaudeville was not any one song or tune, but the totality of the performance and the collective effort required to produce it.

All of this may seem a bit like a detour on the way to a discussion of creative fragmentation. But if we want to understand this practice, then we need to know more about music in vaudeville, especially the claims that were made by performers to justify certain techniques or effects as essential to their success, and the response that audiences made to them.[19] It is worth pausing here, then, to reiterate David Ewen's observation about the relationship between the music publishers, the songwriters, and vaudeville: "It was to vaudeville, more than any other branch of musical theatre, that the Tin Pan Alley [composers and publishers] of 1890 and the early 1900's owed [their] greatest debt. The history of vaudeville and Tin Pan Alley overlaps so frequently that it is hardly possible to speak of one without discussing the other."[20]

In chapters 5 and 6, I set out the structural relationships between these different aspects of show business and claimed that a more effective way to understand their overlapping history was to see performers, composers, publishers, booking agents, lyricists, playwrights, advertisers, and so on, as part of a single entertainment structure with a unique set of artistic values. I now want to explore the same structural connections at the level of musical concepts and practices by focusing on Irving Berlin's approach to songwriting. As I noted above, a large proportion of Berlin's earliest songs were written for the vaudeville stage, and his conception of songwriting was in many ways a response to the particular demands that the circuits and continuous vaudeville placed on performers.

The central claim that Berlin consistently made was that his songs were based on the ordinary phrases, melodies, rhythms, and images he encountered in daily life. "I get an idea," he said, "either a title or a phrase or a melody, and hum it out to something definite. . . . I am working on songs all of the time, at home and outside and in the office. I gather ideas, and then I usually work them out between eight o'clock at night and five in the morning."[21] This working method was by no means unusual for songwriters, although Berlin was often singled out as an exemplary figure because he wrote so many hit songs, and wrote so prodigiously.[22] As with most of the songwriters and arrangers who wrote for vaudeville, Berlin was responding to the performers' constant demand for new songs for their acts. At the same time, however, he claimed that writing a hit song depended on reformulating existing melodies. "Our work," he once claimed, "is to connect the old phrases in a new way, so that they will sound like a new tune." For him, "the real originality in song writing consists in the construction of the song rather than in the actual melodies."[23]

For Berlin, songs derived their meaning from the way in which they allowed for recognition on the part of the listener, while at the same time opening up the possibility of transforming that familiarity, whether through modulation, lyrical additions, or changes in tempo. As he once remarked of his most famous song, "Alexander's Ragtime Band," from 1911: "Its opening words, emphasized by immediate repetition—'Come on and hear! Come on and hear!'—were an invitation to 'come,' to 'join in,' and 'hear' the singer and his song. And that idea of inviting every receptive auditor within shouting distance became a part of the happy ruction—an idea pounded in again and again throughout the song in various ways—was the secret of the song's tremendous success."[24] Berlin's emphasis on the democracy of the event, the pleasures of collective repetition, the happy ruction, and the great call to participate in the show reached back to Barnum's idea of Ballyhoo, Stephen Foster's collective vision of the popular song, and the massed musical festivals associated with the bandleader Patrick S. Gilmore.[25] In his view, a good song invited its listeners into the public experience of music and enabled them to inhabit a different reality.

Berlin's theory of song writing received critical support from Brett Page, who frequently cited him in *Writing for Vaudeville*. For example, he quotes Berlin as saying that certain songs lent themselves more readily to effective staging, turning them into what he called production songs. "For instance," Berlin notes,

> "Alexander's Ragtime Band" could be—and often was—put on with a real band. The principal character could sing the first verse and the chorus alone. The chorus girls could come out in regimentals, each one "playing" some instrument—the music faked by the orchestra or produced by "zobos"—and when they were all on stage, the chorus could be played again with rousing effect. During the second verse, sung as a solo, the girls could act out the lines. Then with the repetition of the chorus, they could produce funny characteristic effects on the instruments. And then they could all exit—waiting for the audience to bring them back for the novelties the audience would expect to be introduced in an encore.[26]

Berlin's songs were thus constructed to allow for a continuous variation of singers, groups, situations and styles, and no single performance was meant to be the original or definitive one. It was the performance that made the song, and not the other way around.[27]

The production song was in many ways the product of vaudeville's tabloid form, (see chap. 6). The term *tabloid*, or "tab," as Page uses it, referred to that process of condensing existing material to fit the time limits of a vaudeville bill, but also related to the qualities he associated with vaudeville's elementary appeal. This included the sequences of disconnected images or subplots, the practice of rearranging familiar parts and characters onto a new act, and the emphasis on slapstick comedy. This mostly involved what Page calls "punch." "Punch," he writes, "comes from a certain strong human appeal. Punch is the thing that makes the pulse beat a little quicker, because the heart has been touched. Punch is the precise moment of the dramatic. It is the second in which the revelation flashes upon the audience."[28]

This dramatic moment both amplified and extended the theatrical effect of the song in the shortest possible time. "Ten notes may be the secret of a popular song success," Anatol Friedland observes.

> If I can make my listeners remember ten notes of a song that's all I ask. . . . This is the music punch, and it depends on merit alone. . . . To make a punch more punchy still, we repeat it at least once, and some-times oftener, in a song. You may start your chorus with it, repeat it in the middle, or repeat it at the end. Rarely is it repeated in the verse. High-brow composers call it the theme. For the popular song composer, it's the punch. Clever repetition that makes the strain return with de-lightful satisfaction is one of the tricks of the trade—as well as of the art of popular music.[29]

In this formulation, popular music has no intrinsic content; it refers only to a practice of putting a song or tune together, and to the possibility of keep-ing the audience members involved in each dramatic situation as the per-formances unfold across the course of a show. Jeffrey Magee confirms the centrality of this practice in Berlin's early songs. "On the vaudeville stage a song had to tell a complete story and create a vivid character through which to tell that story," he argues. "In this context Berlin exploited a savvy trick: what might be called the *reinterpreted refrain*. Songwriting conventions dictated that refrains repeated the same words after every verse. But to avoid stasis or dramatic inertia Berlin found a way to write verses so that the re-curring refrain words took on new meaning with every verse."[30] And this variability meant that the song's meaning was transformed with each new performance as well.

While I have focused almost exclusively on Irving Berlin's theories of song production, the claims on which he based his practices were by no means unique. For instance, William Schafer and Johannes Riedel demon-strate that such practices were also widespread among ragtime composers. Their example is Kerry Mills, who became the most successful writer of cakewalks in the early 1900s. Schafer and Riedel describe him as "a skilful and prolific hack composer capable of writing in any popular idiom and of instantly capitalizing on any fad." They then go on to suggest that Mill's hit song, "At a Georgia Campmeeting," which he wrote in 1897, was success-ful because "it so thoroughly synthesizes musical materials: a regular piano march structure of several strains, with repeats, bridges, and trio effects combined with an old folk tune ("Our Boys Will Shine Tonight") guaranteed to evoke a complex Civil War/Old South/Minstrel nostalgia. All of this—using rhythms reminiscent of minstrel dances like the grand walk-around, with a percussive, banjo-like sonority." Moreover, on the published sheet music, the tune was subtitled: "A characteristic march which can be used effectively as a two-step, polka or cakewalk." For Schafer and Riedel, the song's contents, as well as the performance instructions, demonstrate Mills's "shrewd inventiveness," along with a preference for compositions that were all "equally facile and melodic."[31]

I doubt that Schafer and Riedel's contempt for Mills (and, by association, his audience) offers us much by way of understanding why "At a Georgia Campmeeting" proved so popular in the late 1890s, or why it remained so well into the 1950s (see Sidney Bechet's well-known recording from 1950, for example). However, their analysis does convey (mostly in negative terms) some of the complexity and difficulty of tracing out, and then trying to explain, the particular processes of popular music production on the vaudeville stage. But their discussion also highlights why the methods of analysis developed for the eighteenth- and nineteenth-century European symphonic and chamber-music traditions may not be able to adequately account for what was happening to music on the vaudeville stage; let alone what took place when someone sang it on the street, after a show, or in someone's home, as she or he attempted to find ways of expressing their connection with the melodies heard the evening before. As Paul Charosh puts it, the word *song* may "evoke nothing tangible, but, rather, a memory of a performance, public or private, professional or amateur."[32]

The musical practices that came to define and frame the experience of a vaudeville, from dance acts to a comic monologues, enabled performers to connect the most ordinary or familiar of musical themes, or phrases, or rhythms with the constant search for new ways of producing them. "The easiest thing in the world is to write a song," declares Page, "the most difficult, to write a song that will be popular. I do not mean a 'popular' song, but a song everybody will whistle—for few songs written for the populace really become songs of the people."[33]

CHAPTER NINE

Nothing Succeeds Like Success

I now want to return to the broader issue of popular success in vaudeville. Before I turn to several instances in which performers and critics elaborate their understanding of popular success, I want to outline my theoretical reference points. A more sustained discussion of these references takes place below, and it will involve drawing together a number of the conceptual strands I have been exploring in the previous three chapters. It is important, however, to begin by putting the concepts in view.

The narratives and images of popular success on the vaudeville stage were an integral part of the broader mythology of modernization that was taking shape in the United States.[1] What I mean by mythology is a story about the past that groups of human beings tell about themselves in order to explain their origins, to confirm their collective identity, and hence to understand what counts as meaningful in their lives. The definition I have found most useful in this regard is the one developed by Richard Slotkin over the course of his three-volume study of the American frontier. "A mythology," he writes, "is a complex of narratives that dramatizes the world vision and historical sense of a people or culture, reducing centuries of experience into a constellation of compelling metaphors."[2] Slotkin's analysis reminds us that, however contested or complicated the frontier myth is, nonetheless it functions as a deep structure within Americans' collective consciousness. This is not to say that it has remained constant, or that it implies a uniform perspective on the world. For while it has provided Americans with a compelling founding narrative for several centuries, it has also been continuously challenged and transformed in response to changing cultural values, political ideas, and social circumstances.[3]

The myth of success was predominantly a late nineteenth-century phenomenon, although it was clearly related to earlier Puritan mythologies

about the work ethic and the virtuous life, as well as the powerful themes
of self-sufficiency that characterized texts such as Benjamin Franklin's influential *Autobiography* and J. Hector St. John de Crèvecoeur's *Letters to
a Young Farmer*.[4] Moreover, as Slotkin suggests, the success literature was
initially a variant of the frontier myth, drawing on well-known themes of
individual self-transformation in a wide-open society, and the New World
promise (or what is now referred to as the American Dream) of unlimited opportunity that was considered to be the birthright of every individual.[5] After
the 1820s, however, it was also a story about the possibility for worldly
success within the new environment of the industrial city. Individuals suc-
ceeded by triumphing over the corrupting institutions and social conditions
of urban life, transforming both themselves and the city in the process. This
explains the appeal of the most influential and enduring expression of the
success myth, which appeared in the series of best-selling dime novels by
Horatio Alger. According to Kenneth Lynn, Alger's novels about the "rag-to-
riches" adventures of street urchins such as Ragged Dick, his most famous
character, and their attempts to achieve security, power, and wealth in the
metropolis through hard work, honesty, and thrift, codified "a scheme of
values, a conception of the world, a way of life, which has in varying degrees
been shared by the great bulk of the American people for over a century."[6]
The success myth thus involves us in some very complicated questions
about what achievement means in modern democratic societies. How do
we know what counts as a genuine success story? How can we measure the
worth of an individual life?

In 1896 George Cohan finally got his big break. A last-minute cancellation
of the headline act the Adams Street Theatre, one of the premier vaudeville theaters in Brooklyn, meant that he and his family were booked as
a "Family Act" to fill the absent spot on the bill. The Cohans had waited
a long time for this moment and quickly made their way to Brooklyn.
When they arrived at the theater, however, their "reception wasn't any too
cordial." The other performers and stagehands disparaged them as lowly
music-hall types, while the stage manager hurried them on to open the
show with only thirty minutes notice. This was not the headline spot they
had been led to expect, nor was it the welcome they felt they deserved. Still,
the family took the stage and launched into their routine, nervous about
their abilities and intensely aware of how much was at stake. As Cohan
put it, "Everything depended on that first performance." To Cohan's surprise the audience responded with more than polite applause. A seventeen-
minute song-and-dance skit turned into twenty-six-minutes, as they paused

for laughter, encores, and extra curtain calls. "Some hit, folks, some hit," the stage manager shouted to them over rapturous cheers and foot stomping as they took their final bow. So impressed were the theater's owners by this rowdy reception that they immediately promoted the Cohan family to the prized fourth spot on the bill and then, three weeks later, to the headline attraction. Until that moment, Cohan confessed, he had not really understood what it meant to succeed.[7]

Cohan's pathway to popular acclaim on Broadway was not instant. As the title of his autobiography indicates—*Twenty Years on Broadway and the Other Twenty It Took to Get There*—narratives about success in vaudeville were equally concerned to highlight the realities of life on the circuits. Although he was born into a show business family, and always involved in some aspect of the business, for over a decade from the mid-1880s Cohan had repeatedly tried to establish himself in the big-time vaudeville. First, as part of the Four Cohans "Family Act," and then as a solo song-and-dance man, he had sought a permanent spot in one of the major New York theaters. Repeatedly, however, Cohan found himself dismissed after an initial "tryout" or side-lined with a "bit part." A habit of criticizing the quality of the shows he was auditioning for and regularly questioning the competence of those for whom he worked did nothing to help his ambitions.

Disillusioned by these early rejections, but unwilling to give up, Cohan turned to writing songs. Initially, the results were no more promising. Week in and week out he traipsed from one music publisher to the next with his song manuscripts. He recalled that "I had about exhausted the entire tin-pan-alley circuit. They all said the same thing. No market for songs of that kind." Cohan offered to write anything at all, on any subject. "'We don't want any right now,' they'd answer." Undeterred by these rejections, however, Cohan became one of the regular "hangers-on" around several music houses. He was set on becoming a songwriter and so practiced verse writing night and day: "The words must jingle, the words must jingle," he repeated over and over, humming different tunes to the same four cords. Within six months, during which he "worked like a trojan to improve my style of melody and learn how to jingle words in rhyme," no less than half a dozen manuscripts had been accepted for publication. He played no favorites with publishers, selling a song wherever he got the price.[8]

As Cohan tells it, his persistence eventually paid off. He began to write songs, comic sketches, and monologues for Lew Dockstader, one of the biggest stars in New York vaudeville.[9] But in spite of a growing demand for his work, what he really wanted was to get back behind the footlights. It was for this reason that his triumph on the stage in Brooklyn was so crucial to his understanding of what success meant and why he thought he wanted it. It enabled him to measure his talent in terms of the other performers, to prove his worth in front of the theater's management and, most significantly, to gain the recognition of the vaudeville audience, whose unreserved approval held the key to his recognition. As Cohan says, "A round of applause from even a dime-museum audience meant far more to me than a fat certified check from a song publisher or sketch team."[10]

The story of Cohan's big break is instructive for comprehending one performer's efforts to reflect on the reasons for his popularity. It is clear from this that the saying "Nothing succeeds like success" was more than just a show biz platitude. It conveyed the interior structure of vaudeville in which a round of applause connected every level of the business, from the barrel-house pianists along the Mississippi Delta, to the stars of major Broadway shows, from small-time promoters in Midwestern towns to the theater critics of the major urban newspapers. As a result, the instant success of Cohan's act in Brooklyn proved to be more than just the break he was looking for. No longer was he just one of the thousands of hangers-on who milled around the stage doors and presented themselves daily at the music publishing houses. He had found his audience, and they, too, had discovered him.

What this section of Cohan's account demonstrates is that vaudeville was a system organized primarily around the production of popular success. Performers, managers, agents, and critics commented frequently, and often at great length, about what it meant to succeed in vaudeville, expounding their theories at every opportunity, as well as continually modifying them in response to their own experiences. "Playing the Palace [Theatre]," writes Marian Spitzer, "spells professional opportunity as well as social success. All the biggest bookers are in the theatre every Monday afternoon and a successful appearance there means more and better work. In addition to that, a large number of Broadway producers have scouts who attend the Palace religiously each week, to catch new acts, and a considerable amount of theatrical history has been made that way."[11] But what were the theatrical bookers or Broadway scouts looking for in an act? When they saw a young comic, Bob Hope, for example, recycling as many jokes as he could borrow from other comedians, or "stealing" a line from a magazine, what was the element or quality in his act that caught a booking agent or Broadway scout's attention?[12] Why did a performer such as Hope achieve such phenomenal and rapid success in the late 1920s while other no less talented standup acts never made it past the Monday morning tryouts at the Palace?

These are complicated questions, and answering them very much depends on how we end up making sense of the way in which performers, managers, agents, and audiences collectively came to understand the significance of a vaudeville act, especially the qualitative distinctions they made between one act and another. As my summary of Cohan's narrative illustrates, success on the vaudeville stage linked audiences, artists, managers, agents, and professional critics via their applause (or the lack of it) to a set of claims about why an act was either good or bad, or more often than not, simply just average. But, equally, those claims, along with the applause that verified them, implied a specific commitment to and an acknowledgment of the developing history of the vaudeville aesthetic. More fundamentally, however, such claims open onto the deeper question highlighted above: how popular performers accounted for their successes and failures.

Where Cohan's autobiography is a model success story in which he set out the general principles of making it in show business, his article on the mechanics of emotion (cowritten with the influential theatre critic George Nathan) tries to address this issue in concrete terms. By focusing on the realities of stagecraft, the authors explored the technical means that were available to vaudeville writers (and the performers who realized their work, from songs to playlets) in order to get their ideas across to their audience, from the things that "act upon the tear ducts" to "some things men laugh at." They argue that the effective use of specific mechanical devices guaranteed a "reflex response" in the audience and, ultimately, encouraged its members to engage with and find renewed pleasure in recognizing, and unconsciously responding to, pre-existing conventions, from comedy to suspense. Ultimately, they claim, the audience came to the theater in order to suspend disbelief and so have its emotions played upon.[13]

For Cohan and Nathan, therefore, successful theatrical practice means using these pre-existing conventions of genre to transform the audience's experience of the show. "If we are normal," they allege,

> we all cry at the same things, laugh at the same things, and are thrilled by the same things, and these expedients are, for the most part, artless and simple—so simple that, under ordinary circumstances, we should indignantly repudiate the suggestion that the could move us. But the playwright knows exactly what they are. He has not invented them; he has inherited them. His predecessors used them over and over again; his successors will use them to the end of time. In his own language he calls them his "bag of tricks," or, sometimes, more dignifiedly, his "tools of emotion." If produced at the right moment and with sufficient skill, they . . . comprise the complete science of the "lump in the throat."[14]

Moreover, these conventions intersect with basic issues of human perception. "At the core of what have become merely mechanical stratagems for the arousing of theatrical emotion," they suggest, "constant, immutable human nature declares itself." While vaudeville was frequently criticized (even among sympathetic critics) for its overt reliance on theatrical conventions—well-known plots, familiar routines, recognizable images, stock melodies—Cohan and Nathan believed that, above all, the playwright must make his or her audiences laugh. And as with crying, their predecessors have already laid down the essential formulas. "Here, again," they assert, "the contrivances used are largely mechanical. For years the playwrights have servilely depended on them for 'laughs,' and will unquestionably always do so." Only when writers and performers understood how these essential formulas responded to the audience's unconscious emotional reflexes, would they begin to realize that the "secret of stage effectiveness rests in the impression of the moment."[15]

Nora Bayes made a similar argument for the impression of the moment through access to emotion. Although I have already discussed her theory, I want to underline once more her central claim: popular success in vaudeville was based on the artist achieving a particular kind of intimate identification with the audience. For Bayes, as we have seen, her audience was her most valuable relationship. "My performances," she proclaims, "are exactly like an intimate chat with one or two close friends, who sit around the table and enjoy themselves." The artist who really has something to say, who feels they have something to give to others, in her view "really confides a secret. That is to say, the ideas of artistic value are in themselves the outcome of inner feeling or thought."[16] For Bayes, theatrical success was contingent on overcoming the limits of the stage and connecting with an audience's deepest emotional experiences, whether through laughing or crying, or a mixture of both.

I now want widen our perspective slightly. While recent studies of vaudeville have tended to sidestep McLean's focus on the success myth, or criticized him for emphasizing cultural consensus at the expense of multiple class, gendered, or race-based perspectives, I want to suggest that this mythical dimension is in fact as typical of popular entertainment in vaudeville as it is of other art forms.[17] But let's first remind ourselves of the basic tenets of the myth. According to Calvin Colton, writing in 1844, the United States was a country of "self-made men" where a person with "merit and industry" could rise to the top from the lowliest of beginnings.[18] Through hard work, thrift and perseverance, a person could realize economic independence, material well-being, and individual happiness despite the manifold constraints of modern society. As we have already seen, in songs such as "I Work Eight Hours . . ." themes of an escape were central to performers' self-understanding of their art, even as they also emphasized the life-long effort that went into developing their talents. In most cases, they consistently referred to themselves as experienced troupers, whose rise to the top resulted from many years on the circuits performing under the most adverse conditions. Success was a consequence of such a life. "A young man asked me recently what spelled success on the stage," the comedian Will Cressy informed readers of his guide to the circuits. "I told him the only way I had ever found of spelling it was W-O-R-K."[19]

According to McLean, American vaudeville was primarily a social ritual. Participation in its ritual structure thus provided the vast majority of Americans with a captivating and accessible cultural form through which to make sense of their rapidly changing society. "What is most transparently clear about American vaudeville," he suggests, "is that it worshipped success."[20] This was evident in the development of the star system, the lavish design of the big-time theaters, and the regular stories in the press celebrating the daily exploits of the performers, the high-profile entrepreneurs, and the major syndicates. "What vaudeville could do for the myth," he continues, "which the [Horatio Alger] stories could not, in spite of their persistence in journalism and juvenile literature, was to provide the compelling aesthetic experience far more powerful than abstract idea or discursive thought. . . . That surge of magical power evoked by brassy rhythms, the staccato wise-cracks, the poised charm of the 'star,' or the mastery over reality demonstrated by a juggler or animal trainer, were all more immediately assimilated by the mass audience than were the legends of Horatio Alger and his imitators."[21] It was the immediacy of the show, he argues, more than any other aspect, which explains vaudeville's enormous attraction to audiences throughout the United States.

As a collective experience it was all encompassing. Audiences were immersed in a sensory extravaganza that was specifically designed to transform the realities of their day-to-day existence. "In this ritual," McLean notes, "cause-and-effect relationships were completely bypassed, the question of ultimate ends was never raised, and the problem of higher values could be submerged in waves of pathos and humour. Not the happy ending but the happy moment, not fulfilment at the end of some career rainbow but a sensory, psychically satisfying here-and-now were the results of a vaudeville show. Its concern was not the making of money but the enjoyment of it. It offered, in symbolic terms, the sweet fruits of success, but as an accessible right for all those participating in the new life of the cities."[22] The emphasis on reproducing a mythic consciousness in vaudeville opened up a space for new kinds of aesthetic experiences and practices to emerge.

As we saw in previous chapters Sophie Tucker's autobiography offers a particularly insightful perspective on what success meant for performers, as well as highlighting some of the tensions that existed between them. Theatrical triumph depended in her case on whether an act was able to negotiate the many relationships within the space of the theater. A successful artist's ability to "wow" an audience required a deep awareness of how much success was reliant on the largely invisible group of people who supported an act, including stage hands, orchestra leaders, and, most important, the songwriters.

"For all the years I have been in show business," she reflects, "to singers who have asked my advice I have said: 'Get new songs. Pay a writer to write them for you. Get songs that you can make your own. Don't copy other singers. Don't sing their songs. Don't do their stunts. Don't make your act a carbon copy of someone else's. Not if you want to succeed. And not if you want to stay in show business more than a season or two. Put off buying that mink coat or the diamond bracelet and buy songs instead. They'll pay dividends and cost nothing for insurance or storage.'"[23]

As with many other examples of success literature, Tucker's narrative connected her popularity on stage to the general conduct of her life as a trouper. One continually reinforced the other, as her comments about Nora Bayes confirm. "Knowing Nora taught me another lesson," she explains to her readers, "to live modestly. Nora was extravagant in all that she did. She loved life and living. She traveled with a staff of secretaries, servants, pianists, and manager. She adopted three lovely children and added them and a governess to her train. And she was always surrounded by hangers-on. Her party filled several suites in the hotels. . . . When I would meet Nora in some city she would always fuss with me: 'Sophie, you must take a suite. You must live well. It helps your prestige. People take notice of you. It makes you important.'"[24]

Tucker also devoted several sections of her book to the booking agent William Morris, with whom she had a long professional relationship and who influenced many of her most important decisions. According to Tucker, Morris was the archetypal show biz manager, whose commitment to his artists was based on a powerful empathy with what audiences wanted from a show, and an intuitive understanding of the intrinsic value of popular entertainment. "He could see changes coming along before other people knew a change was possible. There was one thing, though, he kept telling me never changed. That was the customers' response to an entertainer who met them at their own level; who was one of them." She then quotes Morris. 'It isn't that the public doesn't like success. It does. But if the performer's success, and what she does with it, separates her from the life of the folks who plunk down their dollar bills to see her and hear her, something happens to her that kills her work.'"[25]

While she was profoundly invested in Morris's ideal of the popular artist, ultimately, however, the structure of vaudeville was organized around the priorities of the managers. "I suppose more careers were made and more hearts broken in that one theatre [the New York Palace] than in all the other houses of the entire Orpheum and Keith circuits," Tucker recalls. "Your success in show business depended on how you went over at the Palace. At a Monday matinee there were more upset stomachs backstage than at a Metropolitan opening. Would the czar of vaudeville, Mr. E. F. Albee, see your act and would he like it? Would Mr. J. J. Murdoch okay the price you asked for it after the matinee? Every booker in New York, and many in London, would be standing in the back of the theatre at a Monday matinee. So were all the 'legitimate' managers and producers, scouting for talent. The Palace was like an auction block."[26] Tucker's comments reveal just how complicated the issue of success was for performers, as they negotiated competing values and expectations about what constituted a successful act—seeking empathy and intimacy on the one hand, and theatrical distance on the other.[27]

Jane Feuer has described the way in which the "multiple levels of performance and multiple levels of audience [in a Hollywood musical] combine [self-reflexively] to create a myth about musical entertainment permeating ordinary life."[28] Within this mythology, vaudeville was identified with a pure experience of entertainment, in which performers' success was derived from their complete identification with the audience and with the show. Entertainment was their whole world; they lived for it. No film makes this point so compellingly as Michael Curtiz's *Yankee Doodle Dandy*, the 1942 biopic about George M. Cohan. Featuring James Cagney as the "Man Who Owned Broadway," it presents a complicated argument about success, only to resolve the question of what it means to entertain an audience into a story about the triumph of democracy. In a crucial scene halfway through the film, Cohan is trying to convince a reluctant Fay Templeton (played by Irene Manning) to star in his next show. Worried that she is going to turn the offer down, Abe Erlanger (played by George Barbier), the owner of the theater and one of the new corporate managers discussed in chapter 5, makes the case for Cohan's importance as a writer, songwriter, and performer:

> "Have you thought it over, Fay?" Erlanger asks her as she walks offstage.
>
> "I'm not interested in Mr. Cohan or his plays," she replies dismissively.
>
> "Now you're making a great mistake," counters Erlanger. "He's the most original thing that ever hit Broadway. You know why? Because he's the whole darn country squeezed into one pair of pants. His writing, his songs, why even his walk and his talk. They all touch something way down here in people [pointing to his stomach]. Now don't ask me why it is, but it happens every time the curtain goes up. It's pure magic."
>
> "I'm bored by magic," retorts Templeton. "I know his formula. A fresh young sprout gets rich between 8:30 and 11 pm."
>
> "Yes, that's just it, Fay," says Erlanger. "George M. Cohan has invented the success story. And every American loves it because it happens to be his own private dream. He's found the mainspring in the ante clerk: ambition, pride, patriotism. That's why they call him the Yankee Doodle Boy. If you take a tip from me, Fay, you'll do just what I'm doing; you'll hitch your wagon to his star right now."[29]

The film spends a lot of time showing us the way in which popular entertainment merges art and life into a single moment of collective possibility. For example, in another scene, Cohan and his wife, Mary (played by Joan Leslie), are having dinner in a café. Outside on the street, crowds of revelers are celebrating the arrival of the New Year, and as he looks out at them, he remarks, "Welcome to the greatest show on earth: the people." To which his wife replies, raising her glass: "To the people."[30] The larger claim the film makes is that the spontaneous performer is the true image of democratic society, as the final scene of *Yankee Doodle Dandy* so effectively attests. Having received the Congressional Medal of Honor from President Roosevelt (played by Captain Jack Young, a noted lookalike), Cohan, almost speechless (as he jokes, "for once in my life"), comments: "But this medal is for people who've given their lives to their country, or done something big. I'm just a song and dance man, everybody knows that."

To which Roosevelt replies: "A man can give his life to his country in many different ways Mr. Cohan. And quite often he isn't the best judge of how much he has given. Your songs were a symbol of the American spirit. 'Over There' [Cohan's 1917 hit song, which became an unofficial war anthem] was just as powerful as any canon, as any battleship we had in the First World War. Today we're all soldiers; we're all on the front. We need more songs to express America. I know that you and your comrades will give them to us."

As the orchestra begins to play Cohan's most famous song, "Yankee Doodle Boy," he leaves the Oval Office, glances momentarily at a portrait of George Washington at the top of the White House stairs, and then begins a slow walk down them, dropping a stair in time to the song's jaunty rhythm. Halfway down, as if struck by a magnificent thought, he breaks into a tap routine, reminding us perhaps that for a "plain guy" like him, at least one who has come to embody the spirit of the nation, there is nothing so natural as to break out into a dance, and nothing that unites the people so much as a good song.

Commenting on Cohan's theatrical innovations, his biographer, John McCabe, maintains that no other playwright in American popular culture used theater so consistently as "a stratagem of entertainment and, ultimately, as a symbol for life itself."[31] In his 1906 play *Popularity*, for example, a scene that was set backstage in a theater used the actual backstage of the Wallace Theatre, where the play was being produced. In the same production, Cohan included a note in the program inviting the audience to "holler for [the main character] Rand when the lights go out in Act II."[32] In both these examples, Cohan's fundamental claim was that popular success required the dissolution of all artificial barriers between the artist and his audience and therefore between the world of show business and the world outside the theater.

The same claim was central to the themes explored in George Cukor's 1954 film *A Star Is Born*, featuring Judy Garland and James Mason. The film charts the rise of one screen star, Esther Blodgett (played by Garland), and the fall of another, Norman Maine (played by Mason). Early in the film, after Maine hears Blodgett singing with her friends in an after-hours bar off Sunset Boulevard in Los Angeles, he tries to describe "that little jolt of pleasure" that comes from the encounter with natural talent:

> "You're a great singer," declares Maine.
>
> "Who me?" Blodgett responds, somewhat taken aback.
>
> "Hasn't anyone ever told you that before?" asks Maine.
>
> "No, Mr. Maine. No one's ever told me that before. Maybe you're not quite as sober as we both thought you were. But thank you," she replies.
>
> "I'm as sober as a judge and I know exactly what I'm saying," Maine retorts.

"You've got that little something extra that Ellen Terry talked about. Ellen Terry, great actress, long before you were born. She said that star quality was that little something extra. Well, you've got it. Now what are you doing wasting your time singing with this band?"

"Wasting my time?" Blodgett objects. "I'm not wasting my time. You don't know how many years it's taken me to get this far. I'm doing fine, Mr. Maine. Just great."

"You're wasting your time," insists Maine.[33]

This exchange between Maine, the already established star, and Blodgett, the aspiring singer, sets up the central problem of the film (and the larger problem of modern art). How do we know what counts as a genuine performance? What are the values by which we measure success in popular entertainment? Is it many years hard work, as Esther suggests, or, as Maine claims, that little "something" extra? As with earlier Garland films about show business (such as *Babes in Arms* with Mickey Rooney in 1939 or *Me and My Gal* with Gene Kelly in 1942) the tension is between two versions of the myth of success.[34] It is not until the famous "Born in a Trunk" sequence, however, when Esther (now renamed Vicki Lester by the studio manager, in a further complication of the main character's theatrical identity) appears in her first screen triumph, that the film attempts to explore what this contradiction means for understanding popular success. Unlike the character of Norman Maine, who is incapable of reconciling his on-screen star persona with his off-screen personal life, and so ultimately destroys himself and his career (he finally kills himself so that Esther can triumph), the film is trying to show us that Esther Blodgett's life (and Garland's along with it) *is* show business. Because she was "born in a trunk" there *is* in fact no contradiction for her. Her life and her art are the same.

The narrative in this famous sequence is very similar to Gene Kelly's "Broadway Melody" sequence from *Singin' in the Rain*. Esther tells the story of a young singer's struggle for theatrical success following her maturation as a vaudeville performer. As with Kelly's entrance to the world of New York entertainment, she begins with the booking agents, none of whom are interested in her. She then finds work in a burlesque chorus, which allows her to eat, but little else. From there she receives a call to perform in New York, which she imagines means a shot at the big-time, but instead, it turns out to be a small-time club in which she has to contend nightly with a drunken patron's request for the same song . . . over and over again. Finally, however, she finds a benefactor, who hears her singing Ernie Burnett and George Norton's song, "Melancholy Baby" and, as a result, offers to produce

her first Broadway show. The scene then cuts to Esther starring in that new
show, leading a lavish production number based on George Gershwin's 1919
hit, "Swanee," which (in another theatrical twist) went on to become one of
Garland's signature songs.

What we are being asked to consider in this sequence is how someone
like Esther, whose identity was inseparable from the world of show business, could ever become the star she was born to be. This is complicated
by the fact that we are watching the character of Esther watching herself
on a film-within-a-film playing a character who resembles not just herself,
but Garland as well. Following several scenes in which we see her singing
about performing as part of her parents' vaudeville two-act, celebrating all
the tricks she has learned from them, and finally leaving to go out on her
own, Esther sounds a note of warning: "And with the tricks, I learned traditions, and the hardest one of all, is that no matter what, the show must go
on."[35] Which takes us back to one of Sophie Tucker's most enduring claims
about her life. "You can see that my story has to be the story of show business during the past thirty years," she declares in the opening pages of *Some
of These Days*. "Show business has been my life. I wouldn't have had any
other. It is the life I always wanted."[36]

CHAPTER TEN

Applause

Beginning with what I called vaudeville's ritual question—"How did a person get started in show business?"—I have been suggesting that one way of understanding the significance of vaudeville is to see it as a system for working out the conditions under which those with talent might be recognized as such, but also that the recognition of talent was ultimately left up to the audience to determine for themselves.[1] In the last two chapters I focused on how this system for producing popular success affected issues of performance practice and popular music production. In particular, I suggested that performers' understanding of what it meant to be a popular artist derived from their claim to speak directly to their audiences, and that this self-awareness was primarily mediated by their songs. I want to conclude by setting these same issues in the wider context of the emergence of cultural distinctions between popular and serious music in the United States.

This is a large and complicated issue, and directs us toward the deeper problem of the origins and implications of mass culture. As historians such as William Leach, T. Jackson Lears, Richard Ohmann, and Janice Radway demonstrate, the four decades from 1880 through to 1920, during which the vaudeville system was consolidated, were decisive for the immense transformations that took place in Americans' cultural ideas and practices,.[2] From magazine subscriptions to department stores, advertising to reading practices, the society that emerged in this period was founded on a new vision of the good life in which consumption, desire, novelty, and pecuniary reward were principal values. "From the 1880s onward," Leach claims, "a commercial aesthetic of desire and longing took shape to meet the needs of business. And since that need was constantly growing and seeking expression in wider and wider markets, the aesthetic of longing and desire was everywhere and took many forms. After 1880 this aesthetic appeared

in show windows, electrical signs, fashion shows, advertisements, and billboards; as free services and sumptuous consumer environments; and as the
artifacts or commodities themselves."[3]

At the center of this process were the corporations. "Unlike entrepre-
neurial firms," Leach continues, "which were (and are) owned and con-
ducted by individuals or partners, corporations were legal entities designed
to provide limited liability and to ensure continuity of ownership beyond
the lifetime of the original owners. They were social organizations marked
by administrative hierarchies, managing machines, tools, and labor. But
they were above all economic institutions, created to generate capital
through private and public stock ownership and, through consolidation
and often mergers, to seize market control in behalf of making profits."[4]
These changes in the structure of business institutions, which affected all
aspects of industry, including manufacturing, finance, banking, sales, communications, and accounting, also saw the emergence of a new business
class: a powerful group of managers, experts, and professionals who increasingly controlled these institutions and played a central role in making these
transformations possible.[5] Their innovations involved the vertical integration of production as well as the comprehensive management of the selling
process, which, as Richard Ohmann points out, had "previously been left
to chance and a variety of middlemen with interests different from those of
the manufacturers."[6]

Vaudeville was inseparable from this process. This accounts not only
for the importance of the transcontinental syndicates such as the Keith-
Orpheum organization, which dramatically altered the cultural experiences
of musicians and their audiences in unprecedented ways. But, equally, it
underlines the significance of the larger movement toward corporate control in all aspects of show business, from the centralization of the booking
process to song production, from the corporate reform of management to
the mass circulation of trade newspapers such as *Billboard* and *Variety*.
The influence of vaudeville on the practices and forms of American popular
music, however, has in my view not been sufficiently understood. The more
specific problem this highlights, and the one I want to discuss in this final chapter, is how to assess vaudeville's place within the historical debate
about music's cultural value. Before returning to the problem of applause, I
want to briefly summarize that debate.

Writing in the 1840s, after a long period spent reflecting on his travels in
the United States, Alexis de Tocqueville observed that if you want to understand a society undergoing a democratic revolution, study its dramatic pro-

ductions. The theater, he claimed, is the true medium of democracy. "If the effect of democracy is generally to question the authority of all literary rules and conventions," he remarks in the second volume of *Democracy in America*, "on the stage it abolishes them altogether and puts in their place nothing but the caprice of each author and each public." Democratic audiences, he notes, go to the theater not for "pleasures of the mind, but the keen emotion of the heart." They delight in novelty, surprise, and invention above all, regardless of the dramatic rules. "You may be sure," he concludes, "that if you [the artist] succeed in bringing your audience into the presence of something that affects them, they will not care by what road you brought them there."[7] Tocqueville's more general claim was that in democratic societies audiences related to the theatrical experience in ways that were radically different from the art of aristocratic cultures. Even when cultural distinctions were reasserted in these societies, as when the genius of a particular artist was celebrated, Tocqueville believed that among those peoples most committed to equality, this phenomenon was not likely to last. The theater was thus a space in which such distinctions were called into question and, ultimately, transformed.

No scholar has had a greater influence on how we think about these issues than the historian Lawrence Levine.[8] By focusing on the emergence of the distinctions between high, low, popular, and mass cultural forms, Levine sets out to demonstrate that by the late nineteenth century the experience of going to the theater, an opera, or a symphony concert was increasingly antithetical to the kind of democratizing process highlighted by de Tocqueville. The revolutionary idealism that had characterized American society during the 1830s and 1840s, and which formed the basis for Tocqueville's claims, was being challenged by an emerging, and increasingly powerful, middle class in favor of a new set of social, political, and cultural beliefs and alliances. This raises some tricky questions. Why, for example, did the egalitarianism that was so central to the political and cultural debates of Jacksonian democracy and which led finally to the abolition of slavery reverse itself when it came to the arts? Why did a new type of cultural hierarchy founded on a reified concept of high culture appear in the North and, paradoxically, among the very class of people who had benefited most from the political equality won through civil war? In a society founded on principles of equality and independence, why then did concepts such as refinement and cultivation come to describe not only the experience of going to the opera, hearing a symphony, seeing a play, or reading a novel, but also the ideals for society as a whole?[9]

Shakespeare's plays provide Levine with his starting premise. Noting their prevalence in all aspects of mid-nineteenth-century American culture, he argues that Shakespeare was performed "not merely alongside popular entertainment as an elite supplement to it; Shakespeare was performed as an integral part of it. Shakespeare *was* popular entertainment in nineteenth-century America."[10] The gradual divorce of Shakespeare from everyday culture in the later part of the century by treating his plays as unique works of art signaled the end of a shared public culture. Attendance at performances of his plays was transformed from a right open to all to a privilege that had to be earned. No longer was the theater a microcosm of society, a kaleidoscopic, democratic institution responsive to the egalitarian energy of the whole society. Instead, it became the exclusive property of an educated, wealthy elite who insisted on the aesthetic properties of Shakespeare's plays and on their author's unquestionable brilliance. The transformation of Shakespeare from poet of the people to artistic genius was, for Levine, sure proof that Americans' democratic ideals were undergoing a challenge from within.

He then extends his analysis to opera and symphonic music and finds that the same process was at work. As with nineteenth-century performances of Shakespeare, opera in this period, he claims, was "an art form that was *simultaneously* popular and elite. That is, it was attended both by large numbers of people who derived great pleasure from it and experienced it in the context of their normal everyday culture, *and* by smaller socially and economically elite groups who derived both pleasure and social confirmation from it." As Americans had domesticated Shakespeare, so too did they embrace opera as "part of the world around them."[11] This meant changing the texts or music as it suited performers, often by inserting well-known airs or minstrel songs or sentimental ballads into operas in the place of the existing arias, and translating whole works from Italian, French, or German into English.

By the last decades of the nineteenth century, however, this democratic approach to the arts had been replaced by a highly selective ethos. Verdi's operas, Mozart's symphonies, and Mendelssohn's songs, along with Shakespeare's plays, were all systematically removed by the upper classes from the public sphere and installed into a sacred realm for which "aesthetic and spiritual elevation rather than entertainment was the goal." Levine summarizes his findings as follows: "In the world of instrumental music as in the world of theatrical performance, then, the nineteenth century was much more fluid, much less rigidly hierarchical than the century that was to follow." Ultimately, the process he describes as the sacralization of the arts was, he notes, "rooted in a quest for intellectual and cultural authority" by

a new social elite, in alliance with the older patrician class.[12] The outcome
of this process was a cultural world both stratified and rigid in its separation
of classical music, opera, and dramatic theater from the lives of ordinary
Americans.

Other studies come to the same conclusions. DiMaggio, for example,
describes how Boston's upper classes "institutionalized a view and vision
of art that made elite culture less and less accessible to the vast majority
of Boston's citizens."[13] Likewise, Bruce McConachie maintains that by the
1850s opera going had become one of the principal contexts within which
upper class New Yorkers acquired "the class consciousness and highly rationalized training necessary to manipulate the social order of a moderniz-
ing America."[14] Both authors claim that the distinction between high and
popular culture "emerged in the period between 1850 and 1900 out of the
efforts of urban elites to build organizational forms that, first, isolated high
culture and, second, differentiated it from popular culture."[15] The institutions that emerged from this process—symphony orchestras, opera companies, chamber music groups, a specialist music press, music schools, artistic foundations, and exclusive performance venues—were inseparable from
the values and interests of the social classes that supported them.[16] From
this perspective, the arts were unequivocally instruments of class rule, and
regulating the experiences associated with them became an essential aspect
of class identity.

Studies such as these have generated significant opposition, especially among classical music scholars. "Those who take a primarily social-
historical or sociological approach to the institutionalization of 'high culture' in America," contends Ralph Locke, "sometimes go too far in their
attempt to stress the ways in which the monied classes bought (and buy) art
music and thus made it their own." While Locke concedes that the metropolitan upper classes were engaged in an active restructuring of musical life
in the late nineteenth century, he rejects the idea that the process was essentially a negative one. No doubt at all, he says, that the new institutions
of musical high culture were primarily established and supported by people
who occupied positions of social, political, and economic power. But this
did not prevent them from working toward a musical life that would be
widely shared within the community and insisting on making the experience of art music "as aesthetically gratifying as possible."[17]

The real challenge for Locke is to discover why works of art are meaningful in this way. The solution, however, is not to treat them as simply
mechanisms for social control and therefore merely a function of class
rule and class identity. "There must," he insists, "be some way to address

the class-bound framing of the musical performance and consumption in various historical situations without erasing the specifically musical aspects of the experience."[18] Paradoxically, Levine, too, urges us to learn more about the categories we use to describe cultural experiences, and so avoid reifying particular genres or traditions at the expense of others. He also makes it clear that he is not attacking the notion of cultural hierarchy per se: "Obviously we need to make distinctions within culture as within every other realm of human endeavor. But at this point, debating the question of hierarchy concerns me less than examining the *nature* of the hierarchy we are debating."[19] And, by all accounts, this hierarchy was anything but fixed.

Which brings us back, finally, to the subject of this book. Given his explicit attention to the origins of late nineteenth-century cultural conflict, it is perhaps surprising to discover that Levine hardly mentions vaudeville at all. "The transition I have been describing," he briefly observes, "was not confined to concert halls, museums, and opera houses. The standards of these emporia of high culture [concert hall, opera house, theatre and museum] extended to what was quickly becoming the world of popular entertainment." What follows are little more than two pages that deal with the vaudeville entrepreneurs' efforts to attract middle class (especially female) patrons by imposing order and decorum on the "undisciplined, raucous behaviour [of audiences] that had been so dominant in the nineteenth century."[20] Where once spectators had been consenting participants, actively involved in, and sometimes even directing, the course of the performance, by the early decades of the twentieth century they had, in Levine's view, been as culturally disenfranchised as they were politically excluded, reduced to mere passive receptors of the new products of mass commercial culture. Vaudeville became just another instance of ruling class power and social control based on the sacralization of culture.

In an influential autobiography documenting fifty years in show business management, booking agent Michael Leavitt writes that there

> is more humanity, more of homely, every-day life in a vaudeville show, than in almost any other form of entertainment. A little of everything cannot be found in the average play, but there is in vaudeville singing, dancing, conversations, laughter, tears, animals, acrobats, contortionists, and usually, one or two good plays, well written and acted. Some of these little plays crowd as much life and action into twenty minutes as we find in the more pretentious Broadway productions of three hours.

And all is seen and heard in vaudeville for half or one-quarter of the price
of a Broadway theatre ticket.[21]

Leavitt's view was not at all uncommon. Caffin, too, makes a similar point
in her book. Vaudeville, she writes, was "as limitless as humanity itself."[22]
Its particular form, she insists, resulted from a long historical process that
began with the great Puritan revolutions in Europe and ended with the
people eventually replacing princes and princesses, kings and queens, and
soldiers and statesmen, as the true subjects of democratic theater.

This uncertainty about vaudeville's significance opened it up to a multiplicity of cultural values and meanings. Performers understood it as a context
for realizing popular success as well as developing their artistic talent; they
frequently complained about conditions on the circuits, especially on the
small-time routes, but then declared that they wanted no other life than the
one they had chosen. For audiences, too, the experience was multilayered.
Familiarity and repetition among small-time routines were just as valued as
the novelty, surprise, and invention associated with high-class acts. Daily
reports from theater managers on the circuits indicate just how complicated
their position was as well. Not only did they have to mediate the competing demands of the owners and the artists, but they also had to understand
the changing composition and character of their audiences. In her study of
the Elinore Sisters, an Irish comic act, Alison Kibler demonstrates that although Keith and Albee wanted to control audience behavior in order to attract middle- and upper-class female patrons to their theaters by appealing to
principles of cultural refinement, what this meant in practice was subject to
continual conflict and negotiation, even among those female audience members who were most likely to benefit from these new policies.[23]

This multiplicity was also central to the aesthetic dimension of show,
as demonstrated in preceding chapters. In the case of music, for example,
this involved a huge diversity of practices and genres, none of which were
guaranteed to find audience approval. "We, of the vaudeville audience, all
love music," Caffin notes. "Individually we may differ as to what particular
variety of noise we honor with the name of music, but our own brand
we each love fervently. In vaudeville, we are offered a gorgeous variety of
brands: from melody extracted from the unwilling material of xylophones
and musical glasses through varying offerings of singers and instrumental-
ists, both comic and serious, to the performances of high-class chamber
music or the singing of an opera diva."[24]

Caffin then goes on to make a critical distinction between the value of music in the concert hall and what audiences might expect from a vaudeville show. "Let it be admitted," she argues,

> that the vaudeville house is not the place in which the musical connoisseur looks for music of the highest rank. There is no aim to compete with the Philharmonic Society or the Boston Symphony Orchestra. But for all that there are some good music and fine musicians and no lack of appreciation for them. Perhaps it is not to be denied that the strange and curious are as highly favored as the artistic; and a violinist may excite as much applause by playing "Swanee River" on one string as by the most exquisite rendering of a violin Fantasia by Brahms.[25]

As we can see from her observations, music in vaudeville was neither simply a medium of social control, through which the managers imposed an elitist vision of cultural hierarchy on their passive audiences, nor a pure representation of a shared public culture in which the sources of value were derived solely from what the audience wanted. It was a space within which performers and audiences and managers continually negotiated between, and responded to, their different understandings of the cultural value and meaning of diverse music styles and practices, all of which were simultaneously coalescing and differentiating in relation to each other. While powerful distinctions were clearly at work within the course of a show, from the persistence of blackface minstrel acts to the presence of what were described as high-class turns, equally, these same acts were continually being revised, or sometimes revived, in response to the changing sensibilities of audiences.

While there are many examples of this process, on closer inspection three stand out. To begin with, most accounts of the origins of the blues mention vaudeville only in passing, and then only as an example of the commercial distortion of the music's African American folk origins. The story of the blues we are most familiar with is probably the one that says it is old, rural, and acoustic. More recently, however, scholars such as Lynn Abbott, Bruce Bastin, David Monod, Doug Seroff, and Elijah Wald have begun to question this narrative. "A more important, but far less explored, platform for the blues' commercial ascendency," claim Abbott and Seroff, "was the African American vaudeville stage."[26] The very different story that these scholars have begun to explore is that the blues was more a product of urban life than it was an expression of rural folkways. This history begins not on the porch of an African American sharecropper's house, but with professional entertainers on the southern vaudeville circuits. As Monod points out, the blues seemed to have evolved as a musical form and as a performance practice over the course of the second decade of the [twentieth] century. This would suggest that the blues did not arrive on vaudeville fully formed, as folk import. Although elements of the blues are certainly traditional—the call and response pattern, the blues (or barbershop) chords, the caesura that commonly divides the line, and possibly even the blue note—there is no evidence that the elements were assembled together prior to the development of commercial blues.[27]

In this context, we might say that the blues emerged in response to new and rapidly changing historical conditions for professional entertainers. Moreover, its development as a form, as well as its dissemination, took place primarily via touring vaudeville acts. Bessie Smith's early career provides ample evidence of this. Most biographies of the singer repeat some version of Chris Albertson's claim that until 1912, when she successfully auditioned for Moses Stokes's traveling show, Smith "had been singing for nickels and dimes on Chattanooga's Ninth Street to the guitar accompaniment of her brother Andrew since she was about nine."[28] Abbott and Seroff demonstrate, however, that her career began much earlier than this, and that by 1912 she was already a veteran of the circuits. "Portions of Bessie Smith's biography seem to have been abandoned to the province of American folklore," they argue, focusing on a series of reports in the African American press that place her regularly in high-profile vaudeville venues such as the Monogram Theatre in Chicago and the Booker T. Washington Theatre in St. Louis, and that her performing career really began around 1909. In these reports she is billed variously as the "Tennessee coon shouter," as a backup singer, dancer, and comic performer, and "the girl with the big voice."[29] A later report in the *Indianapolis Freeman*, from December 8, 1915, underlines the complex environment in which her singing style developed. "The Florida Blossoms Company have started the one-night stand again," the report notes,

after playing week stands at popular prices. The show opens with a very pleasing musical comedy featuring Mrs Ethel Cox, singing "Down in Tennessee," assisted by the following soubrettes: Misses Princella Barrenger, Bertha Schaffer, Katie Price, Bessie Smith, followed by King Williams and his dogs, Nellie Matthews, the girl contortionist, the Great Adams, the trick bicyclist, Clint Taylor and Rastus Williams, sketch team. The show closing with a very laughable after-piece "Milady's Wedding Day." The show can truthfully boast of having one of the best bands and orchestras on the road.[30]

It is clear from this account, and many others like it, that the first generation of blues singers such as Smith consolidated the basic elements of the blues form within, and not independently of, the vaudeville circuits. Their music emerged from within the medium's all-encompassing aesthetic, and took shape in response to the demands of continuous performance and the pressures of year-round touring.

In addition, the same process that we find with the blues happened also to jazz. As Lawrence Gushee shows us in his pioneering study of the Creole Jazz Band, the story of New Orleans jazz is far more complicated than we might expect. "The foundations of jazz history as they have been constructed by three generations of writers, scholars, and critics, and, more recently, technically descriptive analysts, centre unequivocally on sound recordings," he observes.[31]

This has meant the continual neglect of groups such as the Creole Jazz Band, whose career unfolded outside of New Orleans and primarily as performers on the vaudeville circuits. This is how it begins. On August 17, 1914, the *Los Angeles Tribune* included the following report. "Last week at Vernon, during the progress of the Cross-Rivers engagement, Alex Pantages [the manager of the Pantages circuit] discovered a new vaudeville attraction, a colored ragtime band with a style of comedy-music all their own. The vaudeville magnate believes he secured a unique attraction, and to try public opinion before sending it over the circuit, will present the band as an added attraction with this week's show [at Pantages' Los Angeles Theatre]."[32] This brief notice marked the start of nearly four years during which the group was booked on vaudeville bills across the United States and Canada, including several appearances in Chicago and New York. In the course of their time criss-crossing the continent, they were mostly billed as a "plantation act" and appeared alongside a huge diversity of performers, including coon shouters, two-acts, ventriloquists, and traveling revues such as the Schubert's famous Town Topics. None of this sits well with conventional accounts of jazz history, which favors a sequence that follows the musicians from New Orleans to New York via Chicago, and focuses almost exclusively on evaluating particular emblematic recordings (King Oliver, Louis Armstrong's Hot Fives and Sevens, Jelly Roll Morton's Rhythm Kings, and so on).

Mark Berresford makes a similar argument about the clarinetist Wilbur Sweatman, whose career intersected with and had an important influence

on many of the musicians that Gushee discusses, as well as several of the
blues performers featured in Abbott and Seroff's studies. "As we enter the
second century of jazz history," he writes, "it is becoming increasingly difficult to evaluate the earliest years of its development. . . . In researching
and writing this book, it became apparent early on that the roles of black
theatre, tented touring shows, circus sideshows, and vaudeville played a
much greater part in the early development of jazz than has generally been
acknowledged." The vaudeville circuits, he claims, along with tent shows
and black minstrel shows, provided the new syncopated dance music with
a platform upon which its practitioners could reach a national audience and
engage with the most creative developments in popular music, theater, and
dance.[33] He, too, points out that the bias toward sound recordings, the lack
of interest in performers from outside New Orleans, and, furthermore, the
distaste for anything connected to show business among many jazz writers,
scholars, and critics, has misrepresented our understanding of the context
in which jazz took shape.[34]

The third instance I want to discuss is the movement of classical musicians and opera singers into vaudeville. In a 1901 article in *Cosmopolitan*,
the critic Norman Hapgood notes that the lines separating opera, theater,
and classical music from vaudeville were increasingly blurred. "A famous
American singer," he observes,

> for years one of the most popular attractions of light opera, last year went
> into vaudeville, and naturally was asked by the reporters how she liked
> it. "I don't mind," she said, in effect, "appearing between a cat circus and
> an aggregation of trained monkeys, since the animal artists are the best
> of their kind." . . . This was partly a difference between two individu-
> als, but perhaps even more a change in the times. The lines between the
> legitimate and vaudeville have been shattered of late, owing mainly to
> that greatest of stimulants, money, but partly to improved surroundings
> in the vaudeville world, and to the introduction of the one-act play. The
> salaries paid to successful performers in the music halls and continuous
> houses are almost absurdly large compared with those paid most of our
> best-known stars and leading men and women.[35]

The process described here by Hapgood is one in which on the vaudeville
stage, European musical forms were being stripped of their content, cast
aside for the new entertainment forms, such as ragtime or the blues, even
as the older forms continued to stand as the highest expressions of human
achievement. On a standard weekly bill, as Hapgood demonstrates, dis-

tinctions between high and low, rural and urban, modern and ancient, Old World and New, and human and animal performers, were continually reconstructed, even as they were being dissolved. The principle of heterogeneity thus tended to level all cultural forms, depriving them of their existing claims to legitimacy or authenticity, while multiplying the slightest differences between them through an appeal to the greatest possible response from the audience. Vaudeville thus opened up a space in which artistic distinctions were not merely expressed, but also continually questioned and, ultimately, transformed. In this, vaudeville anticipated or in some measure laid the groundwork for the claim that was later to be made for the movies, in which their highest and most ordinary instances appealed to, and to a large extent relied on, the same audiences.[36]

In *The Seven Lively Arts* Gilbert Seldes makes an even stronger case for understanding vaudeville in these terms. Here was a cultural form, he suggested, in which the question of cultural meaning and value was raised explicitly each and every day of the week: by the co-existence of so many different kinds of acts within a single show; by the daily repetition of acts, not to mention the repetition of their contents from week to week and season to season; by the simultaneous emphasis on familiarity and novelty as principles of vaudeville practice; by the fast-paced delivery and time constraints, which required performers to connect immediately with their audiences or risk getting booed off the stage; and by the relentless promotion of major stars alongside the permanent celebration, on and off the stage, of vaudeville's rank-and-file. This is how he describes the process:

> I shall arrive in a moment at the question of refined vaudeville, a thing I dislike intensely; there is another sort of refinement in vaudeville which demands respect. It is the refinement of technique. It seems to me that the unerring taste of Fanny Brice's impersonations is at least partly due to, and has been achieved through, the purely technical mastery she has developed; I am sure that the vaudeville stage makes such demands upon its artists that they are compelled to perfect everything. They have to do whatever they do swiftly, neatly, without lost motion; they must touch and leap aside; they dare not hold an audience more than a few minutes, at least not with the same stunt; they have to establish an immediate contact, set a current in motion, and exploit it to the last possible degree in the shortest space of time. They have to be always "in the picture," for though the vaudeville stage seems to give them endless freedom and innumerable opportunities, it holds them to strict account; it permits no fumbling, and there are no reparable errors. The materials they use

are trivial, yes; but the treatment must be accurate to a hair's breadth; the wine they serve is light, it must fill the goblet to the very brim and not a drop must spill over. There is no great second act to redeem a false entrance; no grand climacteric to make up for even a moment's dullness. The whole question of the material must be subsumed in the whole of the presentation, every page has to be written, every scene rendered, every square inch of the canvas must be painted, not daubed with paint.[37]

Rather than conceive of vaudeville as simply another instrument of class rule, Seldes reframed the debate about vaudeville's significance in terms of its specific and, at the same time conflicting, cultural values and principles. The distinctions that were reinforced in the course of any given show were much too complex and unstable to reduce them to an opposition between high culture and popular culture, or between democratic participation and elite control. And no one was more aware of this than the managers. "Now that we have abandoned the straight legitimate and are resolved to go the vaudeville way," Frederick Proctor informed a reporter, "as I am sure we must go if we are to give the masses what they want—we must bring into vaudeville better and more varied talent."[38]

Opera was in many ways paradigmatic of this problem of fixing cultural distinctions around such terms as *high* and *low*, or *serious* and *popular*, and deriving social significance from them. As DiMaggio contends, "The boundaries of opera were open to contestation, and the movement of managers, designers, and even soloists back and forth between grand opera, light opera, musical comedy, and vaudeville did nothing to clarify them."[39] "I played opera for Mr. Albee," recalled Raymond Hitchcock, "and when I say opera, I mean opera. We played it eleven times a day. We began at 10 o'clock in the morning and played as long as there was anyone present."[40] Opera's cultural value, and the performance practices that defined it, were consistently altered by its inclusion in the continuous format, even as it remained a symbol of a specific kind of aesthetic experience and a particular type of listener.

What is evident from these examples is that the incorporation of blues, jazz, opera, symphonic music, or Shakespearean drama into vaudeville, whether as part of an existing routine, or as an act in its own right, was more about the fluidity and uncertainty of the boundaries between these categories than it was evidence of an attempt to impose a model of sacralization and refinement on the emerging institutions of popular culture. As we have seen, by incorporating diverse cultural practices and forms into a continuous format, and thereby highlighting the often-conflicting cultural

values and meanings that characterized them while also promoting the novelty of their presence on the bill, vaudeville created a social space in which
the older distinctions were resolved into a multiplicity of new expressive
possibilities, even as those new possibilities were themselves transformed
by their presence there.

In *What Made Pistachio Nuts?*, the film scholar Henry Jenkins argues that
vaudeville provided the basis for an essential, and yet neglected, counter-
tradition within classic Hollywood cinema. Without acknowledging this
counter-tradition, he suggests, we not only risk misunderstanding the development of early cinematic practice, most especially sound comedy, but
we may also have no way of recognizing vaudeville's significance as a medium for new aesthetic experiences. The same could be said for popular
music. Although there are frequent references to vaudeville in most
accounts of early twentieth-century popular music, as we have seen, it is
perhaps surprising to see so little discussion of what having this experience
in common might actually have meant for the performers in those styles.
The problem is even more acute when we extend it to classical music, opera, or ballet because of the complicated relationship these forms have tra-
ditionally had with show business.[41]

In order to draw the several themes of this book to a close, I want to
pick up Jenkins's claims about the vaudeville aesthetic and relate it to these
broader issues, especially as they relate to the artist's search for an audience.
"Vaudeville's player-centered mode of production," he writes, "resulted in
a constant foregrounding of the performer's status as an entertainer; variety
audiences valued attempts to command the spotlight and produce a strong
impression. The vaudevillian, as the master of the act from conception to
execution, sought material tailored to particular performance skills. Performers were never subservient to the script; rather, narrative, where it
existed at all, facilitated their familiar tricks." This emphasis on presenting
modular acts made up of diverse material, and delivered in twenty minutes
or less, involved a shift in artistic principles, from inner logic and aesthetic
consistency to endless novelty and infinite variety. Programming, according
to Jenkins, was based on "the selection, juxtaposition, and coordination of
preconceived units, not on direction or creation." Vaudeville's primary aesthetic value was its immediacy, which was achieved through an emphasis
on an infinite diversity within endless combinations of novelty acts.[42]

Central to this aesthetic was the audience's applause. It was no good
trying to wow an audience if nothing happened in response, if no member
of the audience made a sound, or if no one watching or listening in some

way confirmed that what they had just experienced affected them in some way. What defined the success of an act was the communicative value of applause as part of the larger dynamics of the show. "The [vaudeville performer] works with the idea of an immediate response from the audience, and with regards to its demands," claimed critic Vadim Uraneff. "By cutting out everything—every line, gesture, movement—to which the audience does not react and by improvising new things, he establishes unusual unity between the audience and himself. . . . Stylization in gesture, pose, mise-en-scène and make-up follows as a result of long experimentation before the primitive spectator whose power as judge is absolute."[43] This power to judge through applause, and the other ways in which audience members expressed approval or disapproval, whether by stomping, shouting, whistling, or booing, emphasized the contingency of each show—no act's success was ever fully guaranteed in advance—as well as its variable form. The artist's appeal to her audience was thus active and continuous, much like the format within which she had to perform.

This was what playwright and drama critic Mary Cass Canfield is trying to convey when she notes some of the techniques used by performers to mobilize their audience. She writes:

> A vaudeville comedian in American is as close to the audience as Harlequin and Punchinello were to the Italian publics of the eighteenth century. He is, like them, an apparent, if not always actual improviser. He jokes with the orchestra leader, he tells his hearers fabricated, confidential tales about the management, the other actors, the whole entrancing world behind the scenes; he addresses planted confederates in the third row, or the gallery, and proceeds to make fools of them to the joy of all present. He beseeches his genial, gum-chewing listeners to join the chorus of his song; they obey with a zestful roar. The audience becomes part of the show.[44]

This involvement in the show underlined the extent to which vaudeville was ultimately a paradigm of evaluative activity, in that every decision that was made by the performers, or taken by the managers, was dependent on the audience's participation and, ultimately, its approval.

This last point is made very effectively in "What's Up Doc?," a 1949 Looney Tunes cartoon. Bugs Bunny plays a Hollywood movie star, lounging by his pool, who gets a telephone call. It is a journalist from the "Dis-Associated Press," contacting him because the public is demanding his life story. This is how he describes it:

First I was born, which goes without saying. But, even in the hospital, on the day I arrived, I knew I was different from the other kids. I couldn't figure out why at first. The suddenly it came to me. I was a rabbit in a human world. I soon displayed a talent for music. My parents gave me a toy piano to play with and I took to it right away. When I was a little older I was sent to dancing school. At school recitals I was always selected to demonstrate various dances. After graduation, I was ready for the Big Time, and offers poured in. After much consideration, I finally accepted an important part in a hit show, "Girl of the Golden Vest." Then came "Wearing of the Grin." Then my big smash, "Rosie's Cheeks."

The joke here lies in the juxtaposition of Bugs' voice-over with reality of his life as an entertainer. As with Gene Kelly in the "Harry the Hoofer" sequence of *Singin' in the Rain*, the rabbit's career in vaudeville involves him repeating the same chorus—"We are the boys of the chorus, we hope you like our show. We know you're rooting for us, but now we have to go"—in each of the acts he appears in. Finally his big chance comes. "The Star was sick," he tells the reporter, "and I was to take his place. That night I gave my all." His 'all' turns out to be a song-and-dance routine, with some juggling thrown in for good measure. The finale involved him mounting some steps, leaping from them, and then landing in the splits to the deafening sound of (wait for it) . . . crickets. The famous hooked stick comes out from left stage and pulls him off. So much for his big break. "I'm through with show business," Bugs declares, "until I get the right part."

Out of work and down on his luck, he ends up on a park bench with several other penniless performers, until one day Elmer Fudd, that "big vaudeville star," walks by, looking for a new partner for his act. The other performers try out their acts—Al Jolson sings "Mammy," while Bing Crosby croons Harry Warren and Johnny Mercer's song, "You Must Have Been a Beautiful Baby." Fudd is singularly unimpressed, until he sees Bugs. "Bugs Bunny!" Fudd cries out. "Why you hanging around with these guys? They'll never amount to anything. You've got too much talent. I need you in my act. I'll give you equal billing, You'll be a star. You're great. You're wonderful. I need you. What do you say?" Bugs agrees to join Fudd in his act, and the two of them open in Peoria, Illinois. Again we then see the same jokes and songs repeated over and over, in theater after theater, from Buffalo to New York, until Bugs decides to make some changes to their routine. Instead of playing the straight man, he makes Fudd the object of the comedy, first by throwing a pie at him, then squirting him with water, and finally beating him inside his hat. Fudd is so enraged that he returns to the stage with his gun. The rabbit starts sweating, begins to back off, and as he faces the prospect of being shot, asks innocently, 'What's up, Doc?" A pause. Then Bugs notices that the audience is laughing and whispers to Fudd, "Hey, we got something Doc. Let's do it again." And with that one move they were a smash hit. "And then came Hollywood, and Warner Brothers," says Bugs, "where I was launched on my film career."[45]

While there are a number of important issues raised in this cartoon, two are of immediate concern to us. First, there is the claim that those moments that we tend to identify most powerfully with the experience of going to the movies—Fudd's attempt to get the rabbit once and for all, and Bugs's famous question—have their origins in vaudeville's aesthetics of improvised immediacy and its willingness to use any combination of performers (in this case a classic "animal act") to wow an audience. Second, and in a related sense, the film suggests that this experience is primarily about how we have come to understand the artist's relationship to his audience. One consequence of the movies is that artists no longer depend on the presence of an audience as they had to in vaudeville. Film in "What's Up Doc?" is presented as a solution to the problem of performing night after night for an unpredictable audience that at any point might simply leave the theater, or might never have arrived at all.

We can all walk out of a film of course. Who hasn't? But this doesn't affect the performance, or even the showing of the film, only the box office and the future of its stars. The larger meaning of the story that Bugs tells us, therefore, is really about the cultural and technological triumph of Hollywood and Warner Brothers as the exemplary image of Hollywood entertainment. Equally, however, it is a story about what happens to modern artists when they lose contact with their audience. The life that was once wholly in and of the show, and so defined by the presence of an audience, becomes something that is only ever told to an abstract public by the press after the fact. More famous than ever, but with nothing to do but sit by his pool, Bugs is left with no one to talk to but himself. "What's Up Doc?" thus confronts us with the question I began with: what does it mean to entertain an audience?

Toward the end of her book, Sophie Tucker suggests one possible answer. "I'll never forget the last show at the Palace in New York," she says, reflecting on the last days of vaudeville.

It was ghastly. Everyone knew the theatre was to be closed down, and a landmark in show business would be gone. That feeling got into the acts. The whole place, and even the performers, stank of decay. I seemed to

smell it. It challenged me. I went out on that stage determined to keep
my mind on the future—not on the past. I was determined to give the
audience the idea: why brood over yesterday? We have tomorrow. As I
sang I could feel the atmosphere change. The gloom began to lift, the
spirit which had formerly filled the Palace and which made it famous
among vaudeville houses in the world came back. . . . That's what an
entertainer can do.[46]

So even as the show biz world that had sustained her for so many decades
had disappeared, and the values and practices it had made possible no longer
seemed relevant or meaningful, her songs continued to offer her a way to
live and those who participated in them a new knowledge of reality. That
was their wonder.

NOTES

INTRODUCTION

1. David Ewen, *The Life and Death of Tin Pan Alley: The Golden Age of American Popular Music* (New York: Funk and Wagnalls Company, 1964), 25.

2. David Nasaw, *Going Out: The Rise and Fall of Public Amusements* (Cambridge, MA: Harvard University Press, 1999), 3.

3. Albert F. McLean, *American Vaudeville as Ritual* (Lexington: University of Kentucky Press, 1965), 3.

4. Ibid., 15.

5. Ibid., 222.

6. John E. DiMeglio, *Vaudeville U.S.A.* (Bowling Green: Bowling Green University Popular Press, 1973), 198, 199.

7. See Richard Butsch, *The Making of American Audiences: From Stage to Television, 1750–1990* (Cambridge: Cambridge University Press, 2000); Susan Glenn, *Female Spectacle* (Cambridge, MA: Harvard University Press, 2002); Henry Jenkins, *What Made Pistachio Nuts? Early Sound Comedy and the Vaudeville Aesthetic* (New York: Columbia University Press, 1992); M. Alison Kibler, *Rank Ladies: Gender and Cultural Hierarchy in American Vaudeville* (Chapel Hill: University of North Carolina Press, 1999); Nasaw, *Going Out*; Kathryn J. Oberdeck, *The Evangelist and the Impresario: Religion, Entertainment, and Cultural Politics in America, 1884–1914* (Baltimore: Johns Hopkins University Press, 1999); Robert W. Snyder, *The Voice of the City: Vaudeville and Popular Culture in New York* (Chicago: Ivan Dee, 2000).

8. Oberdeck, *Evangelist and the Impresario*, 10.

9. Michael Kammen, *American Culture American Taste: Social Change and the 20th Century* (New York: Basic Books, 1999).

10. William Dean Howells, "The Editors Easy Chair," reprinted in *American Vaudeville as Seen by Its Contemporaries*, ed. Charles W. Stein (New York: Alfred Knopf, 1984), 77.

1. THAT'S ENTERTAINMENT

1. For a summary of Nora Bayes's career see Anthony Slide, *The Encyclopedia of Vaudeville* (Jackson: University of Mississippi Press, 2012), 27–30; and Frank Cullen, *Vaudeville Old and New: An Encyclopedia of Variety Performers*, vol. 1 (New York: Routledge, 2006), 81–84.

2. Philip S. Foner, "Songs of the Eight Hour Movement," *Labor History* 13, no. 4 (1972).

3. Roy Rosensweig, *Eight Hours for What We Will: Workers and Leisure in an Industrial City, 1870–1920* (New York: Cambridge University Press, 1983), 1.

4. Charles Beaumont Davis, "The Vaudeville Club," *Harpers Weekly* 37 (February 1893): 116. Davis is quoted in Lewis A. Erenberg, *Steppin' Out: New York Nightlife and the Transformation of American Culture, 1890–1930* (Chicago: University of Chicago Press, 1981), 38.

5. Edwin Milton Royle, "The Vaudeville Theatre," reprinted in *American Vaudeville*, ed. Stein, 33.

6. In formulating these ideas, I have benefited greatly from the following studies: Rick Altman, *The American Film Musical* (Bloomington: Indiana University Press, 1987); Leo Braudy, *The World in a Frame: What We See in Films* (New York: Anchor/Doubleday, 1976); Stanley Cavell, *Philosophy the Day after Tomorrow* (Cambridge, MA: Belknap/Harvard University Press, 2005); Richard Dyer, *Only Entertainment* (London: Routledge, 1992); Jane Feuer, *The Hollywood Musical* (Houndsmills: Macmillan, 1993); Gerald Mast, *Can't Help Singin': The American Musical on Stage and Screen* (Woodstock, NY: Overlook Press, 1987); and Jacques Ranciere, *The Emancipated Spectator* (London: Verso, 2009).

7. Stanley Cavell, *Themes Out of School: Causes and Effects* (Chicago: University of Chicago Press, 1984), 3–26.

8. Gene Kelly and Stanley Donen, dir., *Singin' in the Rain*, MGM, 1951.

9. Ibid.

10. Vincente Minnelli, dir., *The Band Wagon*. Warner Brothers, 1953.

11. Minnelli is asking his audience to consider whether the loss of faith in oneself and the world, and the possibilities for the renewal of belief, can happen through a medium that appears to undermine any kind of truth-claim. See Cavell, *Philosophy the Day after Tomorrow*, 6–27 and 61–82. My debt to Cavell's thinking here should be obvious. See also Geoffrey Nowell-Smith, "The Band Wagon," in *Vincente Minnelli: The Art of Entertainment*, ed. Joe McElhaney (Detroit: Wayne State University Press, 2009), 175–84.

12. As was also the case with *An American in Paris* (1951) Minnelli is telling us that what we are about to see is a working through of the problem of entertainment's relationship to art, along with related issues of celebrity, recognition, talent, anonymity, the crowd, the press, romance, seriousness, comedy, theatricality, and so on.

13. In an influential study of blackface minstrelsy, Michael Rogin argues that Astaire's routine simply perpetuates the racism upon which the American entertainment industry was founded, describing the "Shine on Your Shoes" sequence as a case of "acknowledgment as domination." Michael Rogin, *Blackface, White Noise: Jewish Immigrants in the Hollywood Melting Pot* (Berkeley: University of California Press, 1996),

204. Cavell's detailed analysis of the sequence is in part a response to Rogin's claim. Cavell, *Philosophy the Day after Tomorrow*, 69–82. Cavell's point is that the relationship between Daniels and Astaire in this scene is more complicated than Rogin's theory allows.

14. Minnelli, *The Band Wagon*.

15. Snyder, *Voice of the City*, xx.

16. Frederick W. Snyder, "American Vaudeville-Theatre in a Package: The Origins of Mass Entertainment" (PhD dissertation, Yale University, 1970).

17. Snyder, *Voice of the City*, 160.

18. Ibid., xxv.

19. A good summary of this story, in all its various versions, is found in Patrick Brantlinger, *Bread and Circuses: Theories of Mass Culture as Social Decay* (Ithaca, NY: Cornell University Press, 1983).

20. Snyder, *Voice of the City*, 127.

21. Ibid., 161. For a critique of concept of a living image, see Ann Kibbey, *Theory of the Capitalist Image: Capitalism, Contemporary Film, and Women* (Bloomington: Indiana University Press, 2005), 6–44.

22. Altman, *American Film Musical*, 204.

23. Ibid., 349.

24. Jacques Rancière, *The Emancipated Spectator*, trans. Gregory Elliot (London: Verso, 2009), 17.

25. Anonymous, "Tryout Nights for Aspirants to Broadway's Favor," *Literary Digest*, June 30 1928, reprinted in *American Vaudeville*, ed. Stein, 165.

26. George Gottlieb, "Psychology of the American Vaudeville from the Manager's Point of View," *Current Opinion*, no. 60 (April 1916), reprinted in *American Vaudeville*, ed. Stein, 181.

27. George Gottlieb, cited in Brett Page, *Writing for Vaudeville* (Springfield: Home Correspondence School, 1915), 7–12.

28. Ibid.

29. Walter De Leon, "The Wow Finish," *Saturday Evening Post*, no. 197 (February 1925), cited in *American Vaudeville*, ed. Stein, 194.

2. NO BUSINESS LIKE SHOW BUSINESS

1. Alfred L. Bernheim, *The Business of Theatre: An Economic History of the American Theatre, 1750–1932* (New York: Benjamin Blom, 1964), 31.

2. Joe Laurie, *Vaudeville: From Honky-Tonks to the Palace* (New York: Henry Holt and Company, 1953), 3.

3. Bernheim, *Business of Theatre*, 34–40.

4. B. F. Keith, cited in Albert F. McLean, "Genesis of Vaudeville: Two Letters from B. F. Keith," *Theatre Survey* 1 (1960): 92.

5. Arthur Frank Wertheim, *Vaudeville Wars: How the Keith-Albee And Orpheum Circuits Controlled the Big-Time and Its Performers* (New York: Palgrave Macmillan, 2006), 96–99.

6. Bernheim, *Business of Theatre*, 36–37.

7. Ibid., 35.

8. *Billboard*, December 22, 1900, 8. It also meant that Frohman was spending about US$1000 a week on railroad fares, an issue I discuss below.

9. Bernheim, *Business of Theatre*, 31.

10. Ibid., 31

11. Snyder, *Voice of the City*, 35.

12. Wertheim, *Vaudeville Wars*, 97. Morris Meyerfield, who owned the San Francisco–based Orpheum Circuit, made a similar point: "About the beginning of my activities in the vaudeville business the legitimate theatre was gravitating to the center. . . . Why should not the interests of the scattered vaudeville houses be similarly linked?" (102).

13. *New York Times*, May 30, 1900, 7.

14. Wertheim, *Vaudeville Wars*, 103–5.

15. Bill Smith, *The Vaudevillians* (New York: Macmillan, 1976), 12.

16. *Billboard*, June 11, 1904, 3.

17. Ibid., July 9, 1904, 2.

18. Hartley Davis, "In Vaudeville," *Everybody's Magazine*, August 1905, reprinted in *American Vaudeville*, ed. Stein, 101.

19. Michael Leavitt, *Fifty Years in Theatrical Management* (New York: Broadway Publishing Co., 1912), 190.

20. Royle, "The Vaudeville Theatre," 28.

21. Ibid., 30.

22. Ibid., 33.

23. This theme is set out in detail in Olivier Zunz, *Making America Corporate, 1870–1920* (Chicago: University of Chicago Press, 1990), and Robert Wiebe, *The Search for Order, 1877–1920* (New York: Hill and Wang, 1967).

24. Timothy B. Spears, "'All Things to All Men': The Commercial Traveler and the Rise of Modern Salesmanship," *American Quarterly* 45, no. 4 (1993): 528.

25. Quoted in Zunz, *Making America Corporate*, 184.

26. Spears, "All Things to All Men," 541.

27. Munsterberg, cited in ibid., 546.

28. This breakdown of sales positions is in Zunz, *Making America Corporate*, 179–81.

29. Ibid., 180–81.

30. Jackson Lears, *Fables of Abundance: A Cultural History of Advertising in America* (New York: Basic Books, 1994), 63–74.

31. Ibid., 99–101; and Zunz, *Making America Corporate*, 181.

32. Bennet Musson, "A Week of One Night Stands" reprinted in *American Vaudeville*, ed. Stein, 45, 52.

33. *Billboard*, April 20, 1901, 4.

34. Sherman Dudley, quoted in Athelia Knight, "He Paved the Way for T.O.B.A," *Black Perspective in Music* 15, no. 2 (1987): 174. See also Cullen, *Vaudeville Old and New*, 332–33.

35. Russell, quoted in Knight, "He Paved The Way for T.O.B.A.," 165.

36. Ibid., 165–71. See also Henry T. Sampson, *Blacks in Blackface: A Sourcebook on Early Black Musical Shows* (Lanham, MD: Scarecrow Press, 2014), 28–36.

37. Quoted in Sampson, *Blacks in Blackface*, 32.

38. Ibid., 36.

39. Sophie Tucker, *Some of These Days: The Autobiography of Sophie Tucker* (New York: Doubleday, 1945), 1.

40. Ibid., 36.

41. Ibid., 42.

42. Harpo Marx, *Harpo Speaks*, in *American Vaudeville*, ed. Stein, 286–87.

43. Ibid.

44. Ethel Waters with Charles Samuels, *His Eye Is on the Sparrow* (London: W. H. Allen, 1951), 75.

45. Gavin Bushell, *Jazz from the Beginning* (New York: Da Capo, 1998), 46.

46. Notable examples are Alfred Bernheim, "The Facts of Vaudeville" (1923), and Walter J. Kingsley, "Vaudeville Is Reconstructed and Establishes Its Own Court" (1919), both of which are reproduced in *American Vaudeville*, ed. Stein. For a fuller political account of the artist-management relationship when vaudeville was the dominant medium for entertainment, see George Fuller Golden, *My Lady Vaudeville and Her White Rats* (New York: Broadway Publishing Co., 1909).

47. Hartley Davis, "The Business Side of Vaudeville," *Everybody's Magazine*, October 1907 cited in *American Vaudeville*, ed. Stein, 120

3. RITES OF PASSAGE

1. McLean, *American Vaudeville as Ritual*, 6.

2. Ibid., 91–105.

3. Warren I. Susman, *Culture and History: The Transformation of American Society in the Twentieth Century* (New York: Pantheon, 1984), 271–85.

4. Roberto DaMatta, *Carnivals, Rogues, and Heroes: An Interpretation of the Brazilian Dilemma*, translated by John Drury (Notre Dame: University of Notre Dame Press, 1991), 16, 20–22, 25

5. Tucker, *Some of These Days*, 4, 5. My italics.

6. Ibid., 6.

7. Ibid.

8. Ibid., 8.

9. Ibid., 10–11, 19.

10. DaMatta, *Carnivals, Rogues, and Heroes*, 21.

11. Ibid., 22.

12. Gillian Rodger, "When Singing Was Acting: Song and Character in Variety Theatre," *Musical Quarterly* 98, nos. 1–2 (2015): 57–80; and Philip Auslander, "Musical Personae," *Drama Review* 50, no. 1 (2006): 100–119.

13. Tucker, *Some of These Days*, 22.

14. Glenn, *Female Spectacle*, 5.

15. Parsons, quoted in ibid.

16. Lillian Russell, "Reminiscences" in *American Vaudeville*, ed. Stein, 12–13.

17. Ibid., 11.

18. Tucker, *Some of These Days*, 62.

19. Ibid.

20. Ibid., 63.

21. Irving Howe, *The World of Our Fathers: The Journey of the Eastern European Jews to America and the Life They Found and Made There* (New York: Harcourt Brace Jovanovich, 1976), and Rogin, *Blackface, White Noise.* See also Janet Brown, "The 'Coon-Singer' and the 'Coon-Song,'" *Journal of American Culture* 7, nos. 1–2 (1984): 1–8; Kathleen B. Casey, "'The Jewish Girl with the Colored Voice': Sophie Tucker and the Sounds of Race and Gender in Modern America," *Journal of American Culture* 38, no. 1 (2015): 16–26; Armand Fields, *Sophie Tucker: First Lady of Show Business* (Jefferson: McFarland and Co., 2003); Lori Harrison-Kahn, *Literature, Minstrelsy, and the Black-Jewish Imaginary* (New Brunswick, NJ: Rutgers University Press, 2011), 16–57; Grace Overbeke, "Subversively Sexy: The Jewish 'Red Hot Mamas': Sophie Tucker, Belle Barth and Pearl Williams," *Studies in American Humor* 3, no. 25, 2012, 35–58; and Jon Stratton, *Jews, Race and Popular Music* (London: Routledge, 2009).

22. Tucker, *Some of These Days*, 33, 34.

23. Victor Turner, *The Ritual Process: Structure and Anti-Structure* (Hawthorn: Aldine de Gruyter, 1995), 95.

24. Brown, "The 'Coon-Singer' and the 'Coon-Song.'"

25. Quoted in Ann Charters, *Nobody: The Story of Bert Williams* (New York: Da Capo, 1983), 16. See also Louis Chude-Sokei, *"The Last Darky": Bert Williams, Black-on-Black Minstrelsy, and the African Diaspora* (Durham, NC: Duke University Press, 2006); and Camille F. Forbes, *Bert Williams: Burnt Cork, Broadway, and the Story of America's First Black Star* (New York: Basic Civitas Books, 2013).

26. Charters, *Nobody*, 18.

27. Ibid., 28.

28. Waters, with Samuels, *His Eye Is on the Sparrow*, 66–67.

29. Ibid., 67.

30. These themes are developed in Erenberg, *Steppin' Out*; Lears, *Fables of Abundance*; Nasaw, *Going Out*; and E. P. Thompson, *Customs in Common* (Harmondsworth: Penguin Books, 1993), 352–403.

31. Charters, *Nobody*, 53.

32. Brown, "The 'Coon-Singer' and the 'Coon-Song'"; and Patricia R. Schroeder, "Passing for Black: Coon Songs and The Performance of Race," *Journal of American Culture* 33, no. 2 (2010): 139–53.

33. Reproduced in Charters, *Nobody*, 135–37.

34. Ibid., 138–39

4. ELEMENTARY STRUCTURES

1. For the history of this type of journalism see Charles L. Ponce de Leon, *Self-Exposure: Human-Interest Journalism and the Emergence of Celebrity in America, 1890–1940* (Chapel Hill: University of North Carolina Press, 2002), 206–40.

2. Tucker, *Some of These Days*, 5

3. Ibid., 11, 12

4. Ibid., 77.

5. Jessel, quoted in Smith, *The Vaudevillians* (New York: Macmillan, 1976), 29.

6. Marshall Sahlins, *What Kinship Is . . . and Is Not* (Chicago: University of Chicago Press, 2013), 2 and 21.

7. Sahlins, *What Kinship Is,* 13. "My sister, Adele," Astaire said in an unscripted speech to the American Film Institute in 1981, "was mostly responsible for my being in show business. She was the whole show, she really was. In all the vaudeville acts we had and the musical comedies we did together, Delly was the one that was the shining light and I was just there pushing away." Quoted in Toni Bentley, "Two Step," *New York Times,* June 3, 2012, BR32.

8. George M. Cohan, *Twenty Years on Broadway, and the Years It Took to Get There* (Westport, CT: Greenwood Press, 1971).

9. Ibid., 8–9.

10. Ibid., 14.

11. Ibid., 15.

12. Ibid., 28.

13. B. F. Keith in ibid., 45.

14. Ibid., 56.

15. Ibid., 55, 56.

16. Sahlins, *What Kinship Is,* 22–23.

17. Cohan, *Twenty Years on Broadway,* 73.

18. Ibid., 75–76.

19. Josie Cohan, quoted in ibid., 107.

20. Ruth Finnegan, *The Hidden Musicians: Music-Making in an English Town* (Middletown, CT: Wesleyan University Press, 2007), 306.

21. Ibid., 308.

22. Ibid., 310.

23. My thinking here has been shaped by Maurice Godelier, *The Metamorphosis of Kinship,* translated by Nora Scott (London: Verso, 2011), 479–519.

24. Paul DiMaggio, "Cultural Entrepreneurship in Nineteenth-Century Boston: The Creation of an Organizational Base for High Culture in America," *Media, Culture and Society* 4, no. 4 (1982): 46

25. Sven Beckert, *The Monied Metropolis: New York City and the Consolidation of the American Bourgeoisie, 1850–1896* (Cambridge: Cambridge University Press, 2001), 33, 267.

26. Marian Spitzer, *The Palace* (New York: Athenaeum, 1969), 44.

27. Ibid., 174.

28. Laurie, *Vaudeville,* 144.

29. Ibid., 154.

30. Sahlins, *What Kinship Is,* 28.

31. Cohan, *Twenty Years on Broadway,* 7.

32. Alan Dale, quoted in Susan A. Glenn, "'Give an Imitation of Me': Vaudeville Mimics and the Play of the Self," *American Quarterly* 50, no. 1 (1998): 49.

33. Ibid., 53.

34. Caroline Caffin, *Vaudeville* (New York: Kennerly, 1914), 21.

35. Marian Spitzer, "The People of Vaudeville" reprinted in *American Vaudeville*, ed. Stein, 228

36. Busby Berkeley, dir., *Babes in Arms*, Warner Brothers, 1939.

37. Martin Rubin, "The Crowd, the Collective, and the Chorus: Busby Berkeley and the New Deal," in *Movies and Mass Culture*, ed. John Belton (London: Athlone, 1999), 59–92.

38. Feuer, *Hollywood Musical*, 17.

5. SHOW ME THE MONEY

1. Martin J. Sklar, *The Corporate Reconstruction of American Capitalism, 1890–1916: The Market, The Law, and Politics* (Cambridge: Cambridge University Press, 1988), 5. Sklar's study is essential to the issues I discuss in this chapter. Other studies that have helped me to formulate the arguments presented here are Lawrence Goodwyn, *Democratic Promise: The Populist Movement in America* (New York: Oxford University Press, 1976), Fredric Jameson, *Representing Capital* (London: Verso, 2011), and Alan Trachtenberg, *The Incorporation of America: Culture and Society in the Gilded Age* (New York: Hill and Wang, 1982).

2. Gabriel Kolko, *The Triumph of Conservatism: A Reinterpretation of American History, 1900–1916* (New York: Free Press, 1963), 3.

3. I should add that historians have found this mythology equally useful, not only as a way of explaining the kinds of distinctions that exist between different artistic forms, but also as a means of justifying their own claims about the political value of popular culture. Their studies take the form of a backstage melodrama, in which the ruling classes—usually represented by an authoritarian manager, conductor, editor, curator, or director—conspire to seize control of the democratic space of the theater or concert hall in order to impose their own elite values on the audience, either by excluding them altogether, or reducing them to passive silence. I will return to this problem in the final chapter.

4. Bluford Adams, *E Pluribus Barnum: The Great Showman and the Making of U.S. Popular Culture* (Minneapolis: University of Minnesota Press, 1997).

5. Lewis, quoted in Neil Harris, *Humbug: The Art of P. T. Barnum* (Chicago: University of Chicago Press, 1981), 55–56.

6. Leo Braudy, *The Frenzy of Renown: Fame and Its History* (New York: Vintage Books, 1986), 499.

7. B. F. Keith, quoted in McLean, "Genesis of Vaudeville," 89.

8. Quoted in Wertheim, *Vaudeville Wars*, 22, 23.

9. Quoted in ibid., 23.

10. Kibler, *Rank Ladies*, 23–54.

11. Walter Richard Eaton, "The Wizards of Vaudeville," *McClure's Magazine* 55, no. 7 (September 1923): 43–49.

12. Ibid., 48.

13. Ibid.

14. Ibid.

15. Albee, quoted in Wertheim, *Vaudeville Wars*, 30.

16. F. F. Proctor, quoted in William M. Marston and John Henry Feller, *F. F. Proctor: Vaudeville Pioneer* (New York: Richard R. Smith, 1943), 31.

17. Reprinted in ibid., 46.

18. Robert Grau, *The Business Man in the Amusement World* (New York: Broadway Publishing Co., 1910), 301.

19. Marston and Feller, *F. F. Proctor*, 46. See T. Jackson Lears, *Rebirth of a Nation: The Making of Modern America, 1877–1920* (New York: HarperCollins, 2009), 336, for a succinct definition of Progressivism.

20. Oberdeck, *Evangelist and the Impresario*, 1–26.

21. Ibid., 3, 25–26.

22. B. F. Keith, "The Vogue of the Vaudeville" reprinted in *American Vaudeville*, ed. Stein, 15–16.

23. Ibid., 16.

24. McLean, *Vaudeville as Ritual*, 203.

25. Laurie, *Vaudeville*, 337–38.

26. Marston and Feller, *F. F. Proctor*, 50.

27. Proctor, quoted in ibid., 31.

28. Ibid., 112, 113.

29. Edward F. Albee, "Twenty Years of Vaudeville" in *American Vaudeville*, ed. Stein, 215.

30. *New York Morning Telegraph*, quoted in editorial, *Billboard*, January 9, 1904, 4.

31. Grau, *Business Man in the Amusement World*, 139.

32. Ibid., 1.

33. Ibid., 323–24.

34. Harry Braverman, *Labor and Monopoly Capital: The Degradation of Work in the Twentieth Century* (New York: Monthly Review Press, 1998), 132.

35. Ibid.

36. Leavitt, *Fifty Years in Theatrical Management*, 196.

6. ON WITH THE SHOW

1. Gerald Mast, *Can't Help Singin': The American Musical on Stage and Screen* (Woodstock, NY: Overlook Press, 1987), 34.

2. Whitney Balliet, "The Three Louis," in *The Sound of Surprise* (London: William Kimber, 1959), 90.

3. Pascal Bonizter, quoted in Thomas Elsaesser, "Film History and Visual Pleasure," in *Cinema Histories, Cinema Practices*, ed. Patricia Mellencamp and Philip Rosen (Frederick, MD: University Publications of America, 1984), 58.

4. Caffin, *Vaudeville*, 61.

5. William J. Mahar, *Behind the Burnt Cork Mask: Early Blackface Minstrelsy and Antebellum Popular Culture* (Urbana: University of Illinois Press, 1999), 36–41; Renee Lapp Norris, "Opera and the Mainstreaming of Blackface Minstrelsy," *Journal for the Society for American Music* 1, no. 3 (2007): 341–65; Ray B. Browne, "Shakespeare in

American Vaudeville and Negro Minstrelsy," *American Quarterly* 12, no. 3 (1960): 374–91; Gillian Rodger, *Champagne Charlie and Pretty Jemima: Variety Theatre in Nineteenth-Century America* (Urbana: University of Illinois Press, 2010).

6. Harris, *Humbug*, 235–76.

7. Eugene Elliot, *A History of Variety-Vaudeville in Seattle from the Beginning to 1914* (Seattle: University of Washington Press, 1944), 41.

8. See Parker R. Zellers, "The Cradle of Variety," *Educational Theatre Journal* 20, no. 4 (1968): 578–58; and Brooks McNamara, *The New York Concert Saloon: The Devil's Own Nights* (Cambridge: University of Cambridge Press, 2007), 1–10.

9. Zellers, "The Cradle of Variety," 578.

10. Reprinted in McNamara, *The New York Concert Saloon*, 59.

11. Laurie, *Vaudeville*, 12.

12. Ibid., 14.

13. Lawrence Senelick, "Variety into Vaudeville: The Process Observed in Two Manuscript Gagbooks," *American Journal of Theatre History* 29, no. 1 (May 1978): 2.

14. Ibid., 2.

15. Ibid.

16. Ibid., 10.

17. Harris, quoted in ibid., 10.

18. Ibid., 12–13.

19. Quoted in McLean, *American Vaudeville as Ritual*, 69.

20. Senelick, "Variety into Vaudeville," 13.

21. Quoted in ibid., 14.

22. Robert Pippin, *The Persistence of Subjectivity: On the Kantian Aftermath* (New York: Cambridge University Press, 2005).

23. Royle, "The Vaudeville Theatre" reprinted in *American Vaudeville*, ed. Stein, 26.

24. Ibid., 26–27.

25. Ibid., 21, 26.

26. Ibid., 33.

27. Ibid.

28. Ibid.

29. Hartley Davis in *American Vaudeville*, ed. Stein, 104.

30. Brooks Atkins, "Vaudeville . . . Is Dead," in *Selected Vaudeville Criticism*, ed. Anthony Slide (Metuchen, NJ: Scarecrow Press, 1988), 248.

31. William Gould, "Vaudeville Versus Musical Comedy" in *American Vaudeville*, ed. Stein, 78.

32. Tucker, *Some of These Days*, 135–36.

33. Ibid., 140.

34. Caffin, *Vaudeville*, 15, 23.

35. Ibid., 226–27.

36. Ibid., 26–27.

37. Ibid., 9, 13.

38. Ibid., 36, 37–38. For an insightful study of the paradoxes of Tanguay's appeal see Andrew L. Erdman, *Queen of Vaudeville: The Story of Eva Tanguay* (Ithaca, NY: Cornell University Press, 2012).

39. Ibid., 39.

40. Ibid., 3, 216–17.

41. Page, *Writing for Vaudeville*, 174, 11.

42. Ibid., 3, 52.

43. Further on in his account, Page actually makes the claim that vaudeville and the short story symbolize the age. Ibid., 74.

44. Ibid., 13, 72.

45. McLean, *American Vaudeville as Ritual*, 91–105.

46. Page, *Writing for Vaudeville*, 129.

47. Ibid., 203.

7. IN SEARCH OF AN AUDIENCE

1. "Boorish Treatment of Yvette Guilbert," *New York Times*, October 12, 1909, 9.

2. Ibid.; Caffin devotes several pages to Guilbert in *Vaudeville*, 57–60.

3. See, for example, Snyder, *Voice of the City*, 107

4. Waters, with Samuels, *His Eye Is on the Sparrow*, 73–74.

5. Burns, quoted in Jenkins, *What Made Pistachio Nuts?*, 69

6. Cantor, quoted in ibid., 70.

7. Eddie Cantor, *The Way I See It* (Englewood Cliffs, NJ: Prentice-Hall, 1959), 101.

8. Eddie Cantor, *My Life Is in Your Hands* (New York: Harper and Brothers, 1928), 76.

9. Lydia Goehr, *The Imaginary Museum of Musical Works: An Essay in the Philosophy of Music* (Oxford: Oxford University Press, 2007).

10. Cantor, *My Life Is In Your Hands*, 2.

11. Stanley Cavell, *Music We Mean What We Say?* (Cambridge: Cambridge University Press, 2002), 198.

12. Waters, with Samuels, *His Eye Is on the Sparrow*, 125.

13. Review in *The Standard & Vanity Fair* 155, no. 1075 (March 19, 1910), reprinted in Slide, *Selected Vaudeville Criticism*,157.

14. Caffin, *Vaudeville*, 27.

15. Tucker, *Some of These Days*, 23

16. Ibid., 40.

17. Ibid., 41.

18. Ibid.

19. Ibid., 41, 42.

20. Walter De Leon, "The Wow Finish," in *American Vaudeville*, ed. Stein, 198.

21. Waters, with Samuels, *His Eye Is on the Sparrow*, 166.

22. George Whiting, quoted in Shirley Staples, *Male-Female Comedy Teams in American Vaudeville, 1865–1932* (Ann Arbor: UMI Research Press, 1984), 171.

23. Mae West, *Goodness Had Nothing to Do with It* (London: W. H. Allen, 1960), 39–40.

24. Ibid.

25. Ibid., 47–51.

26. Nora Bayes, "Holding My Audience," *Theatre Magazine*, no. 26 (September 1917): 128.

27. I am paraphrasing the actor Edward Reed, who wrote, "The true vaudevillian was a 'character.' It was the essence of his art to create a stage personality so definite, rounded, unique, and so entirely his own, that he would be recognised and hailed whenever he appeared on stage—in New York or Kalamazoo." Reed, "Vaudeville Again," reprinted in *American Vaudeville*, ed. Stein, 374, and Bayes, "Holding My Audience," 128.

28. West, *Goodness Had Nothing to Do with It*, 51.

29. Glenn, *Female Spectacle*, 66–69.

30. Bayes, "Holding My Audience," 128.

31. Nora Bayes, quoted in Slide, *Selected Vaudeville Criticism*, 17.

32. Ibid.

33. Bayes, "Holding My Audience," 128.

34. Stanley Cavell, *The World Viewed: Reflections on the Ontology of Film* (Cambridge, MA: Harvard University Press, 1979), 230

35. Pippin, *Persistence of Subjectivity*, 20.

36. Keith, "The Vogue of the Vaudeville," reprinted in *American Vaudeville*, ed. Stein, 17.

8. VAUDEVILLE MELODIES

1. Bert Williams, "The Comic Side of Trouble," *American Magazine* 85 (1918), cited in *American Vaudeville*, ed. Stein, 243–44

2. Alec Wilder, *The American Popular Song: The Great Innovators, 1900–1950* (New York: Oxford University Press, 1972), 3

3. Peter Van Der Merwe, *The Origins of the Popular Style: The Antecedents of Twentieth-Century Popular Music* (Oxford: Oxford University Press, 1989), 203.

4. For Van Der Merwe's point about the futility of historical explanation see ibid., 214. It should be obvious from the arguments presented in this book that I disagree with this claim.

5. William W. Austin, *"Susanna," "Jeanie," and "The Old Folks At Home": The Songs of Stephen C. Foster from His Time to Ours* (New York: Macmillan, 1975), xi, x.

6. Ibid., 38.

7. For example, Austin cites a rural worker interviewed by Newman White in 1915 who claimed that "Susanna" had been a slave song. Ibid., 39.

8. Rennold Wolf, "The Boy Who Revived Ragtime," in Charles Hamm, *Irving Berlin: Songs from the Melting Pot: The Formative Years, 1907–1914* (Oxford: Oxford University Press, 1997), 3–4.

9. Ibid., 19

10. Jeffrey Magee, *Irving Berlin's Musical Theatre* (New York: Oxford University Press, 2012), 29.

11. Joseph Horowitz, *Understanding Toscanini: A Social History of American Concert Life* (Berkeley: University of California Press, 1987); and Derek Scott, *Sounds of the Metropolis: The 19th-Century Popular Music Revolution in London, New York, Paris and Vienna* (Oxford: Oxford University Press, 2008).

12. Scott, *Sounds of the Metropolis*, 4.

13. Zellers, "Cradle of Variety," 1; and Dale Cockrell, *Demons of Disorder: Early Blackface Minstrels and Their World* (New York: Cambridge University Press, 1997).

14. Laurie, *Vaudeville*, 61–62.

15. Ibid., 77.

16. Ibid., 44.

17. Ibid., 61.

18. Ibid., 63.

19. Daniel Goldmark explores many of these same cultural practices among Tin Pan Alley songwriters and publishers in two of excellent articles, but from the perspective of the publishers rather than the performers. See Daniel Goldmark, "Creating Desire on Tin Pan Alley," *Musical Quarterly* 90, no. 2 (2007): 197–229, and Goldmark, "'Making Songs Pay': Tin Pan Alley's Formulas for Success," *Musical Quarterly* 98, no. 1–2 (2015): 3–28.

20. Ewen, *Life and Death of Tin Pan Alley*, 25. In *Selling Sounds: The Commercial Revolution in American Music* (Cambridge, MA: Harvard University Press, 2009), David Suisman confirms Ewan's claim about the relationship between Tin Pan Alley and vaudeville. However, his analysis focuses more on the structural changes taking place within the publishing, and nascent recording, industries in the early decades of the twentieth-century, than on vaudeville's formative role in the production of popular music practices and values.

21. Cited in Hamm, *Irving Berlin*, 5.

22. A precedent for this kind of practice was the composer, arranger, and bandleader, David Braham, who worked for several years with Ned Harrigan and Tony Hart's company. "Throughout his career," observes his biographer, John Franceschina, "Braham would compose and arrange hundreds of overtures, some based on his own original melodies, others employing popular tunes, but all were expertly crafted melodies designed to transport the audience into the spirit of the entertainment." See John Franceschina, *David Braham: The American Offenbach* (New York: Routledge, 2003), 35.

23. Hamm, *Irving Berlin*, 10.

24. Ibid., 103.

25. Frank J. Cipolla, "Patrick S. Gilmore: The Boston Years," *American Music* 6, no. 3 (1988): 281–92.

26. Page, *Writing for Vaudeville*, 149–50.

27. Hamm, *Irving Berlin*, 19. Hamm points out that Berlin's emphasis on the production song poses a major challenge for music historians and musicologists, whose insights about musical meaning and significance mostly derive from studying music as a fixed form, whether in the form of a score, a text, or recording.

28. Page, *Writing for Vaudeville*, 136.

29. Cited in ibid., 155.

30. Magee, *Irving Berlin's Musical Theatre*, 30.

31. William J. Schafer and Johannes Riedel, *The Art of Ragtime* (New York: Da Capo, 1977), 30, 31.

32. Paul Charosh, "Studying Nineteenth-Century Popular Song," *American Music* 15, no. 4 (1997): 463.

33. Page, *Writing for Vaudeville*, 152.

9. NOTHING SUCCEEDS LIKE SUCCESS

1. Robert B. Pippin, *Hollywood Westerns and American Myth* (New Haven, CT: Yale University Press, 2010), 62.

2. Richard Slotkin, *Regeneration through Violence: The Mythology of the American Frontier, 1600–1860* (Norman: University of Oklahoma Press, 1973), 6.

3. My attempt to demonstrate what such a transformation might involve can be found in Nicholas Gebhardt, *Going for Jazz: Music Practices and American Ideology* (Chicago: University of Chicago Press, 2001), 77–122.

4. For a sample of the enormous literature dealing with the enormous literature on success in the United States, see John G. Cawelti, *Apostles of the Self-Made Man: Changing Concepts of Success in America* (Chicago: University of Chicago Press, 1968); Jeffrey L. Decker, *Made in America: Self-Styled Success from Horatio Alger to Oprah Winfrey* (Minneapolis: University of Minnesota Press, 1997); Julie Levinson, *The American Success Myth on Film* (New York: Palgrave-Macmillan, 2012); Kenneth S. Lynn, *The Dream of Success: A Study of the Modern American Imagination* (Westport, CT: Greenwood Press, 1972); Daniel T. Rodgers, *The Industrial Work Ethic in America, 1850–1920* (Chicago: University of Chicago Press, 1979); Richard Weiss, *The American Myth of Success: From Horatio Alger to Norman Vincent Peale* (Urbana: University of Illinois Press, 1988); Irvin G. Wyllie, *The Self-Made Man in America: The Myth of Rags to Riches* (New Brunswick, NJ: Rutgers University Press, 1954).

5. Richard Slotkin, *The Fatal Environment: The Myth of the Frontier in the Age of Industrialization, 1800–1890* (Norman: University of Oklahoma Press, 1998), 87, 307.

6. Lynn, *Dream of Success*, 3.

7. Cohan, *Twenty Years on Broadway*, 154–68.

8. Ibid., 86–103.

9. For information on Dockstader see Cullen, *Vaudeville Old and New*, 315–16.

10. Ibid., 112.

11. Marian Spitzer, "The Mechanics of Vaudeville" in *American Vaudeville*, ed. Stein, 172.

12. Adam Kopnik, "Laugh Factory," *New Yorker*, November 17, 2014, 82.

13. George M. Cohan and George J. Nathan, "The Mechanics of Emotion," *McClure's Magazine* 42 (1913): 70.

14. Ibid., 71.

15. Ibid., 74–77.

16. Bayes, "Holding My Audience," 128.

17. Cavell, *The World Viewed*, 213.

18. Calvin Colton, cited in Rodgers, *Industrial Work Ethic in America*, 12.

19. Will M. Cressy, *Continuous Vaudeville* (Boston: Richard G. Badger, 1914), 42.

20. McLean, *American Vaudeville as Ritual*, 7.

21. Ibid., 11.

22. Ibid.

23. Tucker, *Some of These Days*, 77.

24. Ibid., 59.

25. Ibid., 135.

26. Ibid., 150–51.

27. Braudy, *The Frenzy of Renown*, 492.

28. Jane Feuer, "The Self-Reflexive Musical and the Myth of Entertainment," in *The Film Genre Reader II*, ed. Barry Keith Grant (Austin: University of Texas Press, 1995), 443.

29. Michael Curtiz, dir., *Yankee Doodle Dandy*, Warner Brothers, 1942.

30. Ibid.

31. John McCabe, *George M. Cohan: The Man Who Owned Broadway* (New York: Doubleday: 1973), 84.

32. Quoted in ibid., 84.

33. George Cukor, dir., *A Star Is Born*, Warner Brothers, 1954.

34. Feuer, *Hollywood Musical*, 79.

35. Ibid.

36. Tucker, *Some of These Days*, 5.

10. APPLAUSE

1. Tucker, *Some of These Days*, 19.

2. William Leach, *Land of Desire: Merchants, Power and the Rise of a New American Culture* (New York: Vintage Books, 1994); T. Jackson Lears, *Fables of Abundance: A Cultural History of Advertising in America* (New York: Basic Books, 1994); Richard Ohmann, *The Selling of Culture: Magazines, Markets and Class at the Turn of the Century* (London: Verso, 1996); Janice Radway, *A Feeling for Books: Book-of-the-Month-Club, Literary Taste and Middle Class Desire* (Chapel Hill: University of North Carolina Press, 1997).

3. Leach, *Land of Desire*, 9.

4. Ibid., 17–18.

5. Alfred D. Chandler, *The Visible Hand: The Managerial Revolution in American Business* (Cambridge, MA: Harvard University Press, 1977), 132; Beckert, *Monied Metropolis*, 237–72

6. Richard Ohmann, "Epochal Change: Print Culture and Economics," *Proceedings of the American Antiquarian Society* (2003): 358.

7. Alexis de Tocqueville, *Democracy in America*, vol. 2, trans. Henry Reeve (New York: Vintage Books, 1990), 82.

8. Lawrence Levine, *Highbrow/Lowbrow: The Emergence of Cultural Hierarchy in America* (Cambridge, MA: Harvard University Press, 1988).

9. Richard Bushman argues that an ideology based on values of refinement and cultivation appeared in the British American colonies in the 1690s, as part of a European-wide movement. See Richard Bushman, *The Refinement of America* (New York: Vintage, 1992), xi–xix.

10. Levine, *Highbrow/Lowbrow*, 21.

11. Ibid., 86.

12. Ibid., 146, 107, 236.

13. DiMaggio, "Cultural Entrepreneurship in Nineteenth-Century Boston," 39.

14. Bruce McConachie, "New York Operagoing, 1825–1850: Creating an Elite Social Ritual," *American Music* 6, no. 2 (1988): 190.

15. DiMaggio, "Cultural Entrepreneurship in Nineteenth-Century Boston," 33.

16. Paul DiMaggio, "Cultural Entrepreneurship in Nineteenth-Century Boston, Part II: The Classification and Framing of American Art," *Media, Culture and Society* 4, no. 4 (1982): 313.

17. Ralph P. Locke, "Music Lovers, Patrons, and the 'Sacralization" of Culture in America," *19th-Century Music* 17, no. 2 (1993): 154.

18. Ibid., 153.

19. Levine, *Highbrow/Lowbrow*, 8.

20. Ibid., 195, 198

21. Leavitt, *Fifty Years in Theatrical Management*, 186.

22. Caffin, *Vaudeville*, 3.

23. M. Alison Kibler, "Rank Ladies, Ladies of Rank: The Elinore Sisters in Vaudeville," *American Studies* 38, no. 1 (1997): 110–12.

24. Caffin, *Vaudeville*, 76.

25. Ibid., 77.

26. Lynn Abbot and Doug Seroff, "'They Certainly Sound Good to Me:' Sheet Music, Southern Vaudeville and the Commercial Ascendency of the Blues," *American Music* 14, no. 4 (1996): 402

27. David Monod, "'Ev'rybody's Crazy 'bout the Doggone Blues': Creating the Country Blues in the Early Twentieth Century," *Journal of Popular Music Studies* 19, no. 2 (2007): 188.

28. Chris Albertson, *Bessie* (London: Barrie and Jenkins, 1972), 26.

29. Lynn Abbott and Doug Seroff, "Bessie Smith: The Early Years," *Blues and Rhythm* 70 (1992): 8–9.

30. Ibid., 10–11.

31. Lawrence Gushee, *Pioneers of Jazz: The Story of the Creole Jazz Band* (New York: Oxford University Press, 2005), 15.

32. Quoted in ibid., 99.

33. Mark Berresford, *That's Got 'Em! The Life and Music of Wilbur Sweatman* (Jackson: University of Mississippi Press, 2010), xi.

34. William Kenney also demonstrates how inseparable early jazz and vaudeville were. See William Howland Kenney, "The Influence of Black Vaudeville on Early Jazz," *Black Perspective in Music* 14, no. 3 (1986): 233–48.

35. Norman Hapgood, "The Life of a Vaudeville Artist," reprinted in *American Vaudeville*, ed. Stein, 34.

36. Cavell, *The World Viewed*, 5.

37. Gilbert Seldes, *The Seven Lively Arts* (New York: Dover, 2001), 253.

38. F. F. Proctor, quoted in Marston and Feller, *F. F. Proctor*, 49.

39. Paul DiMaggio, "Cultural Boundaries and Structural Change: the Extension of the High Culture Model to Theatre, Opera, and Dance, 1900–1940," in *Cultivating Differences: Symbolic Boundaries and the Making of Inequality*, ed. Michèle Lamont and Marcel Fournier (Chicago: University of Chicago Press, 1992), 31.

40. Raymond Hitchcock, quoted in Wertheim, *Vaudeville Wars*, 26

41. William Weber, "Mass Culture and the Reshaping of European Musical Taste,

1770–1870," *International Review of Aesthetics and Sociology of Music* 8, no. 1 (1977): 5–22.

42. Jenkins, *What Made Pistachio Nuts?*, 63, 64, 68.

43. Vadim Uraneff, "Comedia Dell'Arte and American Vaudeville," *Theatre Arts* (October 1923): 326.

44. Mary Cass Canfield, "The Great American Art," in *American Vaudeville*, ed. Stein, 372.

45. "What's Up Doc?," *Looney Tunes: The Best of Bugs Bunny*, Warner Brothers, 2008.

46. Tucker, *Some of These Days*, 308.

BIBLIOGRAPHY

BOOKS

Abbott, Lynn and Seroff, Doug. "Bessie Smith: The Early Years." *Blues and Rhythm* 70 (1992): 8–11.

———. *Out of Sight: The Rise of African-American Popular Music, 1889–1895*. Jackson: University Press of Mississippi, 2002.

———. *Ragged But Right: Black Traveling Shows, "Coon Songs," and the Dark Pathway to Blues and Jazz*. Jackson: University Press of Mississippi, 2007.

———. "'They Certainly Sound Good to Me'; Sheet Music, Southern Vaudeville and the Commercial Ascendency of the Blues." *American Music* 14, no. 4 (1996): 402–54.

Adams, Bluford. *E Pluribus Barnum: The Great Showman and the Making of U.S. Popular Culture*. Minneapolis: University of Minnesota Press, 1997.

Albertson, Chris. *Bessie*. London: Barrie and Jenkins, 1972.

Allen. Robert C. "B. F. Keith and the Origins of American Vaudeville." *Theatre Survey* 21, no. 2 (1980): 105–15.

Altman, Rick. *The American Film Musical*. Bloomington: University of Indiana Press, 1987.

Auslander, Philip. "Musical Personae." *Drama Review* 50, no. 1 (2006): 100–119.

Austin, William W. *"Susanna," "Jeanie," and "The Old Folks At Home": The Songs of Stephen C. Foster from His Time to Ours*. New York: Macmillan, 1975.

Balliet, Whitney. *The Sound of Surprise*. London: William Kimber, 1959.

Bayes, Nora "Holding My Audience." *Theatre Magazine*, no. 26 (September 1917).

Bentley, Toni. "Two Step." *New York Times*, June 3, 2012, BR32.

Berkert, Sven. *The Monied Metropolis: New York City and the Consolidation of the American Bourgeoisie, 1850–1896*. Cambridge: Cambridge University Press, 2001.

Berman, Ron. "Vaudeville Philosophers: 'The Killers.'" *Twentieth Century Literature* 45, no. 1 (1999): 79–93.

Bernheim, Alfred L. *The Business of Theatre: An Economic History of the American Theatre, 1750–1932*. New York: Benjamin Blom, 1964.

Berresford, Mark. *That's Got 'Em! The Life and Music of Wilbur Sweatman*. Jackson: University Press of Mississippi, 2010.

Brantlinger, Patrick. *Bread and Circuses: Theories of Mass Culture as Social Decay.* Ithaca, NY: Cornell University Press, 1983.

Braudy, Leo. *The World in a Frame: What We See in Films.* New York: Anchor/Doubleday, 1976.

Braverman, Harry. *Labor and Monopoly Capital: The Degradation of Work in the Twentieth Century.* New York: Monthly Review Press, 1998.

Brown, Janet. "The 'Coon-Singer' and the 'Coon-Song.'" *Journal of American Culture* 7, nos. 1–2 (1984): 1–8.

Browne, Ray B. "Shakespeare in American Vaudeville and Negro Minstrelsy." *American Quarterly* 12, no. 3 (1960): 374–91.

Bushell, Gavin. *Jazz from the Beginning.* New York: Da Capo, 1998.

Bushman, Richard. *The Refinement of America.* New York: Vintage Books, 1992.

Butsch, Richard. *The Making of American Audiences: From Stage to Television, 1750–1990.* Cambridge: Cambridge University Press, 2000.

Caffin, Caroline. *Vaudeville.* New York: Kennerly, 1914.

Cantor, Eddie. *The Way I See It.* Englewood Cliffs, NJ: Prentice-Hall, 1959.

———. *My Life Is in Your Hands.* New York: Harper and Brothers, 1928.

Casey, Kathleen B. "'The Jewish Girl with the Colored Voice': Sophie Tucker and the Sounds of Race and Gender in Modern America." *Journal of American Culture* 38, no. 1 (2015): 16–26.

Cavell, Stanley. *Philosophy the Day After Tomorrow.* Cambridge, MA: Belknap/Harvard University Press, 2005.

———. *Themes Out of School: Causes and Effects.* Chicago: University of Chicago Press, 1984.

———. *The World Viewed: Reflections on the Ontology of Film.* Cambridge, MA: Harvard University Press, 1979.

Cawelti, John G. *Apostles of the Self-Made Man: Changing Concepts of Success in America.* Chicago: University of Chicago Press, 1968.

Chandler, Alfred D. *The Visible Hand: The Managerial Revolution in American Business.* Cambridge, MA: Harvard University Press, 1977.

Charosh, Paul. "Studying Nineteenth-Century Popular Song." *American Music* 15, no. 4 (1997): 459–92.

———. "'Popular' and 'Classical' in the Mid-Nineteenth Century." *American Music* 10, no. 2 (1992): 117–35.

Charters, Ann. *Nobody: The Story of Bert Williams.* New York: Da Capo, 1983.

Chude-Sokei, Louis. *"The Last Darky": Bert Williams, Black-on-Black Minstrelsy and the African Diaspora.* Durham, NC: Duke University Press, 2006.

Cipolla, Frank J. "Patrick S. Gilmore: The Boston Years." *American Music* 6, no. 3 (1988): 281–92

Cockrell, Dale. *Demons of Disorder: Early Blackface Minstrels and Their World.* New York: Cambridge University Press, 1997.

Cohan, George M. *Twenty Years On Broadway: And the Years It Took to Get There.* Westport, CT: Greenwood Press, 1971.

Cohan, George M., and George J. Nathan. "The Mechanics of Emotion." *McClure's Magazine* 42 (1913): 69–77.

Cressy, Will M. *Continuous Vaudeville*. Boston: Richard G. Badger, 1914.

Cullen, Frank. *Vaudeville Old and New: An Encyclopaedia of Variety Performers in America*. 2 vols. New York: Routledge, 2006.

DaMatta, Roberto. *Carnivals, Rogues, and Heroes: An Interpretation of the Brazilian Dilemma*. Translated by John Drury. Notre Dame: University of Notre Dame Press, 1991.

Davis, Charles Beaumont. "The Vaudeville Club." *Harpers Weekly*, no. 37 (February 1893).

Decker, Jeffrey L. *Made in America: Self-Styled Success From Horatio Alger to Oprah Winfrey*. Minneapolis: University of Minnesota Press, 1997.

DiMaggio, Paul. "Cultural Boundaries and Structural Change: The Extension of the High Culture Model to Theatre, Opera, and Dance, 1900–1940." In *Cultivating Differences: Symbolic Boundaries and the Making of Inequality*, ed. Michèle Lamont and Marcel Fournier, 21–57 Chicago: University of Chicago Press, 1992.

———. "Cultural Entrepreneurship in Nineteenth-Century Boston: The Creation of an Organizational Base for High Culture in America." *Media, Culture and Society* 4, no. 4 (1982): 33–50.

———. "Cultural Entrepreneurship in Nineteenth-Century Boston, part 2: The Classification and Framing of American Art." *Media, Culture and Society* 4, no. 1 (1982): 303–22.

DiMeglio, John E. *Vaudeville U.S.A.* Bowling Green, OH: Bowling Green University Popular Press, 1973.

Dormon, James H. "Ethnic Cultures of the Mind: The Harrigan-Hart Mosaic." *American Studies* 33, no. 22 (1992): 21–40.

———. "Shaping the Popular Image of Post-Reconstruction American Blacks: The 'Coon Song' Phenomenon of the Gilded Age." *American Quarterly* 40, no. 4 (1988): 450–71.

Dyer, Richard. *Only Entertainment*. London: Routledge, 1992.

Eaton, Walter Richard. "The Wizards of Vaudeville." *McClure's Magazine* 55, no. 7 (September 1923): 43–49.

Elliot, Eugene. *A History of Variety-Vaudeville in Seattle from the Beginning to 1914*. Seattle: University of Washington Press, 1944.

Elsaesser, Thomas. "Film History and Visual Pleasure." In *Cinema Histories, Cinema Practices*, ed. Patricia Mellencamp and Philip Rosen, 47–85 Frederick, MD: University Publications of America, 1984.

Erdman, Andrew. *Blue Vaudeville: Sex, Morals and the Mass Marketing of Amusement, 1895–1915*. Jefferson, NC: McFarland, 2004.

———. *Queen of Vaudeville: The Story of Eva Tanguay*. Ithaca, NY: Cornell University Press, 2012.

Erenberg, Lewis A. *Steppin' Out: New York Nightlife and the Transformation of American Culture, 1890–1930*. Chicago: University of Chicago Press, 1981.

Ewen, David. *The Life and Death of Tin Pan Alley: The Golden Age of American Popular Music*. New York: Funk and Wagnalls Company, 1964.

Feuer, Jane. *The Hollywood Musical*. Houndsmills: Macmillan, 1993.

———. "The Self-Reflexive Musical and the Myth of Entertainment" in *The Film Genre Reader II*, ed. Barry Keith Grant, 441–55 Austin: University of Texas Press, 1995.

Finnegan, Ruth. *The Hidden Musicians: Music-Making in an English Town*. Middletown, CT: Wesleyan University Press, 2007.

Foner, Philip S. "Songs of the Eight Hour Movement." *Labor History* 13, no. 4 (1972): 571–88

Forbes, Camille F. *Bert Williams: Burnt Cork, Broadway, and the Story of America's First Black Star*. New York: Basic Civitas Books, 2013.

Franceschina, John. *David Braham: The American Offenbach*. New York: Routledge, 2003.

Frith, Simon. *Performing Rites: On the Value of Popular Music*. Cambridge, MA: Harvard University Press, 1996.

Garber, Michael. "'Some of These Days' and the Study of the Great American Song Book." *Journal of the Society for American Music* 4, no. 2 (2010): 175–214.

Gebhardt, Nicholas. *Going for Jazz: Music Practices and American Ideology*. Chicago: University of Chicago Press, 2001.

Gilbert, David. *The Product of Our Souls: Ragtime, Race, and the Birth of the Manhattan Musical Marketplace*. Chapel Hill: University of North Carolina Press, 2015.

Gilbert, Douglas. *American Vaudeville: Its Life and Times*. New York: Dover, 1940.

Glenn, Susan A. *Female Spectacle: The Theatrical Roots of Modern Feminism*. Cambridge, MA: Harvard University Press, 2002.

———. "'Give an Imitation of Me': Vaudeville Mimics and the Play of the Self." *American Quarterly* 50, no. 1 (1998): 47–76.

Godelier, Maurice. *The Metamorphosis of Kinship*. Translated by Nora Scott. London: Verso, 2011.

Goehr, Lydia. *The Imaginary Museum of Musical Works: An Essay in the Philosophy of Music*. Oxford: Oxford University Press, 2007.

Golden, George Fuller. *My Lady Vaudeville and Her White Rats*. New York: Broadway Publishing Company, 1909.

Goldmark, Daniel. "Creating Desire on Tin Pan Alley." *Musical Quarterly* 90, no. 2, 2007: 197–229.

———. "'Making Songs Pay': Tin Pan Alley's Formulas for Success." *Musical Quarterly* 98, no. 1–2 (2015): 3–28.

Goodwyn, Lawrence. *Democratic Promise: The Populist Movement in America*. New York: Oxford University Press, 1976.

Grau, Robert. *The Business Man in the Amusement World*. New York: Broadway Publishing Company, 1910.

Gushee, Lawrence. *Pioneers of Jazz: The Story of the Creole Jazz Band*. Oxford: Oxford University Press, 2005.

Hamm, Charles. *Irving Berlin: Songs from the Melting Pot: The Formative Years, 1907–1914*. Oxford: Oxford University Press, 1997.

Harris, Neil. *Humbug: The Art of P. T. Barnum*. Chicago: University of Chicago Press, 1981.

Harrison-Kahn, Lori. *The White Negress: Literature, Minstrelsy, and the Black-Jewish Imaginary*. New Brunswick, NJ: Rutgers University Press, 2011.

Hodin, Mark. "Class, Consumption, and Ethnic Performance in Vaudeville." *Prospects* 22 (1997): 193–210.

Horowitz, Joseph. "Music and the Gilded Age: Social Control and Sacralization Revisited." *Journal of the Gilded Age and Progressive Era* 3, no. 3 (2004): 227–45.

———. *Understanding Toscanini: A Social History of American Concert Life*. Berkeley: University of California Press, 1987.

Howe, Irving. *The World of Our Fathers: The Journey of the Eastern European Jews to America and the Life They Found and Made There*. New York: Harcourt Brace Jovanovich, 1976.

Jameson, Fredric. *Representing Capital*. London: Verso, 2011.

Jenkins, Henry. *What Made Pistachio Nuts? Early Sound Comedy and the Vaudeville Aesthetic*. New York: Columbia University Press, 1992.

Kenney, William Howland. "The Influence of Black Vaudeville on Early Jazz." *Black Perspective in Music* 14, no. 3 (1986): 233–48.

Kibbey, Ann. *Theory of the Capitalist Image: Capitalism, Contemporary Film, and Women*. Bloomington: Indiana University Press, 2005.

Kibler, M. Alison. *Rank Ladies: Gender and Cultural Hierarchy in American Vaudeville*. Chapel Hill: University of North Carolina Press, 1999.

———. "Rank Ladies, Ladies of Rank: The Elinore Sisters in Vaudeville." *American Studies* 38, no. 1 (1997): 97–115.

Knight, Athelia. "He Paved the Way for T.O.B.A." *Black Perspective in Music* 15, no. 2 (1987): 153–81.

Kolko, Gabriel. *The Triumph of Conservatism: A Reinterpretation of American History, 1900–1916*. New York: Free Press, 1963.

Kopnik, Adam. "Laugh Factory." *New Yorker*, November 17, 2014.

Laurie, Joe. *Vaudeville: From Honky-Tonks to the Palace*. New York: Henry Holt and Company, 1953.

Lavitt, Pamela Brown. "First of the Red Hot Mamas: 'Coon Shouting' and the Jewish Ziegfeld Girl." *American Jewish History* 87, no. 4 (1999): 243–90.

Leach, William. *Land of Desire: Merchants, Power and the Rise of a New American Culture*. New York: Vintage Books, 1994.

Lears, T. Jackson. *Fables of Abundance: A Cultural History of Advertising in America*. New York: Basic Books, 1994.

———. *Rebirth of a Nation: The Making of Modern America, 1877–1920*. New York: HarperCollins, 2009.

Leavitt, Michael. *Fifty Years in Theatrical Management*. New York: Broadway Publishing Company. 1912.

Lemons, J. Stanley. "Black Stereotypes as Reflected in Popular Culture, 1880–1920." *American Quarterly* 29, no. 1 (1977): 102–16.

Levine, Lawrence. *Highbrow/Lowbrow: The Emergence of Cultural Hierarchy in America*. Cambridge, MA: Harvard University Press, 1988.

Levinson, Julie. *The American Success Myth on Film*. New York: Palgrave-Macmillan, 2012.

Locke, Ralph P. "Music Lovers, Patrons, and the 'Sacralization' of Culture in America." *19th-Century Music* 17, no. 2 (1993): 149–73.

Lynn, Kenneth S. *The Dream of Success: A Study of the Modern American Imagination*. Westport, CT: Greenwood Press, 1972.

Magee, Jeffrey. *Irving Berlin's Musical Theatre*. New York: Oxford University Press, 2012.

Mahar, William J. *Behind the Burnt Cork Mask: Early Blackface Minstrelsy and Antebellum Popular Culture*. Urbana: University of Illinois Press, 1999.

Marston, William M., and John Henry Feller. *F. F. Proctor: Vaudeville Pioneer*. New York: Richard R. Smith, 1943.

Marx, Harpo. *Harpo Speaks*. Excerpted in *American Vaudeville as Seen by Its Contemporaries*, ed. Charles W. Stein, 285–88 New York: Alfred Knopf, 1984.

Mast, Gerald. *Can't Help Singin': The American Musical on Stage and Screen*. Woodstock, NY: Overlook Press, 1987.

McCabe, John. *George M. Cohan: The Man Who Owned Broadway*. New York: Doubleday: 1973.

McConachie, Bruce. "New York Operagoing, 1825–1850: Creating an Elite Social Ritual." *American Music* 6, no. 2 (1988): 181–92.

McLean, Alfred. F. *American Vaudeville as Ritual*. Kansas City: University of Kentucky Press, 1965.

———. "Genesis of Vaudeville: Two Letters from B. F. Keith." *Theatre Survey* 1 (1960): 82–95.

McNamara, Brooks. "Medicine Shows: American Vaudeville in the Marketplace." *Theatre Quarterly* 4, no. 14 (1974): 19–24.

Mintz, Lawrence E. "Humor and Ethnic Stereotypes in Vaudeville and Burlesque." *Melus* 21, no. 4 (1996): 19–28.

Monod, David. "'Ev'rybody's Crazy 'bout the Doggone Blues': Creating the Country Blues in the Early Twentieth Century." *Journal of Popular Music Studies* 19, no. 2 (2007): 179–214.

Mooney, Jennifer. *Irish Stereotypes in Vaudeville: 1865–1905*. New York: Palgrave-Macmillan, 2015.

Nasaw, Davis. *Going Out: The Rise and Fall of Public Amusements*. Cambridge, MA: Harvard University Press, 1999.

Norris, Renee Lapp. "Opera and the Mainstreaming of Blackface Minstrelsy." *Journal for the Society for American Music* 1, no. 3 (2007): 341–65.

Nowell-Smith, Geoffrey. "The Band Wagon." In *Vincente Minnelli: The Art of Entertainment*, ed. Joe McElhaney, 99–105 Detroit: Wayne State University Press, 2009.

Oberdeck, Kathryn J. *The Evangelist and the Impresario: Religion, Entertainment, and Cultural Politics in America, 1884–1914*. Baltimore: Johns Hopkins University Press, 1999.

Ohmann, Richard. "Epochal Change: Print Culture and Economics." *Proceedings of the American Antiquarian Society*, 2003.

———. *The Selling of Culture: Magazines, Markets and Class at the Turn of the Century*. London: Verso, 1996.

Overbeke, Grace. "Subversively Sexy: The Jewish 'Red Hot Mamas:' Sophie Tucker, Belle Barth and Pearl Williams." *Studies in American Humor* 3, no. 25 (2012): 35–58.

Page, Brett. *Writing for Vaudeville*. Springfield, MA: Home Correspondence School, 1915; Echo Library reprint 2007.

Pippin, Robert B. *Hollywood Westerns and American Myth*. New Haven, CT: Yale University Press, 2010.

———. *The Persistence of Subjectivity: On the Kantian Aftermath.* New York: Cambridge University Press, 2005.

Ponce de Leon, Charles L. *Self-Exposure: Human-Interest Journalism and the Emergence of Celebrity in America, 1890–1940.* Chapel Hill: University of North Carolina Press, 2002.

Radway, Janice *A Feeling for Books: Book-of-the-Month-Club, Literary Taste and Middle Class Desire.* Chapel Hill: University of North Carolina Press, 1997.

Rancière, Jacques. *The Emancipated Spectator.* Translated by Gregory Eliot. London: Verso, 2009.

Rappaport, Roy. *Ritual and Religion in the Making of Humanity.* Cambridge: Cambridge University Press, 1999.

Richards, Jeffrey. *Sir Henry Irving: A Victorian Actor and His World.* London: Hambleton and London, 2005.

Riis, Thomas L. *Just before Jazz: Black Musical Theater in New York, 1890–1915.* Washington, DC: Smithsonian Institution Press, 1989.

Rivers, Larry Eugene and Cantor Brown Jr. "'The Art of Gathering a Crowd': Florida's Pat Chappelle and the Origins of Black-Owned Vaudeville." *Journal of African American History* 92, no. 2 (2007): 169–90.

Rodger, Gillian. *Champagne Charlie and Pretty Jemima: Variety Theatre in the Nineteenth-Century.* Urbana: Illinois University Press, 2010.

———. "When Singing Was Acting: Song and Character in Variety Theatre." *Musical Quarterly* 98, no. 1–2 (2015): 57–80.

Rogers, Daniel T. *The Industrial Work Ethic in America, 1850–1920.* Chicago: University of Chicago Press, 1979.

Rogin, Michael. *Blackface White Noise: Jewish Immigrants in the Hollywood Melting Pot.* Berkeley: University of California Press, 1996.

Rosensweig, Roy. *Eight Hours for What We Will: Workers and Leisure in an Industrial City, 1870–1920.* New York: Cambridge University Press, 1983.

Rourke, Constance. "Vaudeville." *New Republic*, August 27, 1919, 115–16.

Royle, Edwin Milton. "The Vaudeville Theatre." In *American Vaudeville as Seen by Its Contemporaries*, ed. Charles W. Stein, 21–33 New York: Alfred Knopf, 1984.

Rubin, Martin. "The Crowd, the Collective, and the Chorus: Busby Berkeley and the New Deal." In *Movies and Mass Culture*, ed. John Belton, 59–92. London: Athlone.

Russell, Lillian. "Reminiscences." In *American Vaudeville as Seen by Its Contemporaries*, ed. Charles W. Stein, 10–14. New York: Alfred Knopf, 1984.

Sacks, Howard L. "From Barn to the Bowery and Back Again: Musical Routes in Rural Ohio, 1800–1929." *Journal of American Folklore* 116, no. 461 (2003): 314–38.

Sahlins, Marshall. *What Kinship Is . . . And Is Not.* Chicago: University of Chicago Press, 2013.

Saloutos, Theodore. "Alexander Pantages: Theater Magnate of the West." *Pacific Northwest Quarterly* 57, no. 4 (1966): 137–47.

Sampson, Henry T. *Blacks in Blackface: A Sourcebook on Early Black Musical Shows.* Lanham, MD: Scarecrow Press, 2014.

Savran, David. "The Search for America's Soul: Theatre in the Jazz Age." *Theatre Journal* 58, no. 3 (2006): 459–76.

Schafer, William J. and Johannes Riedel. *The Art of Ragtime*. New York: Da Capo, 1977.

Schroeder, Patricia R. "Passing for Black: Coon Songs and the Performance of Race." *Journal of American Culture* 33, no. 2 (2010): 139–53.

Scott, Derek. *Sounds of the Metropolis: The 19th-Century Popular Music Revolution in London, New York, Paris and Vienna*. Oxford: Oxford University Press, 2008.

Seldes, Gilbert *The Seven Lively Arts*. New York: Dover, 2001.

———. "Song and Dance Man–I." *New Yorker*, March 17, 1934, 27–31.

———. "Song and Dance Man–II." *New Yorker*, March 24, 1934, 23–27.

Senelick, Lawrence. "Variety into Vaudeville: The Process Observed in Two Manuscript Gagbooks." *American Journal of Theatre History* 29, no. 1 (May 1978): 1–15.

Singer, Stan. "Vaudeville in Los Angeles, 1910–1926: Theatres, Management and the Orpheum." *Pacific Historical Review* 61, no. 1 (1992): 103–13.

Sklar, Martin J. *The Corporate Reconstruction of American Capitalism, 1890–1916: The Market, the Law, and Politics*. Cambridge: Cambridge University Press, 1988.

Slide, Anthony. *The Encyclopedia of Vaudeville*. Jackson: University Press of Mississippi, 2012.

———, ed. *Selected Vaudeville Criticism*. Metuchen, NJ: Scarecrow Press, 1988.

Slotkin, Richard. *The Fatal Environment: The Myth of the Frontier in the Age of Industrialization, 1800–1890*. Norman: University of Oklahoma Press, 1998.

———. *Regeneration through Violence: The Mythology of the American Frontier, 1600–1860*. Norman: University of Oklahoma Press, 1973.

Smith, Bill. *The Vaudevillians*. New York: Macmillan, 1976.

Smith, Henry Nash. "The Scribbling Women and the Cosmic Success Story." *Critical Inquiry* 1, no. 1 (1974): 47–70.

Snyder, Frederick W. "American Vaudeville-Theatre in a Package: The Origins of Mass Entertainment." Yale University, PhD diss., 1970.

Snyder, Robert W. "The Vaudeville Circuit: A Prehistory of the Mass Audience." In *Audiencemaking: How the Media Create the Audience*, ed. James S. Ettema and D. Charles Whitney, 215–31. Thousand Oaks, CA: Sage, 1994.

———. *The Voice of the City: Vaudeville and Popular Culture in New York*. Chicago: Ivan Dee, 2000.

Sotiropoulos, Karen. *Staging Race: Black Performance in Turn of the Century America*. Cambridge, MA: Harvard University Press, 2006.

Spears, Timothy B. "'All Things to All Men': The Commercial Traveler and the Rise of Modern Salesmanship." *American Quarterly* 45, no. 4 (1993): 524–57.

Spitzer, John. "'Oh! Susanna:' Oral Transmission and Tune Transformation." *Journal of the American Musicological Society* 47, no. 1 (1994): 90–136.

Spitzer, Marian. *The Palace*. New York: Athenaeum, 1969.

———. "The People of Vaudeville" in *American Vaudeville as Seen by Its Contemporaries*, ed. Charles W. Stein, 225–34. New York: Alfred Knopf, 1984.

Staples, Shirley. *Male-Female Comedy Teams in American Vaudeville, 1865–1932*. Ann Arbor: UMI Research Press, 1984.

Stein, Charles W., ed. *American Vaudeville as Seen by Its Contemporaries*. New York: Alfred Knopf, 1984.

Stratton, Jon. *Jews, Race and Popular Music*. London: Routledge, 2009.

Suisman, David. *Selling Sounds: The Commercial Revolution in American Music*. Cambridge, MA: Harvard University Press, 2009.

Susman, Warren I. *Culture and History: The Transformation of American Society in the Twentieth Century*. New York: Pantheon, 1984.

Thompson, E. P. *Customs in Common*. Harmondsworth: Penguin Books, 1993.

Thompson, Frederic. "Amusing the Million." *Everybody's Magazine*, September 1908.

Tocqueville, Alexis de. *Democracy in America*. Vol. 2. Translated by Henry Reeve. New York: Vintage Books, 1990.

Trachtenberg, Alan. *The Incorporation of America: Culture and Society in the Gilded Age*. New York: Hill and Wang, 1982.

Tucker, Sophie. *Some of These Days: The Autobiography of Sophie Tucker*. New York: Doubleday and Company, 1945.

Turner, Victor. *The Ritual Process: Structure and Anti-Structure*. Hawthorn, NY: Aldine de Gruyter, 1995.

Uraneff, Vadim. "Comedia Dell'Arte and American Vaudeville." *Theatre Arts*, October 1923.

Van Der Merwe, Peter. *The Origins of the Popular Style: The Antecedents of Twentieth-Century Popular Music*. Oxford: Oxford University Press, 1989.

Waeber, Jacqueline. "Yvette Gilbert and the Revaluation of the *Chanson Populaire* and *Chanson Ancienne* during the Third Republic, 1889–1914." In *The New Cultural History of Music*, ed. Jane F. Fulcher, 264–306. Oxford: Oxford University Press, 2011.

Waters, Ethel, with Charles Samuels. *Her Eye is on the Sparrow*. London: W. H. Allen, 1951.

Weber, William. "Mass Culture and the Reshaping of European Musical Taste, 1770–1870." *International Review of Aesthetics and Sociology of Music* 8, no. 1 (1977): 5–22.

Weiss, Richard. *The American Myth of Success: From Horatio Alger to Norman Vincent Peale*. Urbana: University of Illinois Press, 1988.

Wertheim, Arthur Frank. *Vaudeville Wars: How the Keith-Albee and Orpheum Circuits Controlled the Big-Time and Its Performers*. New York: Palgrave Macmillan, 2006.

West, Mae. *Goodness Has Nothing to Do with It*. London: W. H. Allen, 1960.

Westcott, William W. "City Vaudeville Classic Blues: Locale and Venue in Early Blues." In *Ethnomusicology in Canada*, ed. Robert Winter, 135–41. Toronto: Institute for Canadian Music, 1990.

Wickes, Edward Michael. *Writing the Popular Song*. Springfield, MA: Home Correspondence School, 1916.

Wiebe, Robert. *The Search for Order, 1877–1920*. New York: Hill and Wang, 1967.

Woods, Leigh. "'The Golden Calf': Noted English Actresses in American Vaudeville, 1914–1916." *Journal of American Culture* 15, no. 3 (1992): 61–71.

———. "Sarah Bernhardt and the Refining of American Vaudeville." *Theatre Research Journal* 18, no. 1 (1993): 16–24.

———. "Two-a-Day Redemptions and Truncated Camilles: The Vaudeville Repertoire of Sarah Bernhardt." *New Theatre Quarterly* 10, no. 37 (1994): 11–23.

Wyllie, Irvin G. *The Self-Made Man in America: The Myth of Rags to Riches*. New Brunswick, NJ: Rutgers University Press, 1954.

Zellers, Parker R. "The Cradle of Variety." *Educational Theatre Journal* 20, no. 4 (1968): 578–85.

Zunz, Olivier. *Making America Corporate, 1870–1920*. Chicago: University of Chicago Press, 1990.

FILMS

Babes in Arms. Dir. Busby Berkeley. Warner Brothers, 1939.

The Band Wagon. Dir. Vincente Minelli. Warner Brothers, 1953.

Looney Tunes: The Best of Bugs Bunny. Dir. Chuck Jones et al. Warner Brothers, 2008.

Singin' in the Rain. Dir. Stanley Donen and Gene Kelly. MGM, 1951.

A Star Is Born. Dir. George Cukor. Warner Brothers, 1954.

Yankee Doodle Dandy. Dir. Michael Curtiz. Warner Brothers, 1942.

INDEX